JANE AUSTEN: THE CRITICAL HERITAGE

THE CRITICAL HERITAGE SERIES

GENERAL EDITOR: B. C. SOUTHAM, M.A., B.LITT. (OXON.)

Formerly Department of English, Westfield College, University of London

Volumes in the series include

JANE AUSTEN

THE CRITICAL HERITAGE

Edited by

B. C. SOUTHAM

LONDON: ROUTLEDGE & KEGAN PAUL

NEW YORK: BARNES & NOBLE INC

Published 1968
in Great Britain
by Routledge & Kegan Paul Limited
and in the United States of America
by Barnes & Noble Inc

SBN 7100 2942 X

Printed in Great Britain
by W & J Mackay & Co Ltd, Chatham

General Editor's Preface

The reception given to a writer by his contemporaries and near-contemporaries is evidence of considerable value to the student of literature. On one side, we learn a great deal about the state of criticism at large and in particular about the development of critical attitudes towards a single writer; at the same time, through private comments in letters, journals or marginalia, we gain an insight upon the tastes and literary thought of individual readers of the period. Evidence of this kind helps us to understand the writer's historical situation, the nature of his immediate reading-public, and his response to these pressures.

The separate volumes in *The Critical Heritage Series* present a record of this early criticism. Clearly, for many of the highly-productive and lengthily-reviewed nineteenth- and twentieth-century writers, there exists an enormous body of material; and in these cases the volume editors have made a selection of the most important views, significant for their intrinsic critical worth or for their representative quality.

For writers of the eighteenth century and earlier, the materials are much scarcer and the historical period has been extended, sometimes far beyond the writer's lifetime, in order to show the inception and growth of critical views which were initially slow to appear.

In each volume the documents are headed by an Introduction, discussing the material assembled and relating the early stages of the author's reception to what we have come to identify as the critical tradition. The volumes will make available much material which would otherwise be difficult of access and it is hoped that the modern reader will be thereby helped towards an informed understanding of the ways in which literature has been read and judged.

B.C.S.

Contents

CONTENTS

ACKNOWLEDGMENTS

I would like to thank Messrs. Basil Blackwell Ltd. for permission to quote from *The Brontës: Lives and Correspondence* (1932) and the Clarendon Press, Oxford, for permission to re-print 'Opinions of *Mansfield Park*' from *Plan of a Novel* (1926), and to quote from the *Letters of Jane Austen* (1952), edited by R. W. Chapman.

I must acknowledge my considerable debt to the account of Jane Austen's early public by Professor C. B. Hogan, listed in the Bibliography, and to Mr. Darrell Mansell, Mr. Charles Murrah and Mr. Ioan Williams for their advice on my Introduction, and my thanks also go to Mr. Roger Morkam for his assistance in the preparation of the text.

NOTE ON THE TEXT

The materials printed in this volume follow the original texts in all important respects. Lengthy extracts from the novels of Jane Austen have been omitted whenever they are quoted merely to illustrate the work in question. These omissions are clearly indicated in the text. Typographical errors in the originals have been silently corrected and the form of reference to titles has been regularized. But when Jane Austen's critics have referred to 'Miss Austin', this indicative spelling has been allowed to stand.

A late addition is item No. 45, an 1818 notice of *Northanger Abbey* and *Persuasion*.

Introduction

I

Anyone who turns to this volume for critical illumination is likely to be disappointed. In many respects the birth and growth of Jane Austen's critical reputation was a dull and long-drawn-out affair. The contemporary reviews are pedestrian and the later nineteenth-century criticism is unenlivened by disputes or by infectious enthusiasm. Nor are there those moments of insight which occur when one great mind is engaged by another—as when Johnson writes on Pope, Blake on Milton, or Coleridge on Shakespeare. Jane Austen's novels have never commanded such a level of attention, such a degree of imaginative empathy. There are no masterpieces of criticism in this volume. That said, however, there are certain, limited claims to be made on behalf of the material collected here. The case of Jane Austen is more than that of a single author. Her novels revealed to the early nineteenth-century reading public that fiction was capable of unsuspected power, that it was to be taken seriously as a form of literature, and that criticism of the novel could itself be a serious intellectual activity. In this respect the documentation of Jane Austen's contemporary reputation is important to our understanding of the rise of the novel in critical esteem.

On the other hand, it is evident enough from this book that the quantity of material is small. Only twelve contemporary reviews and notices are known to us, and even down to 1870 the record is sparse: fewer than fifty articles mention Jane Austen at any length and of these only six take her as the principal subject. After 1870 the situation takes a sudden change. In the space of two years there was a greater quantity of periodical criticism than had appeared in the previous fifty. This change was effected by the first book on Jane Austen, the *Memoir* by her nephew James Edward Austen-Leigh, published in 1870—the terminus date I have chosen for the documents in this volume.

But the 1870 terminus is not merely a matter of convenience, with regard to the quantity of material; it is also a significant date with regard to the quality and kind of attention that Jane Austen received from her Victorian critics and admirers. The *Memoir* draws an engaging portrait of 'dear Aunt Jane', the authoress of charming love-stories spiced with humour. This picture fed a growing interest in the author's life and times and encouraged a cult of appreciation in which biographical details and literary commentary were easily and uncritically mingled. In 1870 there also appeared a totally different view, in an essay by the Shakespearian scholar Richard Simpson. Simpson's Jane Austen is a genius, in outlook essentially critical, limited in her scope, yet remarkable for the power of irony with which she searches the conduct and values of her society. Simpson's view had no antecedents and no immediate following. It awakened no response in Victorian thought and for many years this understanding of the novelist's controlling irony played no part in the discussion of her art.

Pre-1870, Jane Austen was never thought of as a popular novelist nor did she get much attention from the Victorian critics and literary historians. But this is not to say that she went unvalued. From the very beginning, the contemporary reviewers had welcomed the novels as something new, altogether better than the usual run of romantic fiction. During her lifetime Jane Austen knew that her works were fashionable. They enjoyed a reputation for their decorum, their realism and wit and they seem to have been widely read among the upper-middle classes, even in the court of the Prince Regent. And there was no lack of recognition from the few critics capable of grasping her achievement. Scott, in 1815, and Whately, in 1821, saw her as a distinctively 'modern' novelist, the representative of a new school of writing. In the 1840s Lewes and Macaulay hailed her a classic of our literature, to be named in the same breath as Shakespeare. Down to 1870, there is a continuing thread of praise, acknowledging a great writer.

Yet throughout this period Jane Austen remained a critic's novelist—highly spoken of and little read. Nineteenth-century taste was for a literature of scope and power, strongly-drawn and vigorous in the manner of Scott, the Brontës, Thackeray and Dickens, writers who seemed to engage much wider areas of society and deeper levels of human experience. Later in the century, George Eliot's name was also entered as a measure of comparison, as we see in Dallas's remarks on *Felix Holt* (No. 40). By these standards, Jane Austen appeared narrow and provincial, interesting enough as a period writer, a historian of manners, but limited in culture and intellect, unlearned and without a declared seriousness of aim. Beside the other Victorian novelists, the restraint and subtlety of Jane Austen's art were seen at a disadvantage. Her admirers protested, with the complaint that her achievement was not understood. They felt that their first job was to reach an uninformed public with news of a great writer unread.

Such a situation was unfavourable to critical progress. We might hope to find a growing body of criticism, learning from the past, stimulated by the new perspectives of Victorian fiction; what we find instead is a succession of enthusiastic introductory pieces, many of them superficial and derivative, often resting on points already well made by Scott and Whately. Even into the 1870s many critics assume that their readers are in need of detailed plot resumés and character accounts, as if Jane Austen were unknown.

These are purely circumstantial explanations for the slow development and the paucity of the nineteenth-century criticism of Jane Austen. Beyond these arguable and perhaps speculative factors is the simple truth that while Jane Austen is easy to write about, to write about the novels with insight and originality demands critical powers of a high order. Virginia Woolf, admirably equipped for the task, confessed to finding her 'of all great writers . . . the most difficult to catch in the act of greatness', a problem that certainly defeated most nineteenth-century critics. The secret of Jane Austen's art lies in her treatment of materials intrinsically slight. While her critics might recognize this, they had no ready approach to the techniques of narrative and structure, and the mode of irony which the novels involve. So, although it may be disappointing, it is certainly no surprise to find that the body of early writing on Jane Austen is small; and however interesting historically, of only slight value to us as criticism. This is not, however, to dismiss the few exceptional pieces, those by Scott, Whately, Lewes, Mrs. Oliphant, Julia Kavanagh and Simpson. Their views have yet to be bettered or superseded.

II

The first group of documents in this volume includes all the known contemporary reviews and notices for the period 1812 to 1821, complete except for the sometimes lengthy quotations, which have been omitted. This formal criticism is supported by a selection of contemporary private comment, from letters, journals and memoirs, including the views of the stupid and the prejudiced alongside the perceptions of intelligent readers. Most of this fragmentary material is presented within the Introduction, while the more substantial quotations are placed in the body of the volume with the formal reviews and notices.

From the material published between 1821 and 1870 I have chosen the most important critical pieces, together with a selection of articles and notices that characterize the variety of nineteenth-century attitudes towards Jane Austen. As with the contemporary material, the formal published criticism is supported by a small amount of private comment, much of it fragmentary, yet including some important items, notably the extreme 'Romantic' case against Jane Austen, declared so vehemently in the letters of Charlotte Brontë.

THE PUBLICATION OF THE NOVELS

Our understanding of Jane Austen's reception is gained partly through contemporary comments and reviews and partly through the historical and bibliographical details of the novels' publication. It is helpful, too, to recall a few details of Jane Austen's writing career: that when *Sense and Sensibility* was published in 1811, Jane Austen had been writing for about twenty-five years, since the age of eleven, and that before reaching the general public she had enjoyed an immediate audience in her family circle and friends, some of whom were themselves writers in a small way and provided an unusually literate audience, responsive to her satire on gothic and sentimental fiction. The three early novels were begun—*Sense and Sensibility* in 1795, *Pride and Prejudice* in 1796 and *Northanger Abbey* in 1798—at a time when these literary fashions were at their height.

The first step towards publication was taken in November 1797 when her father wrote to the publisher Cadell, offering an early version of *Pride and Prejudice*, but without reply. In 1803, 'Susan', an early version of *Northanger Abbey*, was actually sold to Crosby (for £10) and advertised for publication. But the book never appeared, perhaps because Crosby felt that a skit on gothic fiction might spoil this still profitable market.

Sense and Sensibility was published by Thomas Egerton in November 1811. Egerton was not confident of the book's commercial success, so it was produced at the author's expense. The edition, estimated at about 1,000 copies, was sold out by July 1813, and a second edition was ready in November. In view of this minor success, Egerton bought *Pride and Prejudice* outright for £110, publishing it in January 1813 in an edition of about 1,500 copies. This was sold out by July, a second edition appeared in November, and a third in 1817. *Mansfield Park* was published in May 1814 in an edition of about 1,500 copies. But Egerton must have been doubtful of its popularity, for it came out on the same terms as *Sense and Sensibility*, at the author's expense. In the event, *Mansfield Park* sold out in only six months. Yet Egerton seems to have hesitated over a second edition, which Jane Austen was hoping to arrange in November. He probably shared her private opinion, that 'People are more ready to borrow and praise, than to buy'[1] (as she wrote on the morning of 30 November, before seeing Egerton with her brother Henry to settle the matter). Eventually, she went to a more literary publisher, John Murray, whom she found 'a rogue, but a civil one'.[2] He offered £450 for the copyrights of *Sense and Sensibility*, *Mansfield Park* and her newly-completed *Emma*. But Henry pointed out that his sister had already made more than this out of the one edition of *Mansfield Park* and the even smaller first edition of *Sense and Sensibility*. Murray's offer for the three novels together was refused, but Jane Austen allowed him to bring out the second edition of *Mansfield Park* in February 1816, and to publish *Emma* on ordinary royalty terms. *Emma* appeared in December 1815 in an edition of about 2,000 copies, 1,200 of which were sold within a year. The remaining novels, *Northanger Abbey* and *Persuasion*, were published together by Murray as a four-volume set, in an edition of 2,500 copies, in December 1817 (with 1818 on the title-page) six months after their author's death.

These facts and figures are instructive. Her publishers knew that Jane Austen was no best-seller like Scott, whose *Rob Roy* (1817), for example, sold 10,000 in a fortnight. But sales figures on their own are not a sure guide to the size of Jane Austen's audience, for many of the copies went to the circulating libraries which supplied town and country subscribers. She was keenly interested in the reception of her books. The story of her writing career is that of an author determined to reach a larger audience than her own family and friends. She was prepared to spend years on the writing and revision of the early novels, and to pay for their publication. The two collections of 'Opinions' and remarks in her letters testify to her concern to record how the novels were received. But there is no evidence that she was directly influenced by her readers, either reviewers or friends. The only significant change to any of the published novels was made to the second edition of *Sense and Sensibility*, where a joke about 'a natural daughter', in chapter 13, was cancelled, an omission made perhaps out of respect for public taste.

[1] *Jane Austen's Letters* (1952) second edition, ed. R. W. Chapman, p. 419.
[2] *Letters*, p. 425.

THE REVIEWERS

The patrons of the circulating libraries were mainly women with plenty of time for reading and a feminine taste for romantic fiction. This was the audience which publishers and hack writers had identified long ago, and for which they produced acres of romantic trash (Jane Austen's own word for it) and gothic thrillers, much of it written to a formula. The author of the notice of *Sense and Sensibility* in the *Critical Review* (No. 1) complained of this good-humouredly to his lady readers: the succession of novels with which he was faced

in substance, style, and size, so much alike, that after reading the first three pages, we may with very little difficulty not only know how they will end, but may give a shrewd guess of the various incidents which are to occur, the difficulties and dangers which must accrue, with all the vexations, awkward rencounters, &c. &c. which are so highly necessary to make up a fashionable novel.

In one way, then, this was a time unfavourable to writing which departed from the pattern of commercial success; thus Egerton's caution and the comparatively mild response of Jane Austen's readers, including the reviewers. No one expected to find literature in novels. On the other hand, for readers capable of discrimination, Jane Austen's novels were landmarks in the floods of rubbish. But among the reviewers Scott was alone in recognizing a great writer.

It would be unfair, however, not to concede that whatever their failings as critics, the reviewers were working under difficult conditions. For the most part, their job was merely to provide brief notices, extended with quotations, for the benefit of women readers compiling their library lists and interested only in knowing whether they would like a book for its story, its characters and moral. In chapter 5 of *Northanger Abbey*, Jane Austen jokingly complains about the state of reviewing. But reviewers really did write 'in threadbare strains'; a work of fiction really could be dismissed in a phrase—'it is only a novel!' Almost these very words were used by a family friend, Mrs. Lefroy, who liked *Mansfield Park*, 'but thought it a mere Novel'.[1]

The answer to this was provided by Jane Austen herself. Her own writing was proof enough that the novel could be a distinct and respectable form of literature, and that it could satisfy the classical requirements of amusement and instruction. As Scott and Whately recognized, the novel, at least in the performance of Jane Austen, was

[1] See p. 51.

INTRODUCTION

to be taken seriously as a work of art, and their reviews were evidence
that in turn criticism of the novel could itself be a serious intellectual
activity.

III

Sense and Sensibility and *Pride and Prejudice*

At the time when *Sense and Sensibility* and *Pride and Prejudice* were
published fiction reviewing had no such dignity, and in the light of
prevailing standards the two novels were remarkably well-received.
The reviewers were in no doubt about the superiority of these works.
Although their notices are extremely limited in scope they remark on
points which any modern critic would want to make—the high comedy
of the second chapter of *Sense and Sensibility*, the liveliness of the characterization and the vigour of the writing in *Pride and Prejudice*, the
unnatural abruptness of the change in Darcy, from indifference to
ardour; and, on a more classical note, Jane Austen was commended for
combining amusement and ethical teaching, a point stressed by both
the reviewers of *Sense and Sensibility*.

Apart from a Mrs. Branstone, who thought both novels 'downright
nonsense',[1] most individual readers enjoyed these works. At the end
of November 1811, Lady Bessborough was recommending the newly-
published *Sense and Sensibility* to a friend as 'a clever novel. They were
full of it at Althrop, and tho' it ends stupidly I was much amus'd by it'.[2]
Perhaps it was the marrying-off of Marianne and Colonel Brandon that
Lady Bessborough objected to, an aspect of Jane Austen's ironic scheme
that may have puzzled other readers as well. The 'cleverness' of Jane
Austen's writing was noticed elsewhere. At a dinner party Sheridan
remarked that *Pride and Prejudice* was 'one of the cleverest things he ever
read' and advised his neighbour to buy this new novel immediately.[3]
Jane Austen heard through her brother Henry that Warren Hastings
admired the novel, particularly the character of Elizabeth Bennet,
news which she found 'particularly welcome'.[4] It was 'the fashionable
novel' of the time, according to Annabella Milbanke, the future Lady

1 See pp. 49–50.
2 Letter, 25 November 1811, *Lord Granville Leveson Gower, Private Correspondence*
(1916), ed. Castalia Granville, ii, 418.
3 From an unpublished manuscript in the British Museum, quoted in *Jane Austen:*
A Critical Bibliography (1955), R. W. Chapman, p. 20.
4 Letter, 15 September 1813, to Cassandra Austen, *Letters*, p. 324; and see p. 320.

Byron, who was impressed by its 'strength of character'.[1] At first she
had supposed *Pride and Prejudice* to be the work of a sister of the prolific
novelist Charlotte Smith, but writing to her mother in May 1813 she
had second thoughts:

I have finished the novel called *Pride and Prejudice*, which I think a very superior
work. It depends not on any of the common resources of novel writers, no
drownings, no conflagrations, nor runaway horses, nor lap-dogs and parrots,
nor chambermaids and milliners, nor rencontres and disguises. I really think it
is the *most probable* I have ever read. It is not a crying book, but the interest is
very strong, especially for Mr. Darcy. The characters which are not amiable
are diverting, and all of them are consistently supported. I wish much to know
who is the author or *ess* as I am told.[2]

This is the response of an intelligent reader who understands Jane
Austen's achievement in writing a love-story in which the reader's
sympathies are deeply involved (the meaning here of the word 'interest')
without the melodrama and sentiment commonly found in romantic
fiction. In 1815, William Gifford, the editor of the *Quarterly Review*,
remarked in a similar way upon the novel's probability; he was report-
ing on it for John Murray, the publisher, to whom Jane Austen had
just offered *Emma*:

I have for the first time looked into 'P and P'; and it is really a very pretty thing.
No dark passages; no secret chambers; no wind-howlings in long galleries; no
drops of blood upon a rusty dagger—things that should now be left to ladies'
maids and sentimental washerwomen.[3]

He was relieved to read a story mercifully free from the lumber of
gothic fiction. A second reading, in September 1815, only confirmed
his opinion: 'I have read "P & P" *again*—'tis very good'.[4]

Other experienced readers who thought well of *Pride and Prejudice*
included Jane Austen's fellow-writer Miss Mitford, who read the book
in the autumn of 1814 and found it 'extremely good',[5] and Henry
Crabb Robinson, that tireless diarist and literary correspondent. Although he was keeping his enormous journals and reminiscences
throughout the entire period of Jane Austen's writing career, the

[1] Letter, early 1813, *Life and Letters of Anne Isabella, Lady Noel Byron* (1929), ed. E. C
Mayne, p. 55.
[2] Letter, 1 May 1813, to her mother, *Lord Byron's Wife* (1962), Malcolm Elwin, p. 159.
[3] Letter, September (?) 1815, *A Publisher and his Friends* (1891), ed. Samuel Smiles, i,
282.
[4] Letter, 29 September 1815, i, 282.
[5] Letter, 31 October 1814, *Life of Mary Russell Mitford* (1870), ed. A. G. L'Estrange, i,
293.

novels are not mentioned until as late as 1819. In January of that year, *Pride and Prejudice* kept him up until two in the morning for two nights running. He was particularly impressed by the characterization and 'the perfectly colloquial style of the dialogue' (No. 15a). A few days later he recommended the novel for 'the perfect truth of the painting' (No. 15b).

The novels continued to be praised throughout the nineteenth century for the accuracy and truth of their picture of life. Yet these very qualities could also be viewed with a critical eye. For some readers, Jane Austen's realism was earth-bound, vulgar and uninspiring, as we see in a letter from Lady Darcy, written in May 1813:

'P & P' I do not very much like. Want of interest is the fault I can least excuse in works of mere amusement, and however natural the picture of vulgar minds and manners is there given, it is unrelieved by the agreeable contrast of more dignified and refined characters occasionally captivating attention. Some power of new character is, however, ably displayed, and Mr. Bennett's indifference is in truth not exaggeration.[1]

Lady Darcy's basic complaint is that the novel lacks 'interest'. This word had taken a rather specialized meaning from its use in sentimental literature, where 'interest' invariably meant romantic interest. The force of this meaning to the early nineteenth-century reader comes across clearly in Egerton's advertisement for *Sense and Sensibility*, styling it simply enough an 'INTERESTING NOVEL'.[2] The word's finer shades of meaning are seen in Lady Darcy's comments. The convention of love in sentimental fiction required aristocratic connections for at least one, if not both, of the lovers, and this social elevation was to be matched with the peculiar moral elevation of romantic attachment. By this code, love was always love-at-first-sight, springing from the immediacy of 'first impressions'. The consecration of that love was marriage, but marriage far removed from such mundane considerations as solvency or home-hunting or in-laws or compatibility. Whatever hazards might afflict the lovers, their love itself was an unassailed ideal.

It is easy enough to understand why Lady Darcy found *Pride and Prejudice* so indigestible. The ungentlemanly and unladylike manners of the Bennet family were not the stuff for fiction; nor should young

[1] Letter, 14 May 1813, to Sara Ponsonby, *The Hamwood Papers* (1930), ed. E. M. Bell, p. 351.
[2] *Star*, 27 November 1811.

ladies be so very calculating and thoughtful about their partners and their loved ones; nor should marriage be drawn as a social institution, so deeply involved in ordinary life, so open to petty family quarrels and untragic issues.

These points are worth making at some length. Lady Darcy's reaction is not untypical. It expresses the concern of readers who wanted to preserve literature as a kind of higher, happier reality, and Jane Austen's novels were a particular threat to the greatly-prized unreality of romantic and sentimental fiction. While few readers could deny that they enjoyed reading the novels—for the vitality of the characters, the wit, the accuracy and realism of her picture of society—praise comes grudgingly, fenced round with qualifications: that her characters are socially and morally vulgar, that the novels are simply entertaining, that the 'instruction' (what we might term the adduceable 'moral' of the story) is not inspiring or elevating, that the commonplace is perfectly rendered but the commonplace is not what we look for in literature. These notions of decorum persisted throughout the nineteenth century, and created a particular unease in the reader, the sense on one hand that he was undoubtedly enjoying Jane Austen, but equally a sense that he must temper his admiration, recalling that novels so very worldly and realistic could never be great art.

The next few pages give plentiful evidence of this lurking ambivalence of response. Towards *Pride and Prejudice* it is shown in a letter from Miss Mitford to Sir William Elford, written in December 1814 (No.6). She calls for an improved Jane Austen, a writer with 'more taste', more respect for 'the graceful', a writer, one would say, improved quite out of her truthfulness about the people and society around her. Together with her spoken wish to read an idealizing Jane Austen is Miss Mitford's unspoken wish to have her less of a satirist, less of a critic. This, too, is a reaction shared by other contemporary readers.

Mansfield Park

Rather curiously, *Mansfield Park* went unreviewed. The *British Critic* and the *Critical Review* had noticed the two earlier novels, and they might well have been expected to mention the third. But perhaps the editors were doubtful of the novel's appeal. The love and marriage interest was strong in the previous books, and both open on a note of high comedy; whereas what romantic interest there is in *Mansfield Park* is delayed by the Cinderella story of Fanny's early life, and there is little glamour to her eventual union with Edmund Bertram. The tone of the novel, too, is quite different from the sparkle and wit of *Pride and Prejudice*. On this score, then, it is easy to see why *Mansfield Park* passed unmentioned, a circumstance that Jane Austen probably noticed, just as she was quick to see that Scott also ignored *Mansfield Park* in his review of *Emma* (No. 8), a glaring omission, since he did refer there to the two other novels.

By way of recompense, we are fortunate to have the collection of comments gathered together and transcribed by Jane Austen herself under the title 'Opinions of *Mansfield Park*' (No. 5a). These thirty-eight comments, some only a few words, some a paragraph long, were compiled by Jane Austen from her own correspondence, from hearsay and from remarks passed on to her by members of the family. The manuscript is undated, but external evidence shows that the opinions are those of the novel's first readers in 1814 and 1815. Little allowance need be made for family partiality. The Austens were known for their candour as well as for family pride. What is particularly striking about these comments is their testimony to the readers' involvement in the drama of character and action: their sharp division, for example, on questions of innocence and guilt; whether or not Henry Crawford's elopement with Mrs. Rushworth is 'natural'. Other repeated comments touch on the success of the Portsmouth scenes; the character of the heroine; comparisons, favourable and unfavourable with *Pride and Prejudice*; and the evident moral tendency of the book.

Jane Austen sent a copy of *Mansfield Park* to Maria Edgeworth (the only contemporary novelist that she seems to have admired, apart from Scott). Unfortunately, no reply survives, although we know that Maria Edgeworth found it 'like real life and very interesting'[1] and that her family was 'much entertained'[2] by the book in December 1814. Three months earlier another reader had compared the two authors:

Have you read *Mansfield Park*? . . . I am a great admirer of the two other works by the same author. She has not so much fine humour as your friend Miss Edgeworth, but she is more skilful in contriving a story, she has a great deal more feeling, and she never plagues you with any chemistry, mechanics, or political economy, which are all excellent things in their way, but vile, cold-hearted trash in a novel, and, I piously hope, all of old Edgeworth's putting in.[3]

---

[1] *The Great Maria* (1959), E. I. Jones, p. 124.

[2] Letter, 26 December 1814, to Miss Ruxton, *Memoir of Maria Edgeworth* (1867), F. A. Edgeworth, i, 310.

[3] Letter, 11 August 1814, Earl of Dudley to Helen D'Arcy Stewart, *Letters to Ivy* (1905), ed. S. H. Romilly, p. 250.

The comparison reflects favourably on the integrity of Jane Austen's fiction. It was a familiar trick for novelists to give their stories an added weight or the appearance of authority by inserting chunks of information or propaganda of one kind or another. Jokingly, Jane Austen had suggested to her sister Cassandra that she might do something of this kind in *Pride and Prejudice*, to stretch it out 'here and there with a long chapter of sense, if it could be had; if not, of solemn specious nonsense, about something unconnected with the story'.[1]

Two other comments on *Mansfield Park* share the note of qualified admiration that we met in Miss Mitford on *Pride and Prejudice*. First, a remark of Lady Frampton writing to her daughter in June 1814: 'As I cautioned you against Madame d'Arblay's novel [*The Wanderer*, 1814], now I recommend you *Mansfield Park* if you meet with it. It is not much of a novel, more a history of a family party in the country, very natural, and characters well drawn.'[2] Possibly Lady Frampton wanted a story which was less tame, less static, more in line with the melodrama and often exotic voyaging of romantic novels. Another correspondent, a Miss Anne Romilly, writing to Maria Edgeworth in November 1814, matches Lady Frampton in discounting *Mansfield Park* as a work of literature:

Have you read *Mansfield Park*? It has been pretty generally admired here, and I think all novels must be that are true to life which this is, with a good strong vein of principle running thro' the whole. It has not however that elevation of virtue, something beyond nature, that gives the greatest charm to a novel, but still it is real natural everyday life, and will amuse an idle hour very well in spite of its faults.[3]

'Its faults' are the respects in which *Mansfield Park* fails to touch some higher, ideal reality; while the realism with which it treats everyday life recommends it only as amusement for 'an idle hour'; a critical principle that neatly disposes of Jane Austen as a social satirist.

Emma

Superficially, *Emma* is very different from *Mansfield Park*. High-spirited, full of comic intrigue and misunderstanding, and with a match-making

---

[1] Letter, 4 February 1813, *Letters*, pp. 299–300.

[2] Letter, 15 June 1814, to Mrs. Frampton, *Journal of Mary Frampton* (1885), ed. H. G. Mundy, p. 226.

[3] Letter, 7 November 1814, *Romilly-Edgeworth Letters* (1936), ed. S. H. Romilly, p. 92.

story from start to finish, it was a novel to attract attention, as *Mansfield Park* was not. The publisher John Murray was warm in its praise, and William Gifford, to whom he sent the manuscript for report, answered that he had 'nothing but good to say. I was sure of the writer before you mentioned her'.[1] That was in September 1815. Three months later, Murray wrote to Scott, inviting him to review *Emma* in the *Quarterly Review*, of which he was the founder-proprietor: 'Have you any fancy to dash off an article on *Emma*? It wants incident and romance, does it not? None of the author's other novels have been noticed, and surely *Pride and Prejudice* merits high commendation.'[2] Scott accepted the invitation and produced the first major account of Jane Austen as a novelist (No. 8). Murray blandly assumed Scott's agreement that *Emma* 'wants incident and romance'; nothing could be further from the truth. Scott pointed out that the story has 'cross purposes enough (were the novel of a more romantic cast) for cutting half the men's throats and breaking all the women's hearts'. It is not, as Murray would have it, an *un*romantic novel, but as Scott perceives, an *anti*-romantic novel, in which Jane Austen is playing upon the devices and situations of romantic fiction, adjusting them to a story whose drama and distresses are personal and domestic.

The significance of this review, in the history of criticism as well as in Jane Austen studies, is the breadth of its perspective. Scott draws attention to detail—to the neatness and point of the prose style, to the precision and finish of the character-drawing. He sees the relationship between these aspects of technique and the creation of a fictional world which remains faithful to the events and situations in 'the current of ordinary life'. As a writer himself, he understands what a feat is involved in the imitation of ordinary verifiable reality. And he is able to place this achievement historically, as a turning-point in the progress of fiction. In Jane Austen, he declares, we have 'the modern novel', the antithesis of the sentimental romance in which the nature imitated is *la belle nature*, where the action and characters obey laws remote from the necessities of human existence as we commonly experience it.

What Scott has to say about Jane Austen is stated with confidence and authority. His account wins our consent for its persuasive flair and common sense. It would be perfectly reasonable to assume that Scott's contemporary readers were equally won over, that *la belle nature* had now been shown up once and for all, and that Jane Austen's novels

---

[1] Letter, 29 September 1815, Smiles, i, 282.
[2] Letter, 25 December 1815, Smiles, i, 288.

would thereafter be accepted as setting a standard of artistic truth and reality.

But this would be to underestimate the tenacity with which Scott's readers clung to the 'inspirational' view of literature: that novels, like poetry, should elevate mankind by their depiction of ideal persons, even in defiance of the known realities of ordinary life. This issue is brought out with almost startling clarity in a letter to Scott from Lady Frances Shelley, written in August 1819. Lady Shelley objected to the way in which Diana Vernon ('a common sort of married body' as Scott describes her) was presented in *Rob Roy* (1817), and the force of her criticism seems to attach equally to his review of *Emma*:

It is no argument to say that all this is in accordance with human nature. A novel, like poetry, should have for its hero a person superior to the common herd of men—one who evinces a higher tone of feeling. The same objection may be made to all Jane Austen's novels, and also to most of Crabbe's poetry. Surely works of imagination should raise us above our everyday feelings, and excite in us those *elans passageres* of virtue and sensibility which are exquisite and ennobling, and which, if they are not evanescent, would exalt our poor humanity in the scale of being.[1]

Lady Shelley's appeal for a literature of improvement and inspiration is a not uncommon stand; what is worth remarking on is the exclusiveness of this position, its denial that there can be a literature of 'human nature', of Diana Vernons, and by implication, of Emmas, Mr. Woodhouses and Misses Bates. For some nineteenth-century readers, Jane Austen damned herself by the very fact of writing about ordinary people in ordinary circumstances; beyond this point, however well or badly she wrote was irrelevant; she had denied herself the possibility of great writing. The fallacy here is patently obvious to us today, but it lurks in a great deal of early nineteenth-century criticism, even in the private comments of Scott (No. 17a, c) and, most surprisingly, in so independent a critic as Lewes (see p.166). Implicitly or explicitly, it accounts for a continuing refusal to consider Jane Austen's novels as serious works of art.

The contemporary reviews and the private judgements of *Emma* are trivial beside Scott's article and the issues which it gives rise to. *Emma* attracted more attention than *Mansfield Park*, probably because it seemed immediately amusing and made easier reading; also perhaps for a quite accidental reason, its dedication to the Prince Regent. Jane Austen was informed that he was 'a great admirer of her novels: that he

---

[1] Letter, 16 August 1819, *Diary of Frances, Lady Shelley* (1913), ed. R. Edgcumbe, ii, 64.

often read them, and had a set in each of his residences'.[1] By this time, Jane Austen's authorship was an open secret; 'in the warmth of his Brotherly vanity & Love' Henry Austen had talked about her writing at least two years before, in September 1813.[2]

Generally speaking, the reviewers welcomed *Emma* as light relief. The *British Critic* (No. 11) found it 'amusing, inoffensive and well principled', a change from 'fanatical' books by 'fanatical authoresses'. The *Monthly Review* (No. 10) recommended *Emma* for its simple 'ingredient', 'a strain of genuine natural humour' which made it a 'harmless amusement', a change from 'deep pathos or appalling horrors'. The *Gentleman's Magazine* (No. 12) concluded that it was 'Amusing, if not instructive'.

Two scraps of private comment, both from women novelists, are in the same vein. Writing to a friend, in July 1816, Miss Mitford remarked, 'By-the-way, how delightful is her *Emma*! the best, I think, of all her charming works.'[3] In the same year, Susan Ferrier wrote to a Miss Clavering: 'I have been reading *Emma*, which is excellent, there is no story whatsoever, and the heroine is no better than other people; but the characters are all so true to life, and the style so piquant, that it does not require the adventitious aids of mystery and adventure.'[4]

Our third source of comment on *Emma* is Jane Austen's own collection of 'Opinions' (No. 7); like the collection for *Mansfield Park* it was probably made soon after the book's publication. By this time, Jane Austen's readers had a general sense of the differences among the novels. *Pride and Prejudice* was regarded as the novel of wit, *Mansfield Park* as the novel of morality, with *Emma* somewhere between the two, and *Sense and Sensibility* rather left out of the reckoning, as if unworthy of consideration alongside the others. The views we meet in this collection are not unexpected, the untutored likes and dislikes of ordinary readers, with a preference for this character or that, and praise or criticism for the novel's realism. Her brother Francis valued above all else 'it's peculiar air of Nature throughout' (it is just possible he is referring to its open-airness rather than its imitative nature), whereas a Mrs. Guiton 'thought it too natural to be interesting'. And Jane Austen had long before anticipated criticism of the novel's heroine: 'I am going to take

---

[1] *My Aunt Jane Austen* (1952), Caroline Austen, p. 12.
[2] *Letters*, p. 340.
[3] Letter, 2 July 1816, to Sir William Elford, L'Estrange, i, 331.
[4] Letter, 1816, to Miss Clavering, *Memoir and Correspondence of Susan Ferrier* (1898), J. A. Doyle, p. 128.

a heroine whom no one but myself will much like',[1] was her warning to the family before the novel was begun. Sure enough, Miss Herries 'objected to my exposing the sex in the character of the heroine', an echo of Miss Mitford's disapproval of Elizabeth Bennet as a 'pert' and 'worldly' heroine.

Notably absent from these 'Opinions', as indeed from all the contemporary views of Jane Austen's work, is any sign that her readers were conscious of her satire, an edge turned towards themselves. 'Such good sense, & so very comfortable', said Mrs. Cage of *Emma*. We might well hope to come across some comment on Jane Austen's handling of the story, or on the remarkable structure of the work. But we have to rest content with Mrs. Sclater's praise for the plot, that it was all 'brought ... about very cleverly in the last volume'.

Northanger Abbey and *Persuasion*

These two works were published together in a set of four volumes in December 1817, five months after Jane Austen's death. Her favourite brother, Henry Austen, who had acted for his sister in her publishing transactions, provided a 'Biographical Notice of the Author' (No. 13), the only source of information for her life and writing career until the *Memoir* of 1870.

The 'Notice' is a formal tribute to Jane Austen's private character and Christian virtues, as well as to her activity as a writer. Henry comments that other authors have enjoyed more resounding fame, 'But the public has not been unjust; and our authoress was far from thinking it so.' Scott's review-article had led the rising tide of critical appreciation, continued in the reviews of these two novels. There was a trifling notice in the *Gentleman's Magazine* (July 1818), really an obituary, with only a few lines on the two novels:

The two Novels now published have no connexion with each other. The characters in both are principally taken from the middle ranks of life, and are well supported. *Northanger Abbey*, however is decidedly preferable to the second Novel, not only in the incidents, but even in its moral tendency.[2]

Apart from this, and a notice in *Blackwood's Edinburgh Magazine* (No. 45), there were two substantial reviews, one in the *British Critic* (No. 14) and one by Archbishop Whately in the *Quarterly Review* for January 1821

---

[1] *Memoir of Jane Austen* (1870), J. E. Austen-Leigh, ed. R. W. Chapman (1926), p. 157.
[2] Vol. lxxxviii, 52–53.

(No. 16). The only known contemporary private comment is found in the correspondence of Maria Edgeworth with a Mrs Ruxton. In a letter of February 1818, she found fault with the end of *Northanger Abbey*:

The behaviour of the General in *Northanger Abbey*, packing off the young lady without a servant or the common civilities which any bear of a man, not to say gentleman, would have shown, is quite outrageously out of drawing and out of nature.[1]

The *British Critic* (No. 14) also criticized Jane Austen's portrayal of the General ('not a very probable character . . . not pourtrayed with our author's usual taste and judgement') on much the same basis, that Generals do not behave like this and it is wrong to suggest that they do; and the entire episode of Catherine's visit to the Abbey was held to show 'a considerable want of delicacy'. The continuation of Maria Edgeworth's letter is given to *Persuasion*:

excepting the tangled, useless histories of the family in the first 50 pages—appears to me, especially in all that relates to poor Anne and her lover, to be exceedingly interesting and natural. The love and lover admirably well-drawn: don't you see Captain Wentworth, or rather don't you in her place feel him taking the boistrous child off her back as she kneels by the sick boy on the sofa? And is not the first meeting after their long separation admirably well done? And the overheard conversation about the nut? But I must stop, we have got no further than the disaster of Miss Musgrove's jumping off the steps.[2]

The reading is partial. Affected by the love-story and the sentiment, Maria Edgeworth finds in Jane Austen what she wants, and ignores or dismisses the rest. Here, it is a trivial matter; but it arises more significantly in the *British Critic* review.

The *British Critic* took the occasion to make some general observations on Jane Austen's art. These are much along the lines of its earlier comments (the *British Critic* had noticed the other novels, except *Mansfield Park*), distinguishing these works from gothic romances and epistolary novels, the usual form for sentimental fiction. The reviewer remarked upon Jane Austen's skill in character portrayal, in creating representative types which are finely discriminated, each with a personal idiom of character and speech, and rendered dramatically. Yet he is caught in a dilemma, the problem we have seen before, of feeling admiration for something that other voices tell him he should disapprove of. Good novels, and he includes these under review, are

[1] Letter, 21 February 1818, Edgeworth, ii, 5–6.
[2] *Ibid.*

'among the most fascinating productions of modern literature'; but, in general, the novel form is not sufficiently 'improving' for the reader.

There are other distinct limits to the praise that this reviewer feels able to allow Jane Austen. Our pleasure in her characters, he writes, is wholly on account of their reality, 'the unaccountable pleasure . . . which we derive from a simple imitation of any object'. In themselves, he continues, 'her characters have no kind of merit'. The 'follies' and 'natural imperfections' she portrays are treated with 'good-humoured pleasantry', drawn so accurately that we laugh at 'the ridiculous truth of the imitation, but without ever being incited to indulge in feelings, that might tend to render us ill-natured, and intolerant in society'. Thus, he concludes, Jane Austen is no satirist.

This reviewer seems to glimpse the implications of Jane Austen's critical vision, and, as he does so, to deny it, in an awkwardly contrived argument, whose logic, for what it is worth, runs counter to his obvious enjoyment of her writing. There is an equally artificial or wilful misunderstanding of the meaning of *Persuasion*. He warns his readers against the story's 'moral': 'that young people should always marry according to their own inclinations and upon their own judgement'. Similarly, the *Gentleman's Magazine* hinted darkly at its unwelcome 'moral tendency'. Yet the moral theme of *Persuasion*, in so far as it can be spelt out, is spelt out by Jane Austen in the penultimate chapter with almost painful care, as if she were expecting to be misunderstood.

Why, then, this misreading? Not, I think, because the reviewer in the *British Critic* was an ass, but because the novels of Jane Austen called for a freedom of response which her audience, private readers and critics alike, were not yet ready to give. In particular, I suspect that Jane Austen's contemporary readers were not ready to accept her disconcerting account of the ways and values of their own society. Professor D. W. Harding has suggested that 'her books are, as she meant them to be, read and enjoyed by precisely the sort of people whom she disliked; she is a literary classic of the society which opinions like hers, held widely enough, would undermine'. This is an arguable contention and some modern critics have rejected it. Nonetheless, I believe that it finds support in a number of the quotations and documents presented in this volume. The failure of Jane Austen's contemporaries to identify the force and point of her satire can be attributed in part to their disquiet at its implications. Some of her readers objected to what they could recognize as her attack upon the cherished values of romantic fiction.

Others surely must have recognized that the fools and villains of Jane Austen's novels were uncomfortably close to themselves, their friends and neighbours. This was clear enough to Scott: 'her dramatis personae conduct themselves upon the motives and principles which the reader may recognize as ruling their own and most of their acquaintances' (No. 8).

This account of Jane Austen's immediate reception closes with Whately's review-article of 1821 (No. 16). Following the convention of the *Quarterly Review*, Whately uses the editorial 'we', enabling him to refer freely to Scott's still anonymous 1816 review of *Emma*, in particular to take up Scott's category, the 'modern novel', with its realistic presentation of ordinary middle-class life. Whately argues that with this literary innovation there had come a similar advance in criticism; that the novel could now be taken seriously because it was capable, in its imitative capacity, of giving a 'correct' and instructive view of everyday life: 'it guides the judgment, and supplies a kind of artificial experience'. Whately is careful to explain what he means by a 'correct' view, which turns on the distinction between the terms *natural* and *probable*. It is an Aristotelian argument: the novel is a kind of 'fictitious biography', giving us 'the general, instead of the particular . . . the probable instead of the true', concentrating the result of 'wide experience' into 'small compass'. Had this analysis been read more intelligently, some of the late nineteenth-century critics might not have made the mistake of assuming that the confines of Jane Austen's fictional scene marked the limit of her achievement, the fallacy that novels written about ordinary, everyday life can themselves be no more than ordinary, everyday writing.

Whately's Jane Austen is fundamentally a serious writer whose morality and values are communicated implicitly, wholly in terms of her fiction, quite unlike the didactic method of Maria Edgeworth, which he analyses. Then follows his closely-argued discussion of Jane Austen's technique, these few pages which we meet again and again in later essays, elaborated and re-worded, or sometimes borrowed with little change, especially the sections dealing with her *economy* in the handling of plot and action, and her capacity to effect minute yet significant discriminations amongst a range of similar characters.

Finally, it is interesting to have his estimate of the individual novels. *Northanger Abbey* is dismissed swiftly but not unfairly. While *Mansfield Park* is his favourite, *Persuasion* is for him the finest of Jane Austen's works. Although his commentaries on the extracts from this last novel are perceptive, in his final pages, treating the theme of *Persuasion*, we seem to be led from a review into a sermon, perhaps Whately's highest tribute to his sense of Jane Austen's worth.

IV

1821 TO 1870

In following the example of Scott, Whately seemed to be laying the foundations for a serious critical approach to the novel in general, and to the works of Jane Austen in particular. But there were no critics capable of continuing their ideas. As far as the general public was concerned, the 'society' novels of Lytton and Disraeli, with their snob-appeal and glamour, made Jane Austen's England look dowdy and old-fashioned. Certainly she was less interesting to novel-readers of the '30s and '40s, before whom was opening a new world in Dickens and Thackeray, and later in the century, in Trollope and George Eliot.

Perhaps, then, there are no real grounds for complaint. Jane Austen was virtually ignored because there was too much else to read. In contemporary novels the public could meet the problems of Victorian Britain—its poverty, its social and political inequality, its crisis of belief—areas of experience which were unknown to Jane Austen or which she chose to ignore. Where there is suffering in her novels, it is the suffering of individuals, or at most, of families, and always confined to the personal and domestic crises of the middle classes. Their pangs of love, their shocks of self-discovery and so on are affecting, but relieved of the basic distresses of hunger, of cold, of homelessness, of servitude; their problems are less stark, less typical of the sufferings of ordinary humanity. By this argument, which stands, with some justice, behind much Victorian thinking, Jane Austen was seen to be a relatively un-important writer, drawing the comedy of manners of a past age. That she was a critic of that society was a truth that went unobserved until Simpson's essay of 1870.

The size of Jane Austen's reading public between 1821 and 1870 is difficult to estimate, but we can safely describe it as minute beside the known audience for Dickens and his contemporaries. The novels were relatively successful during her lifetime. Yet after her death, and the publication of *Northanger Abbey* and *Persuasion* in 1817, her popularity seems to have declined almost immediately, the next edition of the novels being in Bentley's *Standard Novels* series, 1833. This was a cheap reprint series at six shillings a volume, compared with the price of 15s.,

18s. or 21s. a three-volume set, the form in which Jane Austen's novels originally appeared, and which the circulating libraries had a vested interest in maintaining, since it encouraged novel-readers to borrow rather than buy.

Jane Austen's inclusion in Bentley's series should not be interpreted as signal recognition. The company was not exceptionally distinguished —Fenimore Cooper, Mary Shelley, Mrs. Inchbald, Mrs. Gore, Bulwer Lytton and Godwin, amongst others. Bentley judged that there was a sufficient market for Jane Austen, although, in the event, the public proved rather smaller than he had thought. The early volumes in the *Standard Novels* series were printed in editions of over six thousand; eighteen months later, with nineteen volumes published, his print number was down to three thousand, presumably because of discouraging sales. We have no figures for Jane Austen's novels, the first of which was *Sense and Sensibility*, number twenty-three in the series, but we can surmise a similar print-number, which probably included the copies also used for a collected edition of Jane Austen, dated 1833. These three thousand copies lasted four years; there was a second collected edition in 1837, later reprinted in 1866 and 1869. Some measure of the relative popularity of the individual novels can be judged from the details set out in the Appendix.

Overall, the history of publication indicates that Jane Austen enjoyed a small but steady following from the 1830s down to 1870, when the *Memoir* provided the public with a highly sympathetic identity for an author whose life-story was hitherto virtually unknown. During most of this period, the criticism of Jane Austen is remarkable only for its missionary zeal, not for its perceptions. The critics were enthusiastic, but weighed down by their sense that Jane Austen was out of fashion, little known, and unjustly undervalued. Few of them were capable of escaping from the formulations of Scott and Whately; fewer still were able to communicate their personal experience of reading the novels. And in the comments of individual readers there is little of interest apart from the 'Romantic' debate, contributed to briefly by Southey, Wordsworth and others during the 1830s, and at greater length by Charlotte Brontë in her correspondence with Lewes and W. S. Williams. Whereas the misunderstandings and even the stupidities of Jane Austen's contemporary audience are historically informative, the misunderstandings which continue down the century are not worth documenting. If the record of these years seems scant, it is because there is little worth preserving.

In terms of critical attention Jane Austen's lifetime was an Indian summer, the reviews of Scott and Whately a false dawn. Whately's review-article of 1821 was the last essay devoted to Jane Austen for thirty years. Her name was mentioned during this period, sometimes highly praised. Yet the references are always incidental, in reviews of other novelists or in essays on the history of fiction. Macaulay and Lewes associated her name with that of Shakespeare, praise that went almost unnoticed, just as earlier the praise of Scott and Whately had failed to arouse any general interest. Jane Austen's reading public remained the small, fashionable, highbrow audience that she had enjoyed in her lifetime. As far as the reviewers were concerned, she was no longer of current interest.

The position is neatly illustrated in the 1820s. To a reviewer in the *Edinburgh Magazine* 1824 (No. 19), she is known as 'Miss Austin', a writer successful with her small 'sketches', yet undoubtedly inferior to such female novelists as Fanny Burney, Susan Ferrier and Maria Edgeworth. In contrast, T. H. Lister put the matter neatly and fairly in the *Edinburgh Review* 1830 (No. 20): what obscures Jane Austen from the public is the self-effacement of great art. Lister argued that

She was too natural for them. It seemed to them as if there could be very little merit in making characters act and talk so exactly like the people whom they saw around them every day. They did not consider that the highest triumph of art consists in its concealment; and here the art was so little perceptible that they believed there was none.

Another Jane Austen enthusiast, writing in the *Retrospective Review* 1823 (No. 18), employs an over-blown rhetoric almost indistinguishable from the purple style of romantic fiction. Although it starts from Scott's sober point about Jane Austen as a 'modern' novelist, the passage becomes an absurd and extravagant eulogy, sailing to rhapsodical heights in contemplation of the saintly Anne Elliot. This is laughable; yet we must admit the critic's strategy in trying to stir an audience which was unlikely to have read the analytical essays of Scott and Whately in the *Quarterly Review*.

Bentley's editions of Jane Austen in 1833 gave the novels a new lease of life and aroused a certain amount of comment amongst readers who can fairly be classified as intellectual, or at least literary. In 1834, Bulwer Lytton reported that the novels 'are generally much admired' and 'enjoy the highest reputation' (No. 22c). He personally liked them for being 'so natural and simple'. At this time the actor-manager William

Macready, a 'sofa' critic, turned to the novels for light reading and found them quite without the 'elevating influence of piety' which he admired in Mrs. Brunton (No. 23a). Other readers were more deeply stirred, either, like Southey, to praise Jane Austen's passages of 'feeling' (No. 22b), an admiration that seems to have been shared by Coleridge (No. 22d), or, like Wordsworth, to admire the fidelity of her picture of life yet to express disappointment at its lack of imagination (No. 22d). The great romantic poet faulted Jane Austen for being without the *sine qua non* of poetry, 'the pervading light of imagination'; and for Wordsworth, Jane Austen's humour was no recompense.[1] It is amusing to see that Newman, too, looked for and was disappointed not to find his own ideal: 'What vile creatures her parsons are: she has not a dream of the high Catholic ἦθος' (ethos). (No. 22e.)

On this evidence, it would be stretching the case to see Jane Austen as a pawn in the Romantic debate; she is an author who usually provokes a sharp response, and the diversity of views can be put down to differing temperaments amongst her audience. Yet there is something we can at least identify as a counter-Romantic taste, which interpreted Jane Austen as a voice of sense, of moral prudence and of its social equivalent, propriety, qualities for which she was praised in *The Athenaeum* 1833 (No. 21). As a complement to her ethical virtues, there was also admiration for her Augustan craftsmanship, expressed rather fulsomely by Viscount Morpeth in a poetical tribute in *The Keepsake for 1835* (No. 24) which begins the myth of Jane Austen the faultless artist. The *Edinburgh Review* 1839 (No. 25) took a mid-way position, nicely balancing the Romantic and Augustan views: Harriet Martineau is credited with 'more eloquence, more poetry', Jane Austen with 'a more exquisite completeness of design and strict attention to probability'. It is interesting to compare that comment with the views of Mary Shelley, who was also writing in 1839 about Harriet Martineau's latest novel, *Deerbrook*: 'Without Miss Austen's humour she has all her vividness & correctness. To compensate for the absence of humour she has higher philosophical views.'[2] Harriet Martineau herself had a deep respect for Jane Austen, as we can glimpse from these passing remarks

---

[1] In a letter to Henry Crabb Robinson, 28 March 1847, Sarah Coleridge remarked on the genius of Carlyle: 'One characteristic of that genius is *humour*, and Mr. Wordsworth never in his life appreciated any genius in which that is a large element. Hence his disregard for Jane Austen's novels, which my Father and Uncle so admired.' (*Correspondence of Crabb Robinson with the Wordsworth Circle* (1927), ed. E. J. Morley, ii, 634.)

[2] Letter, 4 April 1839, to Edward Moxon, *Letters of Mary Shelley* (1944), ed. F. L. Jones, ii, 133.

in her 1837 review of an American novelist, Miss Sedgwick: she describes Jane Austen as the pre-eminent author of fiction 'which, is nearly as possible, a transcript of actual life'. Perhaps of more significance are the words Miss Martineau employs in writing of the novels, any one of which 'may be taken as a specimen of her powers, a manifestation of her mind'.[1] Yet Mrs. Carlyle could find 'Miss Austin . . . Too washy; water-gruel for mind and body.'[2] In the same year, 1843, Macaulay named her with Shakespeare (No. 26). The association of names probably derives from Whately (see p. 98), but this scarcely detracts from the novelty and force of Macaulay's challenge to his readers. The comparison was next taken up by G. H. Lewes in the *New Quarterly Review* 1845 (see p. 124). Tennyson also spoke of Jane Austen 'as next to Shakespeare',[3] for 'the realism and life-likeness'[4] of her characters.

Macaulay's claim was both more and less than it seemed: less, because he urged the comparison only on the grounds of Jane Austen's portrayal of character; more, however, because he treated her achievement as a flight of genius eluding analysis and description. In his 1847 review in *Fraser's Magazine* (No. 27), Lewes glanced at the implications of calling Jane Austen a '*prose* Shakespeare', acknowledging the 'incongruity' of the term without inquiring into it. Lewes is more forthcoming about his own assertion, calculatedly bold, 'that Fielding and Miss Austen are the greatest novelists in our language', a claim which he justifies by defining precisely where Scott (currently the great novelist) falls short—in his lack of 'those two Shakespearian qualities—tenderness and passion'.

Charlotte Brontë was affronted by these claims, perhaps because she felt his admiration for her own novel, *Jane Eyre*, to be the less satisfying when it appeared alongside praise for a writer towards whom she discovered such a profound antipathy. Her correspondence with Lewes (No. 28a), and in 1850 with W. S. Williams (No. 28b), provides the key statement of the Romantic case against Jane Austen, a case determined as much by a personal, temperamental incompatibility as by the moment of history. Charlotte Brontë found her 'only shrewd and observant' and lacking in poetry. 'Can there be a great artist without

---

[1] *Westminster Review* (October 1837), xxviii, n.s. 6, 43–44.
[2] Letter, March 1843, *Letters and Memorials* (1883), i, 186.
[3] Letter, 1860 (?), reported by Mrs. Cameron, *Autobiography of Henry Taylor* (1885) ii, 193.
[4] *Tennyson: A Memoir* (1897), H. Tennyson, ii, 371.

poetry?' she asked. Lewes's side of the exchange has not survived, but we know something of his argument from an article in *Blackwood's Magazine* 1859 (No. 36) that appeared after her death. In this he quotes and answers the objections she had raised in her first letter to him, this document now having been made public in Mrs. Gaskell's *Life of Charlotte Brontë* (1857).

Lewes's exchange with Charlotte Brontë alerted him to some of the ways in which Jane Austen might be misread, under-valued or disliked by the Victorian public, and in the *Westminster Review* 1852 (No. 32) he takes account of the Romantic view, admitting the limits both of Jane Austen's fictional world and the range of experience it contains. Against this, he insisted on her technical mastery and her essentially feminine vision, a point which had been made by Whately (see p. 100). Lewes wrote that he was pleased to be 'echoing an universal note of praise in speaking thus highly of her works'. Yet we should be wary of accepting this as firm evidence of Jane Austen's popularity at the time. Earlier in 1852, the author of an article in the *New Monthly Magazine* (No. 31) complained that Jane Austen had not yet 'reaped her rightful share of public homage'. This writer was well-read in Jane Austen criticism. He quotes Scott, Whately, the *Edinburgh Review* 1830 (No. 20), amongst others, rehashing their views in a piece of smart journalism. Clearly, this is an attempt at popularization; but we should not overlook his references, brief as they are, to Jane Austen's 'felicitous irony', to 'her most caustic passages' and to 'the hardest hits and keenest thrusts of her satire'. This aspect of her writing had never before been described in such suggestive terms.

At this time the *Westminster Review* 1853 (No. 34) classified Jane Austen as an inferior writer, failing to reach the highest realms of fiction, 'the art whose office it is' to face man with the heroic and to elevate his soul. This demand is repeated in *Fraser's Magazine* 1854 (No. 35): nature, indeed, is 'sketched with inimitable skill', but it is nature unexalted, unspiritualized. Mrs. Browning also found the characters soulless. Her comment on the novels was curt: 'perfect as far as they go —that's certain. Only they don't go far, I think.'[1] In the earlier years of the century, Jane Austen was found deficient in romantic idealism; in mid-century, the charge was different, that she lacked the 'high seriousness' which Matthew Arnold and his contemporaries required of great art.

[1] Letter, 5 November 1855, to Ruskin, *Letters of Elizabeth Barrett Browning* (1897), ed. F. G. Kenyon, ii, 217.

By mid-century it was clear that Jane Austen was not a European novelist, nor was she well-known in America. The Englishness of her novels had a certain charm and curiosity value for the stranger—'ou les Caractères Anglais du Siècle' was the sub-title of the French version of *Emma*, published in 1816—but the quality inherent in her tone and style was untranslatable. The only nineteenth-century translations were into French, three of these appearing in Jane Austen's lifetime, although she was quite unaware of them.

The French seem to have received Jane Austen in almost total silence. We have one word from Madame de Staël—'vulgaire', which may have been her opinion of *Pride and Prejudice* (No. 22a). The only person to hail Jane Austen's achievement was an interested party, Madame Isabelle de Montolieu, who added a prefatory puff to her translation of *Persuasion* 1821, following her version of *Sense and Sensibility* in 1815. The first critical mention occurs in the *Revue des deux Mondes* 1842; in an article on the English novel since Scott, Jane Austen merits a few lines together with Fanny Burney and Susan Ferrier:

With these novelists, it is all a matter of nuances and half-tones. Imagination is not their strong point. These delicate and gracious works are ruled by feminine malice, puritan prudery and the social etiquette which goes with it, the traditional morality set down by Richardson, and a slightly morbid study of character and the human heart. They have nothing in common with Fielding, even less with Cervantes. These are the descendants of Richardson.[1]

The neglect of Jane Austen in France may be on account of the texts, some of which are travesties rather than translations. 'Traduit librement' is the warning carried on the title-pages! Mrs. Norris is almost silenced in *Le Parc de Mansfield*; *Orgueil et Prejugé* is a shortened and careless version; and in *Raison et Sensibilité*, the first of the novels to appear, Mme de Montolieu shortens, mistranslates, and even adds to Jane Austen, sentimentalizing to French taste, inventing didactic passages and elaborating the very worst feature of the original novel, the remote side-plot in which Willoughby features as the seducer of Eliza Brandon.

The earliest American response is something we know very little about. The novels were available. *Emma* was published in Philadelphia in 1816 and James Fenimore Cooper's first story, *Precaution, or Prevention is better than Cure* (1820), was modelled on *Persuasion* (although with a counter moral—that choices in marriage should be governed by the

---

[1] Philarete Chasles, 'Du Roman en Angleterre depuis Walter Scott', *Revue des deux Mondes* (15 July 1842), xxxi, serie 4, 194.

parents, not by the young). In 1832–3, the Philadelphia publishers Carey and Lea brought out a complete edition of the six novels. *Elizabeth Bennet; or, Pride and Prejudice* appeared first, in August 1832, in an edition of 750 copies. This sold briskly enough for the publishers to follow it with *Persuasion* in November, *Mansfield Park* in December, and the three other novels in 1833, all these in editions of 1,250. These facts suggest a Jane Austen following, but the evidence is scanty, even negative. At Harvard in 1826, the lawyer John Story read a paper on the female novelists[1]—including Elizabeth Smith, Hannah More, Mrs. Barbauld, Fanny Burney, Mrs. Radcliffe, Mrs. Hermans and Maria Edgeworth, but not Jane Austen. Chief Justice John Marshall, who had just finished reading the six novels, drew the lecturer's attention to this omission, commenting that 'Her flights are not lofty, she does not soar on an eagle's wings, but she is pleasing, interesting, equable, yet amusing.'[2]

In 1834, Jane Austen was treated to a three-hundred word entry in an American reference work, *Female Biography* by Samuel Knapp. She was described as 'a highly gifted and sensible novelist', her works valued for their 'ease, nature, and a complete knowledge of the features which distinguish the domesticity of the English country gentry'. He understood Jane Austen's object to be 'to advocate the superiority of sound principles, unsophisticated manners, and undesigning rectitude, to more splendid and artificial pretensions'. The entry concludes with a conventional flourish of praise: 'her discrimination was acute, her humour easy, and spontaneous, and her power of creating an interest in her characters, by slight and reiterated touches, extraordinary'.[3] If there are hints of Scott, Whately and Lister (No. 20) in these comments, we should remember that there was at this time little that could be identified as a distinctively 'American' school of fiction reviewing and criticism. Until the 1860s and 1870s a large proportion of literary journalism in American periodicals was simply a reprinting of material that had originally appeared in British journals.

Where there is a recognizably 'American' view it is in relation to Jane Austen's portrayal of English society, as we see in a textbook of literature (No. 29) and in a review in the *North American Review* 1853 (No. 33), where 'the narrow limits' and 'almost unbroken level' of that

---

[1] Annual Oration of the Phi Beta Kappa Society, Harvard (1826), *Life and Letters of Joseph Strong* (1851), W. W. Strong, i, 506–07.
[2] Letter, 26 November 1826, *Life of John Marshall* (1919), A. J. Beveridge, iv, 79–80.
[3] *Female Biography* (1834), Samuel Knapp, p. 44.

society are cited as factors which restrict her popularity in America as they do her own country. For Emerson, on the evidence of *Pride and Prejudice* and *Persuasion*, these 'limits' were as much moral and aesthetic as social. The brief entry in his Journal for 1861 records the encounter of a poetic, idealistic temper with an alien mode of imagination:

I am at a loss to understand why people hold Miss Austen's novels at so high a rate, which seem to me vulgar in tone, sterile in artistic invention, imprisoned in the wretched conventions of English society, without genius, wit, or knowledge of the world. Never was life so pinched and narrow. The one problem in the mind of the writer in both the stories I have read, *Persuasion*, and *Pride and Prejudice*, is marriageableness. All that interests in any character introduced is still this one, Has he or [she] the money to marry with, and conditions conforming? 'Tis the 'nympholepsy of a fond despair'[1], say, rather, of an English boarding-house. Suicide is more respectable.[2]

Austenites may be up in arms at this harsh judgement, but at least Emerson must be cleared of blind prejudice. His journeys to England in 1833 and 1847 had given him a thorough enough knowledge of English boarding-houses; and the high estimate of Jane Austen, to which he refers at the opening, is likely to be that he found in English literary society at the time of his visits.

In *Blackwood's Magazine* 1859 there appeared Lewes's last and most important statement on Jane Austen (No. 36), written on behalf of an author 'very widely read', respected by 'the better critics', but whose unobtrusive 'excellence' is unseen by the public at large. Lewes rises to the occasion with an authoritative plea, surveying the author's life, the opinions of her important critics and bringing together many of the ideas which he had aired elsewhere in his occasional pieces. He was careful not to overstate his case. He points to what he sees as her lack of sympathy for the 'picturesque and passionate', to the prosiness of her authorial comment, the inferiority of her 'culture, reach of mind, depth of emotional sympathy' (this in comparison with George Eliot). In effect, Lewes's fairness is unfair; he claims too little, not too much. Notwithstanding his admiration for her characters and her technical skill, he is unaware of much else. And, surprisingly, at the end of the essay he

---

[1] Byron, *Childe Harold*, IV, cxv.

[2] *Journals of Ralph Waldo Emerson: 1856–1863* (1913), edd. E. W. Emerson and W. E. Forbes, ix, 336–7.

appeals to the 'hierarchy of subject': as he puts it, 'the nature of the subject will determine degree in art'. This is a test in which Jane Austen fares badly. Her dramas are 'of homely common quality'. They cannot meet the Victorian definition of high art, in Lewes's phrasing, that it should fill 'the soul with a noble aspiration', brighten it with 'a fine idea'.

Lewes's superiority to his fellow-critics is in no doubt when we compare his 1859 article with a better-than-average contemporary piece by William Pollock (No. 37) which treats the novels simply as neat entertainments. Equally, Lewes's limitations are shown up when we turn to the chapters on Jane Austen in *English Women of Letters*, 1862 (No. 39), by Julia Kavanagh. At first sight, any comparison would seem to favour Lewes, for Mrs. Kavanagh was simply concerned to provide a readable, unpretentious introduction for ordinary readers, whose tastes she knew well enough as a popular novelist. There is no obvious critical method. She is writing 'cabinet' criticism, a mixture of biographical and historical chit-chat, with lengthy plot resumés and character accounts, set down brightly and easily for light reading.

Where Mrs. Kavanagh scores off Lewes, and indeed, off any of Jane Austen's previous critics, is in conveying to us a personal experience of reading the novels. Her comments arise from an intelligent, sympathetic and unselfconscious response. Whereas Scott and Whately were bent on welcoming a new truth and realism in fiction, a movement as well as an author, and Lewes was burdened with a sense of responsibility for Jane Austen's cause, Mrs. Kavanagh gives the impression of writing out of enjoyment. *English Women of Letters* may have been designed as a money-spinner; whatever its purpose, there is no hint of task-work in her response.

Mrs. Kavanagh is particularly acute in gauging the measure of Jane Austen's detachment, the distance the novelist preserves from her material in the force of her ironic vision. She is the first critic to quote and analyze passages from the text in examining the technique of the satire, with its 'touch so fine we often do not perceive its severity'. She is the first critic to challenge the reader with an interpretation of Jane Austen's experience of life—'she seems to have been struck especially with its small vanities and small falsehoods, equally remote from the ridiculous or the tragic' and with a reading of the novels altogether different from the accepted account: 'If we look under the shrewdness and quiet satire of her stories, we shall find a much keener sense of disappointment than of joy fulfilled. Sometimes we find more than disappointment.' Has any critic ever hinted more tactfully and perceptively at the nature of the experience, for Jane Austen a creative experience, out of which the novels were written?

Mrs. Kavanagh was successful in writing critically at a popular level without any undue concession to popular taste. She resisted, as many other critics failed to do, pressures of the time, such as the demand for a literature of inspiration or piety, and, a particular requirement of the 1860s and '70s, a literature fit for home reading, obedient to current standards of decency, good-taste and politeness. According to the *Englishwoman's Domestic Magazine* 1866 (No. 41), whose very title suggests what interests were involved, Jane Austen was to be recommended. The qualities of her writing are duly defined in social terms: her humour is of 'a refined and amiable kind', the comedy is 'genteel', the morality is 'elegant', the taste of the author 'delicate' and 'lady-like'. She is made something of a cult figure, an author not for the general public but for 'minds of the highest culture', for the reader capable of appreciating her 'subtle strokes of character, delicate shafts of satire . . . dry wit . . . fineness of workmanship'. These are the earliest signs of an unwelcome feature in the later nineteenth-century view of Jane Austen, her elevation as a kind of cultural shibboleth.

Another use to which Jane Austen was put was to reassure Victorian England as to its progress and enlightenment. The contributor to the *St. Paul's Magazine* 1870 (No. 43) admired the novels as reading-matter for 'men of thought and literary education' rather than for 'the girls', yet insisted on their limitation, a limitation consequent as much upon their age as on their author. The 'narrowness of life and thought' in the novels, the attention to the 'follies, vulgarities, vanities and baseness' of 'ordinary life' are seen as a condition of Jane Austen's world, and the reviewer is able to rejoice that times have changed. There is, however, no Whiggism or condescension in Mrs. Oliphant's fine essay in *Blackwood's Magazine* (No. 42) that same year. Like Mrs. Kavanagh, she acknowledges a writer of 'subtle power, keenness, finesse, and self-restraint'. Mrs. Oliphant distinguishes in Jane Austen a 'fine vein of feminine cynicism' which she defines as the 'silent disbelief of a spectator . . . who has learned to give up any moral classification of social sins, and to place them instead on the level of absurdities'. This is the new Jane Austen, with a 'fine stinging yet soft-voiced contempt', her outlook 'so calm and cold and keen'. The emphasis on these aspects of Jane Austen may strike us as slightly unbalanced, but it is intended as a corrective to the softened outlines of the portrait in the then just-published 1870 *Memoir*, and to explain why this classic writer should have been so little to public taste and her reputation so slow to develop.

The publication of the *Memoir* was also the occasion for the outstanding piece of nineteenth-century criticism, the article by Richard Simpson (No. 44) referred to at the opening of this Introduction. Earlier critics had spoken of Jane Austen's satire and irony, though without inquiring into the method or scope; they were usually accepted without distinction or definition as ingredients of the novelist's humour. Simpson named irony as the condition of Jane Austen's art. He saw her as a novelist of essentially critical genius, who employed the language and form of the novel as the instruments of her judgement upon society; it is a judgement all-embracing and unspoken. As Simpson put it, Jane Austen's awareness of the writer's authorial control 'gave her a superiority to her subject, which is one element in solving the secret of her wonderful power over it'. Simpson develops his observation of this point, exploring in particular the ironic tension Jane Austen forms between the notions of romantic true-love and the reality of love within the pressures of society:

That predestination of love, that pre-ordained fitness, which decreed that one and one only should be the complement and fulfilment of another's being— that except in union with each other each must live miserably, and that no other solace could be found for either than the other's society—she treated as mere moonshine, while she at the same time founded her novels on the assumption of it as a hypothesis.

In discussing the novels, Simpson is concerned to identify the nature of Jane Austen's development from novel to novel, something that earlier critics had failed to touch upon. He is also revolutionary in rejecting the assumption that her discriminations of character defy analysis. A third new direction is taken in his scrutiny of Jane Austen's claim to be a historian of society. His conclusions on this point are severe but just, and they testify to the vigour of his judgement.

THE CRITICAL TRADITION AFTER 1870

In 'The Lesson of Balzac', a lecture delivered in 1905, Henry James glanced at the vagaries of Jane Austen's reputation: that 'practically overlooked for thirty or forty years after her death' there had come about a 'slow clearance of stupidity' until, at that moment, it was 'a case of popularity . . . a beguiled infatuation, a sentimentalized vision', it was 'our dear, everybody's dear, Jane'. James is smiling at the myth that arose with the *Memoir* of 1870, the myth of the inspired amateur, the homely spinster who put down her knitting-needles to take up her pen. Ready to laugh at one myth, James was equally ready to usher in another, a Jane Austen who defies or evades the embrace of 'the critical spirit'. James speaks of her 'little touches of human truth, little glimpses of steady vision, little master-strokes of imagination'; yet all this is managed with a 'light felicity' that leaves us incurious of 'her process, or of the experience in her that fed it'.[1] She is seen as an unconscious artist; 'instinctive and charming', as he put it in the essay 'Gustave Flaubert' (1902): 'For signal examples of what composition, distribution, arrangement can do, of how they intensify the life of a work of art, we have to go elsewhere.'[2]

But modern critics have thought otherwise. The irony of it, indeed, is that what we have come to know as the Jamesian approach, which regards the novel (in his very words) as 'a work of art', is precisely the direction in which the greatest critical progress has been made, although it was not until *Jane Austen and her Art* (1939) by Mary Lascelles that a serious start was made in the study of Jane Austen's 'art'. Since then the trend has been towards more detailed studies of the individual novels and of the major aspects of the novelist's technique. Our understanding of her achievement has also been advanced with an increasing knowledge of eighteenth-century ideas and the traditions of prose fiction that Jane Austen drew upon and developed.

Where the twentieth century has advanced less is in the analysis of Jane Austen's ironic vision. This, the main instrument of her imagination, finds its expression in her technique as a novelist—in shaping the structure of her works, controlling the tone and feeling, and fashioning the diction and style. Jane Austen's irony defines the relationship between the world within the novels and the world outside—the historical reality upon which the novels provide a profound and decisive commentary. In Richard Simpson's essay is the basis for an approach along these lines. But few have followed—Reginald Farrer in the *Quarterly Review* 1917,[3] D. W. Harding in *Scrutiny* 1940[4] and in

---

[1] 'The Lesson of Balzac' (1905), reprinted in *The House of Fiction* (1957), ed. Leon Edel, pp. 61–63.

[2] 'Gustave Flaubert' (1902), *ibid.*, p. 207.

[3] 'Jane Austen', *Quarterly Review* (1917), ccxxviii, 1–30.

[4] 'Regulated Hatred: an Aspect of the Work of Jane Austen', *Scrutiny* (1940), viii, 346–62.

volume five of *The Pelican Guide to English Literature* 1957,[1] Marvin
Mudrick, *Jane Austen: Irony as Defense and Discovery* 1952, and Lionel
Trilling in his essays on *Emma* and *Mansfield Park*.[2]
    What the twentieth century has failed to provide is an account of
Jane Austen which is historically sound and at the same time satisfying
in its perception of the experience of life that is rendered in the novels.
For this, Jane Austen still awaits her critic.

[1] 'Jane Austen and Moral Judgement', *From Blake to Byron* (1957), pp. 51–59.
[2] 'Emma', Encounter, June 1957; 'Jane Austen and *Mansfield Park*', *The Pelican Guide
to English Literature*, vol. V, 1957, pp. 112–29.

SENSE AND SENSIBILITY

November 1811

1. Unsigned review, *Critical Review*

February 1812, n.s.4, i, 149–57

The lovers of novel reading can have but a very faint idea of the difficulty which we reviewers experience in varying the language with which we are to give our judgment on this species of writing. The numerous novels which are continually presenting themselves to our notice, are in substance, style, and size, so much alike, that after reading the three first pages, we may with very little difficulty not only know how they will end, but may give a shrewd guess of the various incidents which are to occur, the difficulties and dangers which must accrue, with all the vexations, awkward rencounters, &c. &c. which are so highly necessary to make up a fashionable novel.

We are no enemies to novels or novel writers, but we regret, that in the multiplicity of them, there are so few worthy of any particular commendation. A genteel, well-written novel is as agreeable a lounge as a genteel comedy, from which both amusement and instruction may be derived. *Sense and Sensibility* is one amongst the few, which can claim this fair praise. It is well written; the characters are in genteel life, naturally drawn, and judiciously supported. The incidents are probable, and highly pleasing, and interesting; the conclusion such as the reader must wish it should be, and the whole is just long enough to interest without fatiguing. It reflects honour on the writer, who displays much knowledge of character, and very happily blends a great deal of good sense with the lighter matter of the piece.

The story may be thought trifling by the readers of novels, who are insatiable after *something new*. But the excellent lesson which it holds up to view, and the useful moral which may be derived from the perusal, are such essential requisites, that the want of *newness* may in this instance be readily overlooked. The characters of Elinor and Marianne are

35

very nicely contrasted; the former possessing great good sense, with a *proper quantity of sensibility*, the latter an equal share of the sense which renders her sister so estimable, but blending it at the same time with an *immoderate* degree of sensibility which renders her unhappy on every trifling occasion, and annoys every one around her. The wary prudence of John Dashwood and the good nature of Sir John Middleton, the volatile dissipation of Willoughby, and the steady feeling of Colonel Brandon, are all equally well conceived and well executed. We will just give a slight sketch of a work which has so well pleased us.

The family of Dashwood consists of a mother and three daughters, who are introduced to us on the death of their father, whose residence was at Norland Park, Sussex. Mr. Dashwood had not inherited his estate long enough to save much fortune for his three girls, and at his death, it devolved to his only son by a former marriage. To this son (who is married to a woman of fortune), Mr. Dashwood, on his death bed, recommends with the utmost urgency the interest of his mother-in-law and his sisters. Mr. J. Dashwood promises to do all in his power to render them comfortable. This young man is described as, what the world calls, a *worthy respectable* character, that is, he conducts himself with propriety in the discharge of his ordinary duties, goes with the stream, and takes good care of the *main chance*. His resolves in favour of his mother and sisters, the execution of which is postponed till the arrival of his wife, who is a narrow-minded, selfish woman, come of course to nought; and Mrs. Dashwood and her daughters derive no advantage from the *good intentions* of this near relative.

Mrs. Dashwood, the mother of these daughters, possessed an eagerness of mind, which would have hurried her into indiscretions, had it not been somewhat checked by her good disposition and affectionate heart. Elinor, the eldest daughter, has a strong understanding and cool judgment, an amiable temper, with strong feelings, which she knew how to govern. Marianne's abilities are equal to Elinor's: she is sensible and clever, but so terribly impetuous in all her joys and all her sorrows as to know no moderation. She is generous, amiable, interesting, and every thing but prudent. Her *sensibilities* are all in the extreme.

The reader will form a judgment of the character of Mrs. Dashwood and Marianne by the following. On Mr. Dashwood's death,

[quotes ch. 1 'Elinor saw, with concern' to 'similar forbearance.']

Such is the difference exhibited between Sense and Sensibility. We will make another extract on the subject of love, and then our fair readers will have a pretty good idea of what is wanting in the person and sentiments of a lover to please such a romantic enthusiast as Marianne Dashwood, of whom we fear there are too many, but without her elegance and good sense, who play with their feelings and happiness till they lose the latter, and render the former perfectly ridiculous and contemptible.

Marianne and her mother are speaking of a gentleman who is in love with Elinor: her mother asks her if she disapproves her sister's choice.

[quotes ch. 3 ' "Perhaps," said Marianne' to ' "every possible charm".']

Thus argues this fair enthusiast at the wise age of *seventeen*. This lover of her sister, whom Marianne thinks wants so much to make him to her mind, is endowed with sense, goodness, and every qualification which renders a man amiable, except that he could not read Cowper and jump through the ceiling with the violence of his feelings. He also had another fault. He thought, that a person might fall in love more than *once* in his life, which Marianne held an utter impossibility; nor was he any admirer of *dead leaves*, which excited in the breast of Marianne the most transporting sensations. She exclaims: 'How have I delighted as I walked, to see them,' (the *dead leaves*), 'driven in showers about me by the wind! What feelings have they, the season, the air altogether inspired!' The gentleman had, at the same time, no knowledge of the picturesque, which Marianne considered an *indispensable ingredient* in a lover and a husband. He called hills steep, which ought to be bold, 'surfaces strange and uncouth, which ought to be irregular and rugged, and distant objects out of sight, which ought only to be indistinct through the soft medium of a hazy atmosphere.' In the jargon of landscape scenery, Elinor's lover was a mere *ignoramus*; he gave things, objects, and persons, their proper names, a crime which could not be overlooked.

Mrs. Dashwood retires with her daughters into Devonshire, and resides in a house belonging to Sir John Middleton, a relation, who is a good-humoured country gentleman and a keen sportsman. He is perfectly conversant in horse flesh, and has a thorough knowledge of the merits of dogs and the management of the dog kennel, never easy but when his house is full of company, while he is eager in promoting amusement and forming parties of pleasure for young people. His lady is a handsome *stupid* woman of fashion, who piques herself upon the elegance of her person, her table, and her domestic arrangements.

In the friendly attentions of this family and the society they meet at Barton Park (the seat of Sir John), Mrs. Dashwood and her daughters regain their cheerfulness, and, in a short time, our fair Heroine of Sensibility meets with a gentleman, who exactly meets her ideas of perfection.

Mr. Willoughby possesses manly beauty, uncommon gracefulness, superior gallantry, and fascinating manners. In short, Marianne and Willoughby are strikingly alike. They are equally enthusiastic, equally romantic. In the pourtraiture of Marianne's and Willoughby's attachment, the merit of the novel is principally displayed; and it furnishes a most excellent lesson to young ladies to curb that violent sensibility which too often leads to misery, and always to inconvenience and ridicule. To young men who make a point of playing with a young woman's affections, it will be no less useful, as it shows in strong colours the folly and criminality of sporting with the feelings of those whom their conduct tends to wound and render miserable. Such is the conduct of Willoughby after securing the affections of Marianne; being, as far as he is capable, in love with her, and giving herself and her family every reason to think his attachment honourable and unshaken, he finds it inconvenient, from his embarrassed affairs, to marry a girl who has only beauty, sense, accomplishments, and a heart, glowing with the most ardent affection, for her portion. He leaves her with an idea that he will soon return, but afterwards marries a woman for money, that he may continue to enjoy those luxuries which he cannot find it in his heart to relinquish.

The *sensibility* of Marianne is without bounds. She is rendered miserable, and in her peculiar temperament, this misery is extravagantly cherished, whilst Elinor, who has her own love-difficulties to encounter and her own *sensibilities* to subdue, has the painful task of endeavouring to alleviate her sister's grief, which preys upon her health so much, that she is soon reduced to the brink of the grave. The patience and tenderness of Elinor during the long illness of her sister, and the knowledge of her bearing up in so exemplary a manner against the disappointments and mortifications which she has had to endure, sink deep into the mind of Marianne. Her confinement produces reflection, and her good sense at length prevails over her *sensibility*. After a time, she marries a most amiable man, who had long loved her, and whom, in the height of her delirium of sensibility, she could not bear even to think on for the very wise reason, that he was *five* and *thirty*, and consequently in Marianne's ideas of love, had *out-lived* every *sensation* of *that kind.* In her notions, at that period, a man, at the advanced age of *five and thirty*, could not have any thing to do with matrimony. Marianne sees the fallacy of all this nonsense, and becomes a good wife to this *old gentleman* of thirty-five, even though he declares it was necessary for him to wear a flannel waistcoat to prevent a rheumatic affection in one of his shoulders.

We mentioned, that Mr. Dashwood, on his death-bed, requested his son would do something to render his widow and daughters more comfortable, which he had promised to do. And his *first intention* was to present them with a thousand pounds a piece. But as this noble intention was put off from time to time, we will give the following extract, to show our readers how dangerous is the procrastination of liberality, as well as a specimen of a matrimonial tete-a-tete. Mr. Dashwood acquaints his wife with his good intention towards his sisters; but she is shocked at the idea of parting with so vast a sum, though she is rolling in riches.

[quotes ch. 2, 'It was my father's first wish' to end.]

2. Unsigned notice, *British Critic*

May 1812, xxxix, 527

We think so favourably of this performance that it is with some reluctance we decline inserting it among our principal articles, but the productions of the press are so continually multiplied, that it requires all our exertions to keep tolerable pace with them.

The object of the work is to represent the effects on the conduct of life, of discreet quiet good sense on the one hand, and an overrefined and excessive susceptibility on the other. The characters are happily delineated and admirably sustained. Two sisters are placed before the reader, similarly circumstanced in point of education and accomplishments, exposed to similar trials, but the one by a sober exertion of prudence and judgment sustains with fortitude, and overcomes with success, what plunges the other into an abyss of vexation, sorrow, and disappointment. An intimate knowledge of life and of the female character is exemplified in the various personages and incidents which are introduced, and nothing can be more happily pourtrayed than the picture of the elder brother, who required by his dying father, to assist his mother and sisters, first, resolves to give the sisters a thousand pounds a-piece, but after a certain deliberation with himself, and dialogue with his *amiable* wife, persuades himself that a little fish and game occasionally sent, will fulfil the real intentions of his father, and satisfy every obligation of duty. Not less excellent is the picture of the young lady of over exquisite sensibility, who falls immediately and violently in love with a male coquet, without listening to the judicious expostulations of her sensible sister, and believing it impossible for man to be fickle, false, and treacherous. We will, however, detain our female friends no longer than to assure them, that they may peruse these volumes not only with satisfaction but with real benefits, for they may learn from them, if they please, many sober and salutary maxims for the conduct of life, exemplified in a very pleasing and entertaining narrative. There is a little perplexity in the genealogy of the first chapter, and the reader is somewhat bewildered among half-sisters, cousins, and so forth; perhaps, too, the good humoured Baronet, who is never happy but with his house full of people, is rather overcharged, but for these trifling defects there is ample compensation.

PRIDE AND PREJUDICE

January 1813

---

3. Unsigned notice, *British Critic*

February 1813, xli, 189–90

We had occasion to speak favorably of the former production of this author or authoress, specified above, and we readily do the same of the present. It is very far superior to almost all the publications of the kind which have lately come before us. It has a very unexceptionable tendency, the story is well told, the characters remarkably well drawn and supported, and written with great spirit as well as vigour. The story has no great variety, it is simply this. The hero is a young man of large fortune and fashionable manners, whose distinguishing characteristic is personal pride. The heroine, on the first introduction, conceives a most violent prejudice against Darcy, which a variety of circumstances well imagined and happily represented, tend to strengthen and confirm. The under plot is an attachment between the friend of Darcy and the elder sister of the principal female character; other personages, of greater or less interest and importance, complete the dramatis personæ, some of whose characters are exceedingly well drawn. Explanations of the different perplexities and seeming contrarieties, are gradually unfolded, and the two principal performers are happily united.

Of the characters, Elizabeth Bennet, the heroine, is supported with great spirit and consistency throughout; there seems no defect in the portrait; this is not precisely the case with Darcy her lover; his easy unconcern and fashionable indifference, somewhat abruptly changes to the ardent lover. The character of Mr. Collins, the obsequious rector, is excellent. Fancy presents us with many such, who consider the patron of exalted rank as the model of all that is excellent on earth, and the patron's smiles and condescension as the sum of human happiness. Mr. Bennet, the father of Elizabeth, presents us with some novelty of character; a reserved, acute, and satirical, but indolent personage, who sees and laughs at the follies and indiscretions of his dependents, without making any exertions to correct them. The picture of the younger Miss Bennets, their perpetual visits to the market town where officers are quartered, and the result, is perhaps exemplified in every provincial town in the kingdom.

It is unnecessary to add, that we have perused these volumes with much satisfaction and amusement, and entertain very little doubt that their successful circulation will induce the author to similar exertions.

4. Unsigned review, *Critical Review*

March 1813, 4th series, iii, 318–24

Instead of the whole interest of the tale hanging upon one or two characters, as is generally the case in novels, the fair author of the present introduces us, at once, to a whole family, every individual of which excites the interest, and very agreeably divides the attention of the reader.

Mr. Bennet, the father of this family, is represented as a man of abilities, but of a sarcastic humour, and combining a good deal of caprice and reserve in his composition. He possesses an estate of about two thousand a year, and lives at Longbourne, in Hertfordshire, a pleasant walk from the market town of Meryton. This gentleman's estate is made to descend, in default of male issue, to a distant relation. Mr. Bennet, captivated by a handsome face and the appearance of good temper, had married early in life the daughter of a country attorney.

A woman of mean understanding, little information, and uncertain temper. When she was discontented, she fancied herself nervous. The business of her life was to get her daughters married; its solace was visiting and news.

At a very early period of his marriage, Mr. Bennet finds, that a pretty face is but sorry compensation for the absence of common sense; and that youth and the appearance of good nature, with the want of other good qualities, will not make a rational companion or an estimable wife. The consequence of this discovery of the ill effects of an unequal marriage, is the defalcation of all real affection, confidence, and respect on the side of Mr. Bennet towards his wife. His views of domestic comfort being overthrown, he seeks consolation for a disappointment, which he had brought upon himself, by indulging his fondness for a country life and his love for study. Being, as we said, a man of abilities and sense, though with some peculiarities and eccentricities, he contrives not to be out of temper with the follies which his wife discovers, and is contented to laugh and be amused with her want of decorum and propriety.

'This,' as our sensible author remarks, 'is not the sort of happiness which a man would, in general, wish to owe to his wife; but where other powers of entertainment are wanting, the true philosopher will derive benefit from such as are given.'

However this may be, though Mr. Bennet finds amusement in absurdity, it is by no means of advantage to his five daughters, who, with the help of their silly mother, are looking out for husbands. Jane, the eldest daughter, is very beautiful, and possesses great feeling, good sense, equanimity, cheerfulness, and elegance of manners. Elizabeth, the second, is represented as combining quickness of perception and strength of mind, with a playful vivacity something like that of her father, joined with a handsome person. Mary is a female pedant, affecting great wisdom, though saturated with stupidity. 'She is a lady,' (as Mr. Bennet says), 'of deep reflection, who reads great books and makes extracts.' Kitty is weak-spirited and fretful; but Miss Lydia, the youngest,

is a stout, well-grown girl of fifteen, with a fine complexion and good humoured countenance; a favourite with her mother, whose affection had brought her into public at an early age. She had high animal spirits, and a sort of self-consequence.

This young lady is mad after the officers who are quartered at Meryton; and from the attentions of these *beaux garçons*, Miss Lydia becomes a most decided flirt.

Although these young ladies claim a great share of the reader's interest and attention, none calls forth our admiration so much as Elizabeth, whose archness and sweetness of manner render her a very attractive object in the familypiece. She is in fact the *Beatrice* of the tale; and falls in love on much the same principles of contrariety. This family of worthies are informed, that Netherfield Park, which is situated near to the Longbourn estate, is let to a young single gentleman of good fortune. The intelligence puts Mrs. Bennet on the *Qui vive*; or, in a more homely phrase, quite on the *high fidgets*. In her own mind, Mrs. B. augurs not only great good from this occurrence, but secretly determines, that the said gentleman *shall and must* fix upon one of her girls for a wife. She therefore exhorts her husband to visit the new-comer without delay; but perhaps the following conjugal dialogue will exhibit Mr. and Mrs. Bennet to the best advantage.

[quotes ch. 1 ' "My dear Mr. Bennet" ' to ' "visit them all".']

The desired object of Mrs. Bennet's wishes at length arrives; and Mr. Bennet, though he continues to teaze his lady, by refusing to go to Netherfield, is among the first to welcome Mr. Bingley. Mrs. Bennet is delighted to find, that he not only her husband has complied with her wishes; but that Mr. Bingley is a charming handsome man, that he intends to be at the next county ball, and that he is fond of dancing, 'which was a certain step towards falling in love.' At the ball her raptures know no bounds, when Mr. Bingley evidently gives the preference to her eldest daughter before any lady in the room by dancing twice with her in the course of the evening. This is not all; for Mr. Bingley, according to the wishes and desires of Mrs. Bennet, does really and truly fall in love with the beautiful and amiable Jane. Mr. Bingley is, however, prevented from making his proposals of marriage by the interference of his friend, Mr. Darcy, a man of high birth and great fortune. Mr. Darcy represents to his friend the disgrace not only of being allied to a family, who had relations in trade, but particularly where the chief members of it were so wanting in the common forms of decorum and propriety as Mrs. Bennet and her younger daughters were. Mr. Bingley has great respect for his friend's judgment; and, being given to understand, that Jane did not return his passion, absents himself from Netherfield, and leaves Jane to wear the willow.

Mr. Darcy, who has, in his manners, the greatest reserve and hauteur, and a prodigious quantity of family pride, becomes, in spite of his determination to the contrary, captivated with the lively and sensible Elizabeth; who, thinking him the proudest of his species, takes great delight in playing *the Beatrice* upon him; and, finding his manners so very unbending, sets him down as a most disagreeable man. This dislike is heightened almost into hate by her being made acquainted with the part which he took in separating Mr. Bingley from her sister. She is also prejudiced against him for some cruel conduct, of which she believes him guilty towards a young man who was left to his protection. Whilst thinking of him with great bitterness and dislike, and believing herself also to be equally disliked in turn by him, she is surprised by a visit from Mr. Darcy, who formally declares himself her admirer. This gentleman, at the same time, owns, that his pride was hurt by the contemplation of her inferiority; and he acknowledges, that he loves her against his will, his reason, and even his character. This provocation, aided by her fixed dislike, makes her refuse him with very little ceremony. Darcy is highly offended; and, during their conversation, Elizabeth upbraids him for his conduct towards her sister, in separating her from Mr. Bingley. She accuses him also of having, in defiance of honour and humanity, ruined the immediate prosperity, and blasted the prospects of the young man who was left under his protection. Darcy parts from her in anger, and Elizabeth retains her abhorrence of his character.

The next day comes an explanation in a letter of Darcy's conduct, which so entirely exculpates him from the crimes which have been alleged against him, and to which Elizabeth had given credit, that she is obliged to condemn herself for her precipitancy in believing the calumnies to which she had given ear, and exclaims: 'How despicably have I acted! I who have valued myself on my abilities! who have often disdained the generous candour of my sister, and gratified my vanity in useless or blameable distrust.'

From this moment, Elizabeth's prejudice and dislike gradually subside; and the *sly little god* shoots one of his sharpest arrows very dexterously into her heart. On the character of Elizabeth, the main interest of the novel depends; and the fair author has shewn considerable ingenuity in the mode of bringing about the final *eclaircissment* between her and Darcy. Elizabeth's sense and conduct are of a superior order to those of the common heroines of novels. From her independence of character, which is kept within the proper line of decorum, and her well-timed sprightliness, she teaches the man of Family-Pride to know himself. He owns:

[quotes ch. 47 ' "I have been" ' to ' "being pleased".']

The above is merely the brief outline of this very agreeable novel. An excellent lesson may be learned from the elopement of Lydia:—the work also shows the folly of letting young girls have their own way, and the danger which they incur in associating with the officers, who may be quartered in or near their residence. The character of Wickham is very well pourtrayed;—we fancy, that our authoress had Joseph Surface before her eyes when she sketched it; as well as the lively Beatrice, when she drew the portrait of Elizabeth. Many such silly women as Mrs. Bennet may be found; and numerous parsons like Mr. Collins, who are every thing to every body; and servile in the extreme to their superiors. Mr. Collins is indeed a notable object.

The sentiments, which are dispersed over the work, do great credit to the *sense* and *sensibility* of the authoress. The line she draws between the prudent and the mercenary in matrimonial concerns, may be useful to our fair readers—therefore we extract the part.

[quotes ch. 26 'Mrs. Gardiner then rallied' to ' " shall be foolish".']

This also may serve as a specimen of the lively manner in which Elizabeth supports an argument.

We cannot conclude, without repeating our approbation of this performance, which rises very superior to any novel we have lately met with in the delineation of domestic scenes. Nor is there one character which appears flat, or obtrudes itself upon the notice of the reader with troublesome impertinence. There is not one person in the drama with whom we could readily dispense;—they have all their proper places; and fill their several stations, with great credit to themselves, and much satisfaction to the reader.

MANSFIELD PARK

May 1814

5(a). Opinions of *Mansfield Park*: collected and transcribed by Jane Austen

The opinions probably belong to 1814-15. Most of the respondents are members of the Austen family or friends of the family. They are identified by R. W. Chapman in *The Works of Jane Austen: Volume VI Minor Works* (1954), pp. 431-5 and Index II, pp. 467-71.

We certainly do not think it as a *whole*, equal to P. & P.—but it has many & great beauties. Fanny is a delightful Character! and Aunt Norris is a great favourite of mine. The Characters are natural & well supported, & many of the Dialogues excellent.—You need not fear the publication being considered as discreditable to the talents of it's Author.—F.W.A.

Not so clever as P. & P.—but pleased with it altogether. Liked the character of Fanny. Admired the Portsmouth Scene.—Mr K.

Edward & George.—Not liked it near so well as P. & P.—Edward admired Fanny—George disliked her.—George interested by nobody but Mary Crawford.—Edward pleased with Henry C.—Edmund objected to, as cold & formal.—Henry C.s going off with Mrs R.— at such a time, when so much in love with Fanny, thought unnatural by Edward.

Fanny Knight.—Liked it, in many parts, very much indeed, delighted with Fanny;—but not satisfied with the end—wanting more Love between her & Edmund—& could not think it natural that Edmd. shd. be so much attached to a woman without Principle like Mary C.—or promote Fanny's marrying Henry.

Anna liked it better than P. & P.—but no so well as S. & S.—could not bear Fanny.—Delighted with Mrs Norris, the scene at Portsmouth, & all the humourous parts.

Mrs James Austen, very much pleased. Enjoyed Mrs Norris particularly, & the scene at Portsmouth. Thought Henry Crawford's going off with Mrs Rushworth, very natural.

Miss Clewes's objections much the same as Fanny's.

Miss Lloyd perferred it altogether to either of the others.—Delighted with Fanny.—Hated Mrs Norris.

My Mother—not liked it so well as P. & P.—Thought Fanny insipid.—Enjoyed Mrs Norris.

Cassandra—thought it quite as clever, tho' not so brilliant as P. & P.—Fond of Fanny.—Delighted much in Mr Rushworth's stupidity.

My Eldest Brother—a warm admirer of it in general.—Delighted with the Portsmouth Scene.

Edward—Much like his Father.—Objected to Mrs Rushworth's Elopement as unnatural.

Mr B. L.—Highly pleased with Fanny Price— & a warm admirer of the Portsmouth Scene.—Angry with Edmund for not being in love with her, & hating Mrs Norris for teazing her.

Miss Burdett—Did not like it so well as P. & P.

Mrs James Tilson—Liked it better than P. & P.

Fanny Cage—did not much like it—not to be compared to P. & P.—nothing interesting in the Characters—Language poor.—Characters natural & well supported—Improved as it went on.

Mr & Mrs Cooke—very much pleased with it—particularly with the Manner in which the Clergy are treated.—Mr Cooke called it 'the most sensible Novel he had ever read.'—Mrs Cooke wished for a good Matronly Character.

Mary Cooke—quite as much pleased with it, as her Father & Mother; seemed to enter into Lady B.'s character, & enjoyed Mr Rushworth's folly. Admired Fanny in general; but thought she ought to have been more determined on overcoming her own feelings, when she saw Edmund's attachment to Miss Crawford.

Miss Burrel—admired it very much—particularly Mrs Norris & Dr Grant.

Mrs Bramstone—much pleased with it; particularly with the character of Fanny, as being so very natural. Thought Lady Bertram like herself.—Preferred it to either of the others—but imagined *that* might be her want of Taste—as she does not understand Wit.

Mrs Augusta Bramstone—owned that she thought S & S.—and

P. & P. downright nonsense, but expected to like M P. better, & having finished the 1st vol.—flattered herself she had got through the worst.

The families at Deane—all pleased with it.—Mrs Anna Harwood delighted with Mrs Norris & the green Curtain.

The Kintbury Family—very much pleased with it;—preferred it to either of the others.

Mr Egerton the Publisher—praised it for it's Morality, & for being so equal a Composition.—No weak parts.

Lady Rob: Kerr wrote—'You may be assured I read every line with the greatest interest & am more delighted with it than my humble pen can express. The excellent delineation of Character, sound sense, Elegant Language & the pure morality with which it abounds, makes it a most desirable as well as useful work, & reflects the highest honour &c. &c.—Universally admired in Edinburgh, by all the *wise ones*.—Indeed, I have not heard a single fault given to it.'

Miss Sharpe—'I think it excellent— & of it's good sense & moral Tendency there can be no doubt.—Your Characters are drawn to the Life—so *very, very* natural & just—but as you beg me to be perfectly honest, I must confess I prefer P & P.'

Mrs Carrick.—'All who think deeply & feel much will give the Preference to Mansfield Park.'

Mr J. Plumptre.—'I never read a novel which interested me so very much throughout, the characters are all so remarkably well kept up & so well drawn, & the plot is so well contrived that I had not an idea till the end which of the two wd marry Fanny, H. C. or Edmd. Mrs Norris amused me particularly, & Sir Thos. is very clever, & his conduct proves admirably the defects of the modern system of Education.'—Mr J. P. made *two* objections, but only one of them was remembered, the want of some character more striking & interesting to the generality of Readers, than Fanny was likely to be.

Sir James Langham & Mr Sanford, having been told that it was much inferior to P. & P.—began it expecting to dislike it, but were very soon extremely pleased with it— & I *beleive*, did not think it at all inferior.

Alethea Bigg.—'I have read M P. & heard it very much talked of, very much praised, I like it myself & think it very good indeed, but as I never say what I do not think, I will add that although it is superior in a great many points in my opinion to the other two Works, I think it has not the Spirit of P & P., except perhaps the *Price* family at Portsmouth, & they are delightful in their way.'

Charles—did not like it near so well as P. & P.—thought it wanted Incident.

Mrs Dickson.—'I have bought M P.—but it is not equal to P. & P.'

Mrs Lefroy—liked it, but thought it a mere Novel.

Mrs Portal—admired it very much—objected cheifly to Edmund's not being brought more forward.

Lady Gordon wrote 'In most novels you are amused for the time with a set of Ideal People whom you never think of afterwards or whom you the least expect to meet in common life, whereas in Miss A–s works, & especially in M P. you actually *live* with them, you fancy yourself one of the family; & the scenes are so exactly descriptive, so perfectly natural, that there is scarcely an Incident or conversation, or a person that you are not inclined to imagine you have at one time or other in your Life been a witness to, born a part in, & been acquainted with.'

Mrs Pole wrote, 'There is a particular satisfaction in reading all Miss A—s works—they are so evidently written by a Gentlewoman—most Novellists fail & betray themselves in attempting to describe familiar scenes in high Life, some little vulgarism escapes & shews that they are not experimentally acquainted with what they describe, but here it is quite different. Everything is natural, & the situations & incidents are told in a manner which clearly evinces the Writer to *belong* to the Society whose Manners she so ably delineates.' Mrs Pole also said that no Books had ever occasioned so much canvassing & doubt, & that everybody was desirous to attribute them to some of their own friends, or to some person of whom they thought highly.

Adml. Foote—surprised that I had the power of drawing the Portsmouth-Scenes so well.

Mrs Creed—preferred S & S. and P & P.—to Mansfield Park.

5(b). Opinions of *Mansfield Park* recorded by Jane Austen in her correspondence

1814–16

All page references are to the *Letters* edited by R. W. Chapman.

---

2 March 1814, to Cassandra Austen: 'Henry's[1] approbation hitherto is even equal to my wishes. He says it is very different from the other two, but does not appear to think it at all inferior. He has only married Mrs. R. I am afraid he has gone through the most entertaining part. He took to Lady B. and Mrs. N. most kindly, and gives great praise to the drawing of the characters. He understands them all, likes Fanny, and, I think, foresees how it will all be. . . . Henry is going on with *Mansfield Park*. He admires H. Crawford: I mean properly, as a clever, pleasant man.' (pp. 376, 377–8.)

5 March 1814, to Cassandra Austen: 'Henry has this moment said that he likes my M.P. better & better; he is in the 3d volume. I beleive *now* he has changed his mind as to foreseeing the end; he said yesterday at least, that he defied anybody to say whether H.C. would be reformed, or would forget Fanny in a fortnight.' (p. 381.)

9 March 1814, to Cassandra Austen: 'Henry has finished *Mansfield Park*, & his approbation has not lessened. He found the last half of the last volume extremely interesting.' (p. 386.)

26 November 1815, to Cassandra Austen: 'Mr. H.[2] is reading *Mansfield Park* for the first time and prefers it to P. and P.' (p. 437.)

11 December 1815, to James Stanier Clarke:[3] '. . . I am very strongly haunted by the idea that to those readers who have preferred *Pride and*

---

[1] At this time, Jane Austen was staying with her brother Henry Austen in London. He would be reading the proofs.

[2] Charles Haden was a London surgeon, known to her through Henry Austen.

[3] Clarke was Librarian to the Prince Regent. He had intimated to Jane Austen that she might have the honour of dedicating *Emma* to his royal master.

Prejudice it will appear inferior in wit, and to those who have preferred *Mansfield Park* very inferior in good sense.' (p. 443.)

I April 1816, to John Murray:[1] 'I return you the "Quarterly Review" with many thanks. The Authoress of *Emma* has no reason, I think, to complain of her treatment in it, except in the total omission of *Mansfield Park*. I cannot be but sorry that so clever a man as the Reviewer of *Emma* should consider it as unworthy of being noticed.' (p. 453.)

[1] The publisher, who had sent Jane Austen a copy of Scott's review (No. 8).

6. Miss Mitford on Jane Austen

1814

Letter 20 December 1814, to Sir William Elford, *Life of Mary Russell Mitford* (1870), ed. A. G. L'Estrange, i, 300.

Mary Russell Mitford (1787–1855), the novelist and essayist is here continuing a discussion-by-correspondence (the earlier letters of which are not extant). Her qualified admiration for Jane Austen is characteristic of the period (see Introduction, pp. 9–10).

The want of elegance is almost the only want in Miss Austen. I have not read her *Mansfield Park*, but it is impossible not to feel in every line of *Pride and Prejudice*, in every word of 'Elizabeth,' the entire want of taste which could produce so pert, so worldly a heroine as the beloved of such a man as Darcy. Wickham is equally bad. Oh! they were just fit for each other, and I cannot forgive that delightful Darcy for parting them. Darcy should have married Jane. He is of all the admirable characters the best designed and the best sustained. I quite agree with you in preferring Miss Austen to Miss Edgeworth. If the former had a little more taste, a little more perception of the graceful, as well as of the humorous, I know not indeed any one to whom I should not prefer her. There is none of the hardness, the cold selfishness, of Miss Edgeworth about her writings; she is in a much better humour with the world; she preaches no sermons; she wants nothing but the *beau-idéal* of the female character to be a perfect novel writer; and perhaps even that *beau-idéal* would only be missed by such a *petite maîtresse* in books as myself, who would never admit a muse into my library till she had been taught to dance by the Graces.

EMMA

December 1815

7. Opinions of *Emma*: collected and transcribed by Jane Austen

The Opinions probably belong to 1816. Most of the respondents are members of the Austen family or friends of the family. They are identified by R. W. Chapman in *The Works of Jane Austen: Volume VI Minor Works* (1954), pp. 436–9 and Index II, pp. 467–71.

Captain Austen.—liked it extremely, observing that though there might be more Wit in P & P— & an higher Morality in M P—yet altogether, on account of it's peculiar air of Nature throughout, he preferred it to either.

Mrs F. A.—liked & admired it very much indeed, but must still prefer P. & P.

Mrs J. Bridges—preferred it to all the others.

Miss Sharp—better than M P.—but not so well as P. & P.—pleased with the Heroine for her Originality, delighted with Mr K— & called Mrs Elton beyond praise.—dissatisfied with Jane Fairfax.

Cassandra—better than P. & P.—but not so well as M. P.

Fanny K.—not so well as either P. & P. or M P.—could not bear *Emma* herself.—Mr Knightley delightful.—Should like J. F.—if she knew more of her.

Mr & Mrs J. A.—did not like it so well as either of the 3 others. Language different from the others; not so easily read.

Edward—preferred it to M P.—*only.* —Mr K. liked by every body.

Miss Bigg—not equal to either P & P.—or M P.—objected to the sameness of the subject (Match-making) all through.—Too much of Mr Elton & H. Smith. Language superior to the others.

My Mother—thought it more entertaining than M P.—but not so

interesting as P. & P.—No characters in it equal to Ly Catherine & Mr Collins.

Miss Lloyd—thought it as *clever* as either of the others, but did not receive so much pleasure from it as from P. & P— & M P.

Mrs & Miss Craven—liked it very much, but not so much as the others.

Fanny Cage—like it very much indeed & classed it between P & P.— & M P.

Mr Sherer—did not think it equal to either M P—(which he liked the best of all) or P & P.—Displeased with my pictures of Clergymen.

Miss Bigg—on reading it a second time, like Miss Bates much better than at first, & expressed herself as liking all the people of Highbury in general, except Harriet Smith—but could not help still thinking *her* too silly in her Loves.

The family at Upton Gray—all very much amused with it.—Miss Bates a great favourite with Mrs Beaufoy.

Mr and Mrs Leigh Perrot—saw many beauties in it, but could not think it equal to P. & P.—Darcy & Elizabeth had spoilt them for anything else.—Mr K. however, an excellent Character; Emma better luck than a Matchmaker often has.—Pitied Jane Fairfax— thought Frank Churchill better treated than he deserved.

Countess Craven—admired it very much, but did not think it equal to P & P.—which she ranked as the very first of it's sort.

Mrs Guiton—thought it too natural to be interesting.

Mrs Digweed—did not like it so well as the others, in fact if she had not known the Author, could hardly have got through it.

Miss Terry—admired it very much, particularly Mrs Elton.

Henry Sanford—very much pleased with it—delighted with Miss Bates, but thought Mrs Elton the best-drawn Character in the Book.— Mansfield Park however, still his favourite.

Mr Haden—*quite* delighted with it. Admired the Character of Emma.

Miss Isabella Herries—did not like it—objected to my exposing the sex in the character of the Heroine—convinced that I had meant Mrs & Miss Bates for some acquaintance of theirs—People whom I never heard of before.

Miss Harriet Moore—admired it very much, but M. P. still her favourite of all.

Countess Morley—delighted with it.

Mr Cockerelle—liked it so little, that Fanny would not send me his opinion.

Mrs Dickson—did not much like it—thought it *very* inferior to P. & P.

—Liked it the less, from there being a Mr. & Mrs Dixon in it.

Mrs Brandreth—thought the 3d vol: superior to anything I had ever written—quite beautiful!

Mr B. Lefroy—thought that if there had been more Incident, it would be equal to any of the others.—The Characters quite as well drawn & supported as in any, & from being more everyday ones, the more entertaining.—Did not like the Heroine so well as any of the others. Miss Bates excellent, but rather too much of her. Mr & Mrs Elton admirable & John Knightley a sensible Man.

Mrs B. Lefroy—rank'd *Emma* as a composition with S & S.—not so *Brilliant* as P. & P—nor so *equal* as M P.—Preferred Emma herself to all the heroines.—The Characters like all the others admirably well drawn & supported—perhaps rather less strongly marked than some, but only the more natural for that reason.—Mr Knightley Mrs Elton & Miss Bates her favourites.—Thought one or two of the conversations too long.

Mrs Lefroy—preferred it to M P—but like M P. the least of all.

Mr Fowle—read only the first & last Chapters, because he had heard it was not interesting.

Mrs Lutley Sclater—liked it very much, better than M P— & thought I had 'brought it all about very cleverly in the last volume.'

Mrs C. Cage wrote thus to Fanny—'A great many thanks for the loan of *Emma*, which I am delighted with. I like it better than any. Every character is throughly kept up. I must enjoy reading it again with Charles. Miss Bates is incomparable, but I was nearly killed with those precious treasures! They are Unique, & really with more fun than I can express. I am at Highbury all day, & I can't help feeling I have just got into a new set of acquaintance. No one writes such good sense. & so very comfortable.'

Mrs Wroughton—did not like it so well as P. & P.—Thought the Authoress wrong, in such times as these, to draw such Clergymen as Mr Collins & Mr Elton.

Sir J. Langham—thought it much inferior to the others.

Mr Jeffery (of the Edinburgh Review) was kept up by it three nights.

Miss Murden—certainly inferior to all the others.

Capt. C. Austen wrote—'Emma arrived in time to a moment. I am delighted with her, more so I think than even with my favourite Pride & Prejudice, & have read it three times in the Passage.'

Mrs D. Dundas—thought it very clever, but did not like it so well as either of the others.

8. Walter Scott, an unsigned review of *Emma*, *Quarterly Review*

Dated October 1815, issued March 1816, xiv, 188–201

The publisher of *Emma*, John Murray, who was also proprietor of the *Quarterly Review*, invited Scott to review the novel (in a letter dated 25 December 1815). This is the first major critical notice of Jane Austen (see Introduction, pp. 13–14). For other of Scott's views on Jane Austen, see No. 17.

There are some vices in civilized society so common that they are hardly acknowledged as stains upon the moral character, the propensity to which is nevertheless carefully concealed, even by those who most frequently give way to them; since no man of pleasure would willingly assume the gross epithet of a debauchee or a drunkard. One would almost think that novel-reading fell under this class of frailties, since among the crowds who read little else, it is not common to find an individual of hardihood sufficient to avow his taste for these frivolous studies. A novel, therefore, is frequently 'bread eaten in secret;' and it is not upon Lydia Languish's toilet alone that Tom Jones and Peregrine Pickle are to be found ambushed behind works of a more grave and instructive character. And hence it has happened, that in no branch of composition, not even in poetry itself, have so many writers, and of such varied talents, exerted their powers. It may perhaps be added, that although the composition of these works admits of being exalted and decorated by the higher exertions of genius; yet such is the universal charm of narrative, that the worst novel ever written will find some gentle reader content to yawn over it, rather than to open the page of the historian, moralist, or poet. We have heard, indeed, of one work of fiction so unutterably stupid, that the proprietor, diverted by the rarity of the incident, offered the book, which consisted of two volumes in duodecimo, handsomely bound, to any person who would declare, upon his honour, that he had read the whole from beginning to end. But although this offer was made to the passengers on board an Indiaman, during a tedious outward-bound voyage, the *Memoirs of Clegg the Clergyman*, (such was the title of this unhappy composition,) completely baffled the most dull and determined student on board, and bid fair for an exception to the general rule above-mentioned,— when the love of glory prevailed with the boatswain, a man of strong and solid parts, to hazard the attempt, and he actually conquered and carried off the prize!

The judicious reader will see at once that we have been pleading our own cause while stating the universal practice, and preparing him for a display of more general acquaintance with this fascinating department of literature, than at first sight may seem consistent with the graver studies to which we are compelled by duty: but in truth, when we consider how many hours of languor and anxiety, of deserted age and solitary celibacy, of pain even and poverty, are beguiled by the perusal of these light volumes, we cannot austerely condemn the source from which is drawn the alleviation of such a portion of human misery, or consider the regulation of this department as beneath the sober consideration of the critic.

If such apologies may be admitted in judging the labours of ordinary novelists, it becomes doubly the duty of the critic to treat with kindness as well as candour works which, like this before us, proclaim a knowledge of the human heart, with the power and resolution to bring that knowledge to the service of honour and virtue. The author is already known to the public by the two novels announced in her title-page, and both, the last especially, attracted, with justice, an attention from the public far superior to what is granted to the ephemeral productions which supply the regular demand of watering-places and circulating libraries. They belong to a class of fictions which has arisen almost in our own times, and which draws the characters and incidents introduced more immediately from the current of ordinary life than was permitted by the former rules of the novel.

In its first appearance, the novel was the legitimate child of the romance; and though the manners and general turn of the composition were altered so as to suit modern times, the author remained fettered by many peculiarities derived from the original style of romantic fiction. These may be chiefly traced in the conduct of the narrative, and the tone of sentiment attributed to the fictitious personages. On the first point, although

> The talisman and magic wand were broke,
> Knights, dwarfs, and genii vanish'd into smoke,

still the reader expected to peruse a course of adventures of a nature more interesting and extraordinary than those which occur in his own life, or that of his next-door neighbours. The hero no longer defeated armies by his single sword, clove giants to the chine, or gained kingdoms. But he was expected to go through perils by sea and land, to be steeped in poverty, to be tried by temptation, to be exposed to the alternate vicissitudes of adversity and prosperity, and his life was a troubled scene of suffering and achievement. Few novelists, indeed, adventured to deny to the hero his final hour of tranquillity and happiness, though it was the prevailing fashion never to relieve him out of his last and most dreadful distress until the finishing chapters of his history; so that although his prosperity in the record of his life was short, we were bound to believe it was long and uninterrupted when the author had done with him. The heroine was usually condemned to equal hardships and hazards. She was regularly exposed to being forcibly carried off like a Sabine virgin by some frantic admirer. And even if she escaped the terrors of masked ruffians, an insidious ravisher, a cloak wrapped forcibly around her head, and a coach with the blinds up driving she could not conjecture whither, she had still her share of wandering, of poverty, of obloquy, of seclusion, and of imprisonment, and was frequently extended upon a bed of sickness, and reduced to her last shilling before the author condescended to shield her from persecution. In all these dread contingencies the mind of the reader was expected to sympathize, since by incidents so much beyond the bounds of his ordinary experience, his wonder and interest ought at once to be excited. But gradually he became familiar with the land of fiction, and adventures of which he assimilated not with those of real life, but with each other. Let the distress of the hero or heroine be ever so great, the reader reposed an imperturbable confidence in the talents of the author, who, as he had plunged them into distress, would in his own good time, and when things, as Tony Lumpkin says, were in a concatenation accordingly, bring his favourites out of all their troubles. Mr. Crabbe has expressed his own and our feelings excellently on this subject.

> For should we grant these beauties all endure
> Severest pangs, they've still the speediest cure;
> Before one charm be wither'd from the face,
> Except the bloom which shall again have place,

In wedlock ends each wish, in triumph all disgrace.
And life to come, we fairly may suppose,
One light bright contrast to these wild dark woes.

In short, the author of novels was, in former times, expected to tread pretty much in the limits between the concentric circles of probability and possibility; and as he was not permitted to transgress the latter, his narrative, to make amends, almost always went beyond the bounds of the former. Now, although it may be urged that the vicissitudes of human life have occasionally led an individual through as many scenes of singular fortune as are represented in the most extravagant of these fictions, still the causes and personages acting on these changes have varied with the progress of the adventurer's fortune, and do not present that combined plot, (the object of every skilful novelist,) in which all the more interesting individuals of the dramatis personæ have their appropriate share in the action and in bringing about the catastrophe. Here, even more than in its various and violent changes of fortune, rests the improbability of the novel. The life of man rolls forth like a stream from the fountain, or it spreads out into tranquillity like a placid or stagnant lake. In the latter case, the individual grows old among the characters with whom he was born, and is contemporary,—shares precisely the sort of weal and woe to which his birth destined him,— moves in the same circle,—and, allowing for the change of seasons, is influenced by, and influences the same class of persons by which he was originally surrounded. The man of mark and of adventure, on the contrary, resembles, in the course of his life, the river whose mid-current and discharge into the ocean are widely removed from each other, as well as from the rocks and wild flowers which its fountains first reflected; violent changes of time, of place, and of circumstances, hurry him forward from one scene to another, and his adventures will usually be found only connected with each other because they have happened to the same individual. Such a history resembles an ingenious, fictitious narrative, exactly in the degree in which an old dramatic chronicle of the life and death of some distinguished character, where all the various agents appear and disappear as in the page of history, approaches a regular drama, in which every person introduced plays an appropriate part, and every point of the action tends to one common catastrophe.

We return to the second broad line of distinction between the novel, as formerly composed, and real life,—the difference, namely, of the sentiments. The novelist professed to give an imitation of nature, but it was, as the French say, *la belle nature*. Human beings, indeed, were presented, but in the most sentimental mood, and with minds purified by a sensibility which often verged on extravagance. In the serious class of novels, the hero was usually

A knight of love, who never broke a vow.

And although, in those of a more humorous cast, he was permitted a license, borrowed either from real life or from the libertinism of the drama, still a distinction was demanded even from Peregrine Pickle, or Tom Jones; and the hero, in every folly of which he might be guilty, was studiously vindicated from the charge of infidelity of the heart. The heroine was, of course, still more immaculate; and to have conferred her affections upon any other than the lover to whom the reader had destined her from their first meeting, would have been a crime against sentiment which no author, of moderate prudence, would have hazarded, under the old *régime*.

Here, therefore, we have two essential and important circumstances, in which the earlier novels differed from those now in fashion, and were more nearly assimilated to the old romances. And there can be no doubt that, by the studied involution and extrication of the story, by the combination of incidents new, striking and wonderful beyond the course of ordinary life, the former authors opened that obvious and strong sense of interest which arises from curiosity; as by the pure, elevated, and romantic cast of the sentiment, they conciliated those better propensities of our nature which loves to contemplate the picture of virtue, even when confessedly unable to imitate its excellences.

But strong and powerful as these sources of emotion and interest may be, they are, like all others, capable of being exhausted by habit. The imitators who rushed in crowds upon each path in which the great masters of the art had successively led the way, produced upon the public mind the usual effect of satiety. The first writer of a new class is, as it were, placed on a pinnacle of excellence, to which, at the earliest glance of a surprized admirer, his ascent seems little less than miraculous. Time and imitation speedily diminish the wonder, and each successive attempt establishes a kind of progressive scale of ascent between the lately deified author, and the reader, who had deemed his excellence inaccessible. The stupidity, the mediocrity, the merit of his imitators, are alike fatal to the first inventor, by shewing how possible it is to exaggerate his faults and to come within a certain point of his beauties.

Materials also (and the man of genius as well as his wretched imitator must work with the same) become stale and familiar. Social life, in our civilized days, affords few instances capable of being painted in the strong dark colours which excite surprize and horror; and robbers, smugglers, bailiffs, caverns, dungeons, and mad-houses, have been all introduced until they ceased to interest. And thus in the novel, as in every style of composition which appeals to the public taste, the more rich and easily worked mines being exhausted, the adventurous author must, if he is desirous of success, have recourse to those which were disdained by his predecessors as unproductive, or avoided as only capable of being turned to profit by great skill and labour.

Accordingly a style of novel has arisen, within the last fifteen or twenty years, differing from the former in the points upon which the interest hinges; neither alarming our credulity nor amusing our imagination by wild variety of incident, or by those pictures of romantic affection and sensibility, which were formerly as certain attributes of fictitious characters as they are of rare occurrence among those who actually live and die. The substitute for these excitements, which had lost much of their poignancy by the repeated and injudicious use of them, was the art of copying from nature as she really exists in the common walks of life, and presenting to the reader, instead of the splendid scenes of an imaginary world, a correct and striking representation of that which is daily taking place around him.

In adventuring upon this task, the author makes obvious sacrifices, and encounters peculiar difficulty. He who paints from *le beau idéal*, if his scenes and sentiments are striking and interesting, is in a great measure exempted from the difficult task of reconciling them with the ordinary probabilities of life: but he who paints a scene of common occurrence, places his composition within that extensive range of criticism which general experience offers to every reader. The resemblance of a statue of Hercules we must take on the artist's judgment; but every one can criticize that which is presented as the portrait of a friend, or neighbour. Something more than a mere sign-post likeness is also demanded. The portrait must have spirit and character, as well as resemblance; and being deprived of all that, according to Bayes, goes 'to elevate and surprize,' it must make amends by displaying depth of knowledge and dexterity of execution. We, therefore, bestow no mean compliment upon the author of *Emma*, when we say that, keeping close to common incidents, and to such characters as occupy the ordinary walks of life, she has produced sketches of such spirit and originality, that we never miss the excitation which depends upon a narrative of uncommon events, arising from the consideration of minds, manners, and sentiments, greatly above our own. In this class she stands almost alone; for the scenes of Miss Edgeworth are laid in higher life, varied by more romantic incident, and by her remarkable power of embodying and illustrating national character. But the author of *Emma* confines herself chiefly to the middling classes of society; her most distinguished characters do not rise greatly above well-bred country gentlemen and ladies; and those which are sketched with most originality and precision, belong to a class rather below that standard. The narrative of all her novels is composed of such common occurrences as may have fallen under the observation of most folks; and her dramatis personæ conduct themselves upon the motives and principles which the readers may recognize as ruling their own and that of most of their acquaintances. The kind of moral, also, which these novels inculcate, applies equally to the paths of common life, as will best appear from a short notice of the author's former works, with a more full abstract of that which we at present have under consideration.

Sense and Sensibility, the first of these compositions, contains the history of two sisters. The elder, a young lady of prudence and regulated feelings, becomes gradually attached to a man of an excellent heart and limited talents, who happens unfortunately to be fettered by a rash and ill-assorted engagement. In the younger sister, the influence of sensibility and imagination predominates; and she, as was to be expected, also falls in love, but with more unbridled and wilful passion. Her lover, gifted with all the qualities of exterior polish and vivacity, proves faithless, and marries a woman of large fortune. The interest and merit of the piece depend altogether upon the behaviour of the elder sister, while obliged at once to sustain her own disappointment with fortitude, and to support her sister, who abandons herself, with unsuppressed feelings, to the indulgence of grief. The marriage of the unworthy rival at length relieves her own lover from his imprudent engagement, while her sister, turned wise by precept, example, and experience, transfers her affection to a very respectable and somewhat too serious admirer, who had nourished an unsuccessful passion through the three volumes.

In *Pride and Prejudice* the author presents us with a family of young women, bred up under a foolish and vulgar mother, and a father whose good abilities lay hid under such a load of indolence and insensibility, that he had become contented to make the foibles and follies of his wife and daughters the subject of dry and humorous sarcasm, rather than of admonition, or restraint. This is one of the portraits from ordinary life which shews our author's talents in a very strong point of view. A friend of ours, whom the author never saw or heard of, was at once recognized by his own family as the original of Mr. Bennet, and we do not know if he has yet got rid of the nickname. A Mr. Collins, too, a formal, conceited, yet servile young sprig of divinity, is drawn with the same force and precision. The story of the piece consists chiefly in the fates of the second sister, to whom a man of high birth, large fortune, but haughty and reserved manners, becomes attached, in spite of the discredit thrown upon the object of his affection by the vulgarity and ill-conduct of her relations. The lady, on the contrary, hurt at the contempt of her connections, which the lover does not even attempt to suppress, and prejudiced against him on other accounts, refuses the hand which he ungraciously offers, and does not perceive that she has done a foolish thing until she accidentally visits a very handsome seat and grounds belonging to her admirer. They chance to meet exactly as her prudence had begun to subdue her prejudice; and after some essential services rendered to her family, the lover becomes encouraged to renew his addresses, and the novel ends happily.

Emma has even less story than either of the preceding novels. Miss Emma Woodhouse, from whom the book takes its name, is the daughter of a gentleman of wealth and consequence residing at his seat in the immediate vicinage of a country village called Highbury. The father, a good-natured, silly valetudinary, abandons the management of his household to Emma, he himself being only occupied by his summer and winter walk, his apothecary, his gruel, and his whist table. The latter is supplied from the neighbouring village of Highbury with precisely the sort of persons who occupy the vacant corners of a regular whist table, when a village is in the neighbourhood, and better cannot be found within the family. We have the smiling and courteous vicar, who nourishes the ambitious hope of obtaining Miss Woodhouse's hand. We have Mrs. Bates, the wife of a former rector, past every thing but tea and whist; her daughter, Miss Bates, a good-natured, vulgar, and foolish old maid; Mr. Weston, a gentleman of a frank disposition and moderate fortune, in the vicinity, and his wife an amiable and accomplished person, who had been Emma's governess, and is devotedly attached to her. Amongst all these personages, Miss Woodhouse walks forth, the princess paramount, superior to all her companions in wit, beauty, fortune, and accomplishments, doated upon by her father and the Westons, admired, and almost worshipped by the more humble companions of the whist table. The object of most young ladies is, or at least is usually supposed to be, a desirable connection in marriage. But Emma Woodhouse, either anticipating the taste of a later period of life, or, like a good sovereign, preferring the weal of her subjects of Highbury to her own private interest, sets generously about making matches for her friends without thinking of matrimony on her own account. We are informed that she had been eminently successful in the case of Mr. and Miss Weston; and when the novel commences she is exerting her influence in favour of Miss Harriet Smith, a boarding-school girl without family or fortune, very good humoured, very pretty, very silly, and, what suited Miss Woodhouse's purpose best of all, very much disposed to be married.

In these conjugal machinations Emma is frequently interrupted, not only by the cautions of her father, who had a particular objection to any body committing the rash act of matrimony, but also by the sturdy reproof and remonstrances of Mr. Knightley, the elder brother of her sister's husband, a sensible country gentleman of thirty-five, who had known Emma from her cradle, and was the only person who ventured to find fault with her. In spite, however, of his censure and warning, Emma lays a plan of marrying Harriet Smith to the vicar; and though she succeeds perfectly in diverting her simple friend's thoughts from an honest farmer who had made her a very suitable offer, and in flattering her into a passion for Mr. Elton, yet, on the other hand, that conceited divine totally mistakes the nature of the encouragement held out to him, and attributes the favour which he found in Miss Woodhouse's eyes to a lurking affection on her own part. This at length encourages him to a presumptuous declaration of his sentiments; upon receiving a repulse, he looks abroad elsewhere, and enriches the Highbury society by uniting himself to a dashing young woman with as many thousands as are usually called ten, and a corresponding quantity of presumption and ill breeding.

While Emma is thus vainly engaged in forging wedlock-fetters for others, her friends have views of the same kind upon her, in favour of a son of Mr. Weston by a former marriage, who bears the name, lives under the patronage, and is to inherit the fortune of a rich uncle. Unfortunately Mr. Frank Churchill had already settled his affections on Miss Jane Fairfax, a young lady of reduced fortune; but as this was a concealed affair, Emma, when Mr. Churchill first appears on the stage, has some thoughts of being in love with him herself; speedily, however, recovering from that dangerous propensity, she is disposed to confer him upon her deserted friend Harriet Smith. Harriet has, in the interim, fallen desperately in love with Mr. Knightley, the sturdy, advice-giving bachelor; and, as all the village supposes Frank Churchill and Emma to be attached to each other, there are cross purposes enough (were the novel of a more romantic cast) for cutting half the men's throats and breaking all the women's hearts. But at Highbury Cupid walks decorously, and with good discretion, bearing his torch under a lanthorn, instead of flourishing it around to set the house on fire. All these entanglements bring on only a train of mistakes and embarrassing situations, and dialogues at balls and parties of pleasure, in which the author displays her peculiar powers of humour and knowledge of human life. The plot is extricated with great simplicity. The aunt of Frank Churchill dies; his uncle, no longer under her baneful influence, consents to his marriage with Jane Fairfax. Mr. Knightley and Emma are led, by this unexpected incident, to discover that they had been in love with each other all along. Mr. Woodhouse's objections to the marriage of his daughter are overpowered by the fears of house-breakers, and the comfort which he hopes to derive from having a stout son-in-law resident in the family; and the facile affections of Harriet Smith are transferred, like a bank bill by indorsation, to her former suitor, the honest farmer, who had obtained a favourable opportunity of renewing his addresses. Such is the simple plan of a story which we peruse with pleasure, if not with deep interest, and which perhaps we might more willingly resume than one of those narratives where the attention is strongly riveted, during the first perusal, by the powerful excitement of curiosity.

The author's knowledge of the world, and the peculiar tact with which she presents characters that the reader cannot fail to recognize, reminds us something of the merits of the Flemish school of painting. The subjects are not often elegant, and certainly never grand; but they are finished up to nature, and with a precision which delights the reader. This is a merit which it is very difficult to illustrate by extracts, because it pervades the whole work, and is not to be comprehended from a single passage. The following is a dialogue between Mr. Woodhouse, and his elder daughter Isabella, who shares his anxiety about health, and has, like her father, a favourite apothecary. The reader must be informed that this lady, with her husband, a sensible, peremptory sort of person, had come to spend a week with her father.

[quotes ch. 12 'While they were thus' to 'to assist in praising'.]

Perhaps the reader may collect from the preceding specimen both the merits and faults of the author. The former consists much in the force of a narrative conducted with much neatness and point, and a quiet yet comic dialogue, in which the characters of the speakers evolve themselves with dramatic effect. The faults, on the contrary, arise from the minute detail which the author's plan comprehends. Characters of folly or simplicity, such as those of old Woodhouse and Miss Bates, are ridiculous when first presented, but if too often brought forward or too long dwelt upon, their prosing is apt to become as tiresome in fiction as in real society. Upon the whole, the turn of this author's novels bears the same relation to that of the sentimental and romantic cast, that cornfields and cottages and meadows bear to the highly adorned grounds of a show mansion, or the rugged sublimities of a mountain landscape. It is neither so captivating as the one, nor so grand as the other, but it affords to those who frequent it a pleasure nearly allied with the experience of their own social habits; and what is of some importance, the youthful wanderer may return from his promenade to the ordinary business of life, without any chance of having his head turned by the recollection of the scene through which he has been wandering.

One word, however, we must say in behalf of that once powerful divinity, Cupid, king of gods and men, who in these times of revolution, has been assailed, even in his own kingdom of romance, by the authors who were formerly his devoted priests. We are quite aware that there are few instances of first attachment being brought to a happy conclusion, and that it seldom can be so in a state of society so highly advanced as to render early marriages among the better class, acts, generally speaking, of imprudence. But the youth of this realm need not at present be taught the doctrine of selfishness. It is by no means their error to give the world or the good things of the world all for love; and before the authors of moral fiction couple Cupid indivisibly with calculating prudence, we would have them reflect, that they may sometimes lend their aid to substitute more mean, more sordid, and more selfish motives of conduct, for the romantic feelings which their predecessors perhaps fanned into too powerful a flame. Who is it, that in his youth has felt a virtuous attachment, however romantic or however unfortunate, but can trace back to its influence much that his character may possess of what is honourable, dignified, and disinterested? If he recollects hours wasted in unavailing hope, or saddened by doubt and disappointment; he may also dwell on many which have been snatched from folly or libertinism, and dedicated to studies which might render him worthy of the object of his affection, or pave the way perhaps to that distinction necessary to raise him to an equality with her. Even the habitual indulgence of feelings totally unconnected with ourself and our own immediate interest, softens, graces, and amends the human mind; and after the pain of disappointment is past, those who survive (and by good fortune those are the greater number) are neither less wise nor less worthy members of society for having felt, for a time, the influence of a passion which has been well qualified as the 'tenderest, noblest and best.'

9. Unsigned notice, *Literary Panorama*

June 1816, n.s. vi, 418

Emma presents the history of a young lady, who, after allowing her imagination to wander towards several gentlemen, and almost to mislead her affections, fixes them, at last, on the proper object. This we are persuaded, is no uncommon case. The story is not ill conceived; it is not romantic but domestic. To favour the lady, the gentlemen are rather unequal to what gentlemen should be.

10. Unsigned notice, *Monthly Review*

July 1816, lxxx, 320

If this novel can scarcely be termed a composition, because it contains but one ingredient, *that one* is, however, of sterling worth; being a strain of genuine natural humour, such as is seldom found conjointly with the complete purity of images and ideas which is here conspicuous. The character of Mr. Woodhouse, with his 'habits of gentle selfishness,' is admirably drawn, and the dialogue is easy and lively. The fair reader may also glean by the way some useful hints against forming romantic schemes, or indulging a spirit of patronage in defiance of sober reason; and the work will probably become a favourite with all those who seek for harmless amusement, rather than deep pathos or appalling horrors, in works of fiction.

11. Unsigned notice, *British Critic*

July 1816, n.s. vi, 96–98

Whoever is fond of an amusing, inoffensive and well principled novel, will be well pleased with the perusal of *Emma*. It rarely happens that in a production of this nature we have so little to find fault with.

In few novels is the unity of place preserved; we know not of one in which the author has sufficient art to give interest to the circle of a small village. The author of *Emma* never goes beyond the boundaries of two private families, but has contrived in a very interesting manner to detail their history, and to form out of so slender materials a very pleasing tale. The characters are well kept up to the end. The valetudinarian fathers, the chattering village belles, are all preserved to the life. Let us take the following scene.

[quotes ch. 21 ' "I hope every body" ' to ' "saw the letter; well" '.]

We are not the less inclined to speak well of this tale, because it does not dabble in religion; of fanatical novels and fanatical authoresses we are already sick.

12. Unsigned notice, *Gentleman's Magazine*

September 1816, lxxxvi, 248–9

Dulce est desipere in loco;[1] and a good Novel is now and then an agreeable relaxation from severer studies. Of this description was *Pride and Prejudice*; and from the entertainment which those volumes afforded us, we were desirous to peruse the present work; nor have our expectations been disappointed. If *Emma* has not the highly-drawn characters in superior life which are so interesting in *Pride and Prejudice*; it delineates with great accuracy the habits and the manners of a middle class of gentry; and of the inhabitants of a country village at one degree of rank and gentility beneath them. Every character throughout the work, from the heroine to the most subordinate, is a portrait which comes home to the heart and feelings of the Reader; who becomes familiarly acquainted with each of them, nor loses sight of a single individual till the completion of the work. The unities of time and place are well preserved; the language is chaste and correct; and if *Emma* be not allowed to rank in the very highest class of modern Novels, it certainly may claim at least a distinguished degree of eminence in that species of composition. It is amusing, if not instructive; and has no tendency to deteriorate the heart.

[1] 'It is pleasant to indulge in trifles' (Horace, *Odes*, iv, 12, 28).

13. Henry Austen: The Biographical Notice
1817

The *Biographical Notice of the Author* prefaced the four-volume
set *Northanger Abbey and Persuasion* (1818); a slightly altered
version, entitled 'Memoir of Miss Austen', dated October 1832,
prefaced Bentley's edition of *Sense and Sensibility* (1833).

Henry Thomas Austen (1771–1850), soldier, banker and clergyman, the fourth son of George Austen, was Jane Austen's favourite
brother and acted for her in publishing matters. While at Oxford
he edited, with his brother James, *The Loiterer*, a periodical which
ran for sixty numbers between January 1789 and March 1790,
and to which Jane Austen may have contributed. Next to
Cassandra Austen, Henry was the member of the family who
knew most about his sister's writing career. For the first time, these
details were made public.

The following pages are the production of a pen which has already
contributed in no small degree to the entertainment of the public.
And when the public, which has not been insensible to the merits of
Sense and Sensibility, *Pride and Prejudice*, *Mansfield Park*, and *Emma*, shall
be informed that the hand which guided that pen is now mouldering
in the grave, perhaps a brief account of Jane Austen will be read with
a kindlier sentiment than simple curiosity.

Short and easy will be the task of the mere biographer. A life of
usefulness, literature, and religion, was not by any means a life of event.
To those who lament their irreparable loss, it is consolatory to think
that, as she never deserved disapprobation, so, in the circle of her family
and friends, she never met reproof; that her wishes were not only
reasonable, but gratified; and that to the little disappointments incidental to human life was never added, even for a moment, an abatement
of goodwill from any who knew her.

Jane Austen was born on the 16th of December, 1775, at Steventon,
in the county of Hants. Her father was Rector of that parish upwards
of forty years. There he resided, in the conscientious and unassisted

discharge of his ministerial duties, until he was turned of seventy years. Then he retired with his wife, our authoress, and her sister, to Bath, for the remainder of his life, a period of about four years. Being not only a profound scholar, but possessing a most exquisite taste in every species of literature, it is not wonderful that his daughter Jane should, at a very early age, have become sensible to the charms of style, and enthusiastic in the cultivation of her own language. On the death of her father she removed, with her mother and sister, for a short time, to Southampton, and finally, in 1809, to the pleasant village of Chawton, in the same county. From this place she sent into the world those novels, which by many have been placed on the same shelf as the works of a D'Arblay and an Edgeworth. Some of these novels had been the gradual performances of her previous life. For though in composition she was equally rapid and correct, yet an invincible distrust of her own judgement induced her to withhold her works from the public, till time and many perusals had satisfied her that the charm of recent composition was dissolved. The natural constitution, the regular habits, the quiet and happy occupations of our authoress, seemed to promise a long succession of amusement to the public, and a gradual increase of reputation to herself. But the symptoms of a decay, deep and incurable, began to shew themselves in the commencement of 1816. Her decline was at first deceitfully slow; and until the spring of this present year, those who knew their happiness to be involved in her existence could not endure to despair. But in the month of May, 1817, it was found advisable that she should be removed to Winchester for the benefit of constant medical aid, which none even then dared to hope would be permanently beneficial. She supported, during two months, all the varying pain, irksomeness, and tedium, attendant on decaying nature, with more than resignation, with a truly elastic cheerfulness. She retained her faculties, her memory, her fancy, her temper, and her affections, warm, clear, and unimpaired, to the last. Neither her love of God, nor of her fellow creatures flagged for a moment. She made a point of receiving the sacrament before excessive bodily weakness might have rendered her perception unequal to her wishes. She wrote whilst she could hold a pen, and with a pencil when a pen was become too laborious. The day preceding her death she composed some stanzas replete with fancy and vigour. Her last voluntary speech conveyed thanks to her medical attendant; and to the final question asked of her, purporting to know her wants, she replied, 'I want nothing but death.'

She expired shortly after, on Friday the 18th of July, 1817, in the arms of her sister, who, as well as the relator of these events, feels too surely that they shall never look upon her like again.

Jane Austen was buried on the 24th of July, 1817, in the cathedral church of Winchester, which, in the whole catalogue of its mighty dead, does not contain the ashes of a brighter genius or a sincerer Christian.

Of personal attractions she possessed a considerable share. Her stature was that of true elegance. It could not have been increased without exceeding the middle height. Her carriage and deportment were quiet, yet graceful. Her features were separately good. Their assemblage produced an unrivalled expression of that cheerfulness, sensibility, and benevolence, which were her real characteristics. Her complexion was of the finest texture. It might with truth be said, that her eloquent blood spoke through her modest cheek. Her voice was extremely sweet. She delivered herself with fluency and precision. Indeed she was formed for elegant and rational society, excelling in conversation as much as in composition. In the present age it is hazardous to mention accomplishments. Our authoress would, probably, have been inferior to few in such acquirements, had she not been so superior to most in higher things. She had not only an excellent taste for drawing, but, in her earlier days, evinced great power of hand in the management of the pencil. Her own musical attainments she held very cheap. Twenty years ago they would have been thought more of, and twenty years hence many a parent will expect their daughters to be applauded for meaner performances. She was fond of dancing, and excelled in it. It remains now to add a few observations on that which her friends deemed more important, on those endowments which sweetened every hour of their lives.

If there be an opinion current in the world, that perfect placidity of temper is not reconcileable to the most lively imagination, and the keenest relish for wit, such an opinion will be rejected for ever by those who have had the happiness of knowing the authoress of the following works. Though the frailties, foibles, and follies of others could not escape her immediate detection, yet even on their vices did she never trust herself to comment with unkindness. The affectation of candour is not uncommon; but she had no affectation. Faultless herself, as nearly as human nature can be, she always sought, in the faults of others, something to excuse, to forgive or forget. Where extenuation was impossible, she had a sure refuge in silence. She never uttered either a hasty, a silly, or a severe expression. In short, her temper was as polished as her wit.

Nor were her manners inferior to her temper. They were of the happiest kind. No one could be often in her company without feeling a strong desire of obtaining her friendship, and cherishing a hope of having obtained it. She was tranquil without reserve or stiffness; and communicative without intrusion or self-sufficiency. She became an authoress entirely from taste and inclination. Neither the hope of fame nor profit mixed with her early motives. Most of her works, as before observed, were composed many years previous to their publication. It was with extreme difficulty that her friends, whose partiality she suspected whilst she honoured their judgement, could prevail on her to publish her first work. Nay, so persuaded was she that its sale would not repay the expense of publication, that she actually made a reserve from her very moderate income to meet the expected loss. She could scarcely believe what she termed her great good fortune when *Sense and Sensibility* produced a clear profit of about £150. Few so gifted were so truly unpretending. She regarded the above sum as a prodigious recompense for that which had cost her nothing. Her readers, perhaps, will wonder that such a work produced so little at a time when some authors have received more guineas than they have written lines. The works of our authoress, however, may live as long as those which have burst on the world with more éclat. But the public has not been unjust; and our authoress was far from thinking it so. Most gratifying to her was the applause which from time to time reached her ears from those who were competent to discriminate. Still, in spite of such applause, so much did she shrink from notoriety, that no accumulation of fame would have induced her, had she lived, to affix her name to any productions of her pen. In the bosom of her own family she talked of them freely, thankful for praise, open to remark, and submissive to criticism. But in public she turned away from any allusion to the character of an authoress. She read aloud with very great taste and effect. Her own works, probably, were never heard to so much advantage as from her own mouth; for she partook largely in all the best gifts of the comic muse. She was a warm and judicious admirer of landscape, both in nature and on canvass. At a very early age she was enamoured of Gilpin on the Picturesque; and she seldom changed her opinions either on books or men.

Her reading was very extensive in history and belles lettres; and her memory extremely tenacious. Her favourite moral writers were Johnson in prose, and Cowper in verse. It is difficult to say at what age she was not intimately acquainted with the merits and defects of the best essays and novels in the English language. Richardson's power of creating, and preserving the consistency of his characters, as particularly exemplified in *Sir Charles Grandison*, gratified the natural discrimination of her mind, whilst her taste secured her from the errors of his prolix style and tedious narrative. She did not rank any work of Fielding quite so high. Without the slightest affectation she recoiled from every thing gross. Neither nature, wit, nor humour, could make her amends for so very low a scale of morals.

Her power of inventing characters seems to have been intuitive, and almost unlimited. She drew from nature; but, whatever may have been surmised to the contrary, never from individuals.

The style of her familiar correspondence was in all respects the same as that of her novels. Every thing came finished from her pen; for on all subjects she had ideas as clear as her expressions were well chosen. It is not hazarding too much to say that she never dispatched a note or letter unworthy of publication.

One trait only remains to be touched on. It makes all others unimportant. She was thoroughly religious and devout; fearful of giving offence to God, and incapable of feeling it towards any fellow creature. On serious subjects she was well-instructed, both by reading and meditation, and her opinions accorded strictly with those of our Established Church.

London, Dec. 13, 1817

POSTSCRIPT

Since concluding the above remarks, the writer of them has been put in possession of some extracts from the private correspondence of the authoress. They are few and short; but are submitted to the public without apology, as being more truly descriptive of her temper, taste, feelings, and principles than any thing which the pen of a biographer can produce.

The first extract is a playful defence of herself from a mock charge of having pilfered the manuscripts of a young relation.

'What should I do, my dearest E. with your manly, vigorous sketches, so full of life and spirit? How could I possibly join them on to a little bit of ivory, two inches wide, on which I work with a brush so fine as to produce little effect after much labour?'[1]

[1] Letter of 16 December 1816, to James Edward Austen. This extract has been silently changed by Henry Austen; the correct version of these much-quoted lines is given in *Letters*, pp. 468–9.

The remaining extracts are from various parts of a letter written a few weeks before her death.[1]

'My attendant is encouraging, and talks of making me quite well. I live chiefly on the sofa, but am allowed to walk from one room to the other. I have been out once in a sedan-chair, and am to repeat it, and be promoted to a wheel-chair as the weather serves. On this subject I will only say further that my dearest sister, my tender, watchful, indefatigable nurse, has not been made ill by her exertions. As to what I owe to her, and to the anxious affection of all my beloved family on this occasion, I can only cry over it, and pray to God to bless them more and more.'

She next touches with just and gentle animadversion on a subject of domestic disappointment. Of this the particulars do not concern the public. Yet in justice to her characteristic sweetness and resignation, the concluding observation of our authoress thereon must not be suppressed.

'But I am getting too near complaint. It has been the appointment of God, however secondary causes may have operated.'

The following and final extract will prove the facility with which she could correct every impatient thought, and turn from complaint to cheerfulness.

'You will find Captain —— a very respectable, well-meaning man, without much manner, his wife and sister all good humour and obligingness, and I hope (since the fashion allows it) with rather longer petticoats than last year.'

London, Dec. 20, 1817.

[1] The original of this letter has not survived, and the version, obviously a severely edited text, given here is the only known reading. Chapman places it at the end of May 1817 (*Letters*, p. 497).

NORTHANGER ABBEY
and PERSUASION

December 1817

14. Unsigned review, *British Critic*[1]

March 1818, n.s. ix, 293–301

In order to impart some degree of variety to our journal, and select matter suited to all tastes, we have generally made it a point to notice one or two of the better sort of novels; but, did our fair readers know, what a vast quantity of useful spirits and patience, we are for this purpose generally forced to exhaust, before we are able to stumble upon any thing that we can at all recommend to their approbation; what innumerable letters we are compelled to read from the witty Lady Harriet F—— to the pathetic Miss Lucretia G——; through what an endless series of gloomy caverns, long and winding passages, secret trap doors, we are forced to pass—now in the Inquisition, now in a gay modern assembly—this moment in the east wing of an old castle in the Pyrenees; in the next, among banditti; and so on, through all the changes and chances of this transitory life, acquiescing in every thing, with an imperturbable confidence, that he or she, who has brought us into all these difficulties, will, in their own good time, release us from them: sure we are, that even the most resolute foes to all the solid parts of learning, will agree with us in admitting, that the sound and orthodox divinity with which so considerable a portion of our pages is usually filled, and of which we have so often had the mortification to hear many sensible young ladies complain, is nevertheless very far from being quite so dull and exhausting, as are their own favourite studies, when indiscriminately pursued. In return for this concession on their part, we on our's will frankly allow, that a good novel, such, for example, as that at present before us, is, perhaps, among the most fascinating

[1] See No. 45 (p. 266) for another review.

79

productions of modern literature, though we cannot say, that it is quite
so improving as some others.

Northanger Abbey and *Persuasion*, are the productions of a pen, from
which our readers have already received several admired productions;
and it is with most unfeigned regret, that we are forced to add, they
will be the last.

[provides a biographical sketch derived and quoting from the *Biographical Notice* (No. 13).]

With respect to the talents of Jane Austen, they need no other voucher,
than the works which she has left behind her; which in some of the
best qualities of the best sort of novels, display a degree of excellence
that has not been often surpassed. In imagination, of all kinds, she
appears to have been extremely deficient; not only her stories are utterly
and entirely devoid of invention, but her characters, her incidents, her
sentiments, are obviously all drawn exclusively from experience. The
sentiments which she puts into the mouths of her actors, are the sentiments, which we are every day in the habit of hearing; and as to her
actors themselves, we are persuaded that fancy, strictly so called, has had
much less to do with them, than with the characters of Julius Cæsar,
Hannibal, or Alexander, as represented to us by historians. At description she seldom aims; at that vivid and poetical sort of description,
which we have of late been accustomed to, (in the novels of a celebrated
anonymous writer) never; she seems to have no other object in view,
than simply to paint some of those scenes which she has herself seen,
and which every one, indeed, may witness daily. Not only her characters
are all of them belonging to the middle size, and with a tendency, in
fact, rather to fall below, than to rise above the common standard, but
even the incidents of her novels, are of the same description. Her heroes
and heroines, make love and are married, just as her readers make love,
and were or will be, married; no unexpected ill fortune occurs to
prevent, nor any unexpected good fortune, to bring about the events
on which her novels hinge. She seems to be describing such people as
meet together every night, in every respectable house in London; and
to relate such incidents as have probably happened, one time or other,
to half the families in the United Kingdom. And yet, by a singular good
judgment, almost every individual represents a class; not a class of
humourists, or of any of the rarer specimens of our species, but one of
those classes to which we ourselves, and every acquaintance we have,
in all probability belong. The fidelity with which these are distinguished

is often admirable. It would have been impossible to discriminate the characters of the common-place people, whom she employs as the instruments of her novels, by any set and formal descriptions; for the greater part of them, are such as we generally describe by saying that they are persons of 'no characters at all.' Accordingly our authoress gives no definitions; but she makes her *dramatis personæ* talk; and the sentiments which she places in their mouths, the little phrases which she makes them use, strike so familiarly upon our memory as soon as we hear them repeated, that we instantly recognize among some of our acquaintance, the sort of persons she intends to signify, as accurately as if we had heard their voices. This is the forte of our authoress; as soon as ever she leaves the shore of her own experience, and attempts to delineate fancy characters, or such as she may perhaps have often heard of, but possibly never seen, she falls at once to the level of mere ordinary novellists. Her merit consists altogether in her remarkable talent for observation; no ridiculous phrase, no affected sentiment, no foolish pretension seems to escape her notice. It is scarcely possible to read her novels, without meeting with some of one's own absurdities reflected back upon one's conscience; and this, just in the light in which they ought to appear. For in recording the customs and manners of commonplace people in the commonplace intercourse of life, our authoress never dips her pen in satire; the follies which she holds up to us, are, for the most part, mere follies, or else natural imperfections; and she treats them, as such, with good-humoured pleasantry; mimicking them so exactly, that we always laugh at the ridiculous truth of the imitation, but without ever being incited to indulge in feelings, that might tend to render us ill-natured, and intolerant in society. This is the result of that good sense which seems ever to keep complete possession over all the other qualities of the mind of our authoress; she sees every thing just as it is; even her want of imagination (which is the principal defect of her writings) is useful to her in this respect, that it enables her to keep clear of all exaggeration, in a mode of writing where the least exaggeration would be fatal; for if the people and the scenes which she has chosen, as the subjects of her composition, be not painted with perfect truth, with exact and striking resemblance, the whole effect ceases; her characters have no kind of merit in themselves, and whatever interest they excite in the mind of the reader, results almost entirely, from the unaccountable pleasure, which, by a peculiarity in our nature, we derive from a simple imitation of any object, without any reference to the abstract value or importance of the object itself. This fact is notorious in painting;

and the novels of Miss Austen alone, would be sufficient to prove, were proof required, that the same is true in the department of literature, which she has adorned. For our readers will perceive (from the instance which we are now about to present, in the case of the novels before us,) that be their merit what it may, it is not founded upon the interest of a narrative. In fact, so little narrative is there in either of the two novels of which the publication before us consists, that it is difficult to give any thing like an abstract of their contents. *Northanger Abbey*, which is the name of the first novel, is simply, the history of a young girl, the daughter of a country clergyman of respectability, educated at home, under the care of her parents; good kind of people, who taught their large family all that it was necessary for them to know, without apparently troubling themselves about accomplishments in learning of any kind, beyond what our fathers and mothers were instructed in. Our heroine is just such a person, as an education under such circumstances, would lead us to expect; with respect to the hero of the tale, (for every heroine must have a hero) that which fortunately threw one in the way of Catherine, was a journey to Bath which she happily made, in company with the lady of the manor, who was ordered to that place of fashionable resort, for the benefit of her health. The first evening of Catherine's acquaintance with the gaiety of the Bath balls, was unpromising, from the circumstance that neither she, nor Mrs. Allen, her chaperon, had any knowledge of a single individual in the room; and the manner in which our authoress paints the effects of this circumstance upon the feelings and conversation of both, is sufficiently entertaining; but our heroine's second visit, was more favourable; for she was then introduced to a young clergyman, who is the other wheel upon which the interest of the narrative is made to run. The young clergyman's name was Tilney.

The description of our heroine's residence at Bath, is chiefly taken up with an account of her intimacy with a family of the name of Thorpe, consisting of a foolish mother, a foolish son, and four or five foolish daughters; the eldest of whom is a fine handsome girl, thinking of nothing but finery and flirting, and an exact representation of that large class of young women, in the form they assume among the gayer part of the middling ranks of society; for flirts, like all other parts of the animal kingdom, may be divided into two or three species. The character is pourtrayed with admirable spirit and humour; but the impression conveyed by it, is the result of so many touches, that it would be difficult to place it before our readers by means of extracts.

During the time of our heroine's intimacy with this family, the acquaintance with Mr. Tilney goes on; he proves to be the son of a General Tilney, a proud rich man; but who, in consequence of mis-information respecting the circumstances and family of Catherine, acquiesces in Miss Tilney's request of inviting Catherine to pass a few weeks with them, at their family seat of Northanger Abbey. This visit forms the next and only remaining incident in the novel; the result of it was the marriage of Catherine with the son. The circumstance which principally renders the history of our heroine's residence at Northanger Abbey amusing, arises from the mistakes which she makes, in consequence of her imagination, (which had just come fresh from the *Mysteries of Udolpho*,) leading her to anticipate, that the Abbey which she was on the point of adorning by her presence, was to be of the same class and character, as those which Mrs. Radcliffe paints. On her arrival, she was, as may be supposed, a little disappointed, by the unexpected elegance, convenience, and other advantages of General Tilney's abode; but her prepossession was incurable.

[quotes ch. 20 'An abbey!' to 'very distressing', and ch. 6 'The night was stormy' to ' "to alarm one." ']

Catherine, in a few days, was forced to resign all her hopes of dis-covering subterraneous passages, mysterious pictures, or old parch-ments; but, however, she still hoped to be able to detect a hidden secret, in the instance of the General, who having been an unkind husband to his late wife, and being, moreover, of a haughty and supercilious temper, she naturally concluded must have the weight of his wife's untimely end upon his conscience. A thousand little circumstances combined to give strength to her suspicions. But we have no room for extracts; if our readers wish to be entertained with the whole history of our heroine's mistakes in this way, we can safely recommend the work to their perusal. *Northanger Abbey*, is one of the very best of Miss Austen's productions, and will every way repay the time and trouble of perusing it. Some of the incidents in it are rather improbable, and the character of General Tilney seems to have been drawn from imagination, for it is not a very probable character, and is not pourtrayed with our authoress's usual taste and judgment. There is also a considerable want of delicacy in all the circumstances of Catherine's visit to the Abbey; but it is useless to point them out; the interest of the novel, is so little founded upon the ingenuity or probability of the story, that any criticism upon the management of it, falls with no weight upon that which constitutes its appropriate praise, considered as a literary product. With respect to the second of the novels, which the present publication contains, it will be necessary to say but little. It is in every respect a much less fortunate performance than that which we have just been considering. It is manifestly the work of the same mind, and contains parts of very great merit; among them, however, we certainly should not number its *moral*, which seems to be, that young people should always marry according to their own inclinations and upon their own judgment; for that if in consequence of listening to grave counsels, they defer their marriage, till they have wherewith to live upon, they will be laying the foundation for years of misery, such as only the heroes and heroines of novels can reasonably hope ever to see the end of.

15. Henry Crabb Robinson on Jane Austen
1819, 1822, 1839, 1842

Henry Crabb Robinson on Books and their Writers (1938), ed. E. J. Morley.

Robinson (1775–1867) was a voracious reader, a cultivator of literary friendships and an obsessional diarist and recorder.

(a) Extract from diary entry for 12 January 1819: 'I sat up till two, as I did last night, to finish *Pride and Prejudice*. This novel I consider as one of the most excellent of the works of our female novelists. Its merits lie in the characters, and in the perfectly colloquial style of the dialogue. Mrs. Bennet, the foolish mother, who cannot conceal her projects to get rid of her daughters, is capitally drawn. There is a thick-headed servile parson, also a masterly sketch. His stupid letters and her ridiculous speeches are as delightful as wit. The two daughters are well contrasted —the gentle and candid Jane and the lively but prejudiced Elizabeth, are both good portraits, and the development of the passion between Elizabeth and the proud Darcy, who at first hate each other, is executed with skill and effect.' (i, 227.)

(b) Extract from letter, 1 February 1819, to Mrs. William Pattisson: 'During my stay at Bury and on the Sessions journey I read a novel which pleased me very much indeed. If you have not read it I would recommend it to you confidently—*Pride and Prejudice*. The merit lies in the perfect truth of the painting. The dialogue is equisitely in character and the characters, tho' not ideal, are charming. The women especially are drawn after the life and Mrs. Bennet is a very jewel . . . Mr. Collins too, the sneaking and servile parson, is quite a masterpiece. The heroines (for there are a brace of them) are as natural as beauties can be and as beautiful as any successful portrait can be.' (iii, 851.)

(c) Extract from diary entry for 20 April 1822: 'In the evening read the last volume of *Emma*, a novel evincing great good sense, and an acute observation of human life, but it is not interesting. One cares little for Harriet, the kind-hearted girl who falls in love with three men in a year, and yet hers is the best conceived character after all. Emma, the heroine, is little more than a clever woman who does foolish things— makes mistakes for others, and is at last caught unawares herself. We hear rather too much about fools: the kind-hearted but weak father, the silly chattering Miss Bates, who gabbles in the style of polite conversation, and the vulgar impertinence of the Eltons.' (i, 282.)

It is instructive to compare these views with Robinson's comments of twenty years later.

(d) Extracts from diary entries for 13, 22 September 1839: 'I was reading to-day and I have since finished Miss Martineau's *Deerbrook*, a capital novel though it is too full of preaching. It is inferior in execution to Miss Austen's novels in the development of common characters, but is superior in the higher parts.'

'I was reading yesterday and to-day *Sense and Sensibility*, which I resumed at the second volume. The last volume greatly improves on the first, but I still think it one of the poorest of Miss Austen's novels— that is, inferior to *Mansfield Park* and *Pride and Prejudice*, which is all I have read.' (ii, 576.)

(e) Extract from diary entry for 23 September 1842. Robinson had begun *Persuasion* the previous evening: 'I went on with *Persuasion*, finished it, began *Northanger Abbey*, which I have now finished. These two novels have sadly reduced my estimation of Miss Austen. They are little more than galleries of disagreeables and the would-be heroes and heroines are scarcely out of the class of insignificants. Yet I ought to be suspicious perhaps of my own declining judgment.' (ii, 625.)

16. Whately on Jane Austen

1821

Unsigned review of *Northanger Abbey* and *Persuasion*, *Quarterly Review* (January 1821), xxiv, 352–76.

Richard Whately (1787–1863), Archbishop of Dublin, was an experienced reviewer and writer, although this is his only known extensive piece of literary criticism. It takes its point of departure from Scott (No. 8), beside which it ranks as the most important early nineteenth-century statement on Jane Austen (see Introduction, pp. 19–20).

The times seem to be past when an apology was requisite from reviewers for condescending to notice a novel; when they felt themselves bound in dignity to deprecate the suspicion of paying much regard to such trifles, and pleaded the necessity of occasionally stooping to humour the taste of their fair readers. The delights of fiction, if not more keenly or more generally relished, are at least more readily acknowledged by men of sense and taste; and we have lived to hear the merits of the best of this class of writings earnestly discussed by some of the ablest scholars and soundest reasoners of the present day.

We are inclined to attribute this change, not so much to an alteration in the public taste, as in the character of the productions in question. Novels may not, perhaps, display more genius now than formerly, but they contain more solid sense; they may not afford higher gratification, but it is of a nature which men are less disposed to be ashamed of avowing. We remarked, in a former Number, in reviewing a work of the author now before us, that 'a new style of novel has arisen, within the last fifteen or twenty years, differing from the former in the points upon which the interest hinges; neither alarming our credulity nor amusing our imagination by wild variety of incident, or by those pictures of romantic affection and sensibility, which were formerly as certain attributes of fictitious characters as they are of rare occurrence among those who actually live and die. The substitute for these excitements, which had lost much of their poignancy by the repeated and injudicious use of them, was the art of copying from nature as she really exists in the common walks of life, and presenting to the reader, instead of the splendid scenes of an imaginary world, a correct and striking representation of that which is daily taking place around him.'

Now, though the origin of this new school of fiction may probably be traced, as we there suggested, to the exhaustion of the mines from which materials for entertainment had been hitherto extracted, and the necessity of gratifying the natural craving of the reader for variety, by striking into an untrodden path; the consequences resulting from this change have been far greater than the mere supply of this demand. When this Flemish painting, as it were, is introduced—this accurate and unexaggerated delineation of events and characters—it necessarily follows, that a novel, which makes good its pretensions of giving a perfectly correct picture of common life, becomes a far more *instructive* work than one of equal or superior merit of the other class; it guides the judgment, and supplies a kind of artificial experience. It is a remark of the great father of criticism, that poetry (i.e. narrative, and dramatic poetry) is of a more philosophical character than history; inasmuch as the latter details what has actually happened, of which many parts may chance to be exceptions to the general rules of probability, and consequently illustrate no general principles; whereas the former shews us what must naturally, or would probably, happen under given circumstances; and thus displays to us a comprehensive view of human nature, and furnishes general rules of practical wisdom. It is evident, that this will apply only to such fictions as are quite *perfect* in respect of the probability of their story; and that he, therefore, who resorts to the fabulist rather than the historian, for instruction in human character and conduct, must throw himself entirely on the judgment and skill of his teacher, and give him credit for talents much more rare than the accuracy and veracity which are the chief requisites in history. We fear, therefore, that the exultation which we can conceive some of our gentle readers to feel, at having Aristotle's warrant for (what probably they had never dreamed of) the *philosophical character* of their studies, must, in practice, be somewhat qualified, by those sundry little violations of probability which are to be met with in most novels; and which so far lower their value, as models of real life, that a person who had no other preparation for the world than is afforded by them, would form, probably, a less accurate idea of things as they are, than he would of a lion from studying merely the representations on China tea-pots.

Accordingly, a heavy complaint has long lain against works of fiction, as giving a false picture of what they profess to imitate, and disqualifying their readers for the ordinary scenes and everyday duties of life. And this charge applies, we apprehend, to the generality of what are strictly called novels, with even more justice than to romances. When all the characters and events are very far removed from what we see around us,—when, perhaps, even supernatural agents are introduced, the reader may indulge, indeed, in occasional day-dreams, but will be so little reminded of what he has been reading, by any thing that occurs in actual life, that though he may perhaps feel some disrelish for the tameness of the scene before him, compared with the fairy-land he has been visiting, yet at least his judgment will not be depraved, nor his expectations misled; he will not apprehend a meeting with Algerine banditti on English shores, nor regard the old woman who shews him about an antique country seat, as either an enchantress or the keeper of an imprisoned damsel. But it is otherwise with those fictions which differ from common life in little or nothing but the improbability of the occurrences: the reader is insensibly led to calculate upon some of those lucky incidents and opportune coincidences of which he has been so much accustomed to read, and which, it is undeniable, *may* take place in real life; and to feel a sort of confidence, that however romantic his conduct may be, and in whatever difficulties it may involve him, all will be sure to come right at last, as is invariably the case with the hero of a novel.

On the other hand, so far as these pernicious effects fail to be produced, so far does the example lose its influence, and the exercise of poetical justice is rendered vain. The reward of virtuous conduct being brought about by fortunate accidents, he who abstains (taught, perhaps, by bitter disappointments) from reckoning on such accidents, wants that encouragement to virtue, which alone has been held out to him. 'If I were *a man in a novel*,' we remember to have heard an ingenious friend observe, 'I should certainly act so and so, because I should be sure of being no loser by the most heroic self-devotion, and of ultimately succeeding in the most daring enterprises.'

It may be said, in answer, that these objections apply only to the *unskilful* novelist, who, from ignorance of the world, gives an unnatural representation of what he professes to delineate. This is partly true, and partly not; for there is a distinction to be made between the *unnatural* and the merely *improbable*: a fiction is unnatural when there is some assignable reason against the events taking place as described,—when men are represented as acting contrary to the character assigned them, or to human nature in general; as when a young lady of seventeen, brought up in ease, luxury and retirement, with no companions but the narrow-minded and illiterate, displays (as a heroine usually does) under the most trying circumstances, such wisdom, fortitude, and knowledge of the world, as the best instructors and the best examples can rarely produce without the aid of more mature age and longer experience.— On the other hand, a fiction is still *improbable*, though *not unnatural*, when there is no reason to be assigned why things should not take place as represented, except that the *overbalance of chances is* against it; the hero meets, in his utmost distress, most opportunely, with the very person to whom he had formerly done a signal service, and who happens to communicate to him a piece of intelligence which sets all to rights. Why should he not meet him as well as any one else? all that can be said is, that there is no reason why he should. The infant who is saved from a wreck, and who afterwards becomes such a constellation of virtues and accomplishments, turns out to be no other than the nephew of the very gentleman, on whose estate the waves had cast him, and whose lovely daughter he had so long sighed for in vain: there is no reason to be given, except from the calculation of chances, why he should not have been thrown on one part of the coast as well as another. Nay, it would be nothing unnatural, though the most determined novel-reader would be shocked at its improbability, if all the hero's enemies, while they were conspiring his ruin, were to be struck dead together by a lucky flash of lightning: yet many denouements which *are* decidedly un-natural, are better tolerated than this would be. We shall, perhaps, best explain our meaning by examples, taken from a novel of great merit in many respects.[1] When Lord Glenthorn, in whom a most unfavour-able education has acted on a most unfavourable disposition, after a life of torpor, broken only by short sallies of forced exertion, on a sudden reverse of fortune, displays at once the most persevering diligence in the most repulsive studies, and in middle life, without any previous habits of exertion, any hope of early business, or the example of friends, or the stimulus of actual want, to urge him, oustrips every competitor, though every competitor has every advantage against him; this is unnatural.—When Lord Glenthorn, the instant he is stripped of his estates, meets, falls in love with, and is conditionally accepted by the very lady who is remotely intitled to those estates; when, the instant he has fulfilled the conditions of their marriage, the family of the person

---

[1] The work here cited is 'Ennui', one of the *Tales of Fashionable Life* (1809-12), by Maria Edgeworth.

possessed of the estates becomes extinct, and by the concurrence of circumstances, against ever one of which the chances were enormous, the hero is re-instated in all his old domains; this is merely improbable. The distinction which we have been pointing out may be plainly perceived in the events of real life; when any thing takes place of such a nature as we should call, in a fiction, merely improbable, because there are many chances against it, we call it a lucky or unlucky accident, a singular coincidence, something very extraordinary, odd, curious, &c.; whereas any thing which, in a fiction, would be called unnatural, when it actually occurs, (and such things do occur,) is still called unnatural, inexplicable, unaccountable, inconceivable, &c. epithets which are not applied to events that have merely the balance of chances against them.

Now, though an author who understands human nature is not likely to introduce into his fictions any thing that is unnatural, he will often have much that is improbable: he may place his personages, by the intervention of accident, in striking situations, and lead them through a course of extraordinary adventures; and yet, in the midst of all this, he will keep up the most perfect consistency of character, and make them act as it would be natural for men to act in such situations and circumstances. Fielding's novels are a good illustration of this: they display great knowledge of mankind; the characters are well preserved; the persons introduced all act as one would naturally expect they should, in the circumstances in which they are placed; but these circumstances are such as it is incalculably improbable should ever exist: several of the events, taken singly, are much against the chances of probability; but the combination of the whole in a connected series, is next to impossible. Even the romances which admit a mixture of supernatural agency, are not more unfit to prepare men for real life, than such novels as these; since one might just as reasonably calculate on the intervention of a fairy, as on the train of lucky chances which combine first to involve Tom Jones in his difficulties, and afterwards to extricate him. Perhaps, indeed, the supernatural fable is of the two not only (as we before remarked) the less mischievous in its moral effects, but also the more correct kind of composition in point of taste: the author lays down a kind of hypothesis of the existence of ghosts, witches, or fairies, and professes to describe what would take place under that hypothesis; the novelist, on the contrary, makes no demand of extraordinary machinery, but professes to describe what may actually take place, according to the existing laws of human affairs: if he therefore present us with a series of events quite unlike any which ever do take place, we have reason to complain that he has not made good his professions.

When, therefore, the generality, even of the most approved novels, were of this character, (to say nothing of the heavier charges brought, of inflaming the passions of young persons by warm descriptions, weakening their abhorrence of profligacy by exhibiting it in combination with the most engaging qualities, and presenting vice in all its allurements, while setting forth the triumphs of 'virtue rewarded') it is not to be wondered that the grave guardians of youth should have generally stigmatized the whole class, as 'serving only to fill young people's heads with romantic love-stories, and rendering them unfit to mind any thing else.' That this censure and caution should in many instances be indiscriminate, can surprize no one, who recollects how rare a quality discrimination is; and how much better it suits indolence, as well as ignorance, to lay down a rule, than to ascertain the exceptions to it: we are acquainted with a careful mother whose daughters, while they never in their lives read a *novel* of any kind, are permitted to peruse, without reserve, any *plays* that happen to fall in their way; and with another, from whom no lessons, however excellent, of wisdom and piety, contained in a *prose-fiction*, can obtain quarter; but who, on the other hand, is no less indiscriminately indulgent to her children in the article of tales in *verse*, of whatever character.

The change, however, which we have already noticed, as having taken place in the character of several modern novels, has operated in a considerable degree to do away this prejudice; and has elevated this species of composition, in some respects at least, into a much higher class. For most of that instruction which used to be presented to the world in the shape of formal dissertations, or shorter and more desultory moral essays, such as those of the Spectator and Rambler, we may now resort to the pages of the acute and judicious, but not less amusing, novelists who have lately appeared. If their views of men and manners are no less just than those of the essayists who preceded them, are they to be rated lower because they present to us these views, not in the language of general description, but in the form of well-constructed fictitious narrative? If the practical lessons they inculcate are no less sound and useful, it is surely no diminution of their merit that they are conveyed by example instead of precept: nor, if their remarks are neither less wise nor less important, are they the less valuable for being represented as thrown out in the course of conversations suggested by the circumstances of the speakers, and perfectly in character. The praise and blame of the moralist are surely not the less effectual for being bestowed, not in general declamation, on classes of men, but on individuals representing those classes, who are so clearly delineated and brought into action before us, that we seem to be acquainted with them, and feel an interest in their fate.

Biography is allowed, on all hands, to be one of the most attractive and profitable kinds of reading: now such novels as we have been speaking of, being a kind of fictitious biography, bear the same relation to the real, that epic and tragic poetry, according to Aristotle, bear to history: they present us (supposing, of course, each perfect in its kind) with the general, instead of the particular,—the probable, instead of the true; and, by leaving out those accidental irregularities, and exceptions to general rules, which constitute the many improbabilites of real narrative, present us with a clear and *abstracted* view of the general rules themselves; and thus concentrate, as it were, into a small compass, the net result of wide experience.

Among the authors of this school there is no one superior, if equal, to the lady whose last production is now before us, and whom we have much regret in finally taking leave of: her death (in the prime of life, considered as a writer) being announced in this the first publication to which her name is prefixed. We regret the failure not only of a source of innocent amusement, but also of that supply of practical good sense and instructive example, which she would probably have continued to furnish better than any of her contemporaries:—Miss Edgeworth, indeed, draws characters and details conversations, such as they occur in real life, with a spirit and fidelity not to be surpassed; but her stories are most romantically improbable, (in the sense above explained,) almost all the important events of them being brought about by most *providential* coincidences; and this, as we have already remarked, is not merely faulty, inasmuch as it evinces a want of skill in the writer, and gives an air of clumsiness to the fiction, but is a very considerable drawback on its practical utility: the personages either of fiction or history being then only profitable examples, when their good or ill conduct meets its appropriate reward, not from a sort of independent machinery of accidents, but as a necessary or probable result, according to the ordinary course of affairs. Miss Edgeworth also is somewhat too avowedly didactic: that seems to be true of her, which the French critics, in the extravagance of their conceits, attributed to Homer and Virgil; viz. that they first thought of a moral, and then framed a fable to illustrate it; she would, we think, instruct more successfully, and she would, we are sure, please more frequently, if she kept the design of teaching more out of sight, and did not so glaringly press every circumstance of her story, principal or subordinate, into the service of a principle to be inculcated, or information to be given. A certain portion of moral instruction must accompany every well-invented narrative. Virtue must be represented as producing, at the long run, happiness; and vice, misery; and the accidental events, that in real life interrupt this tendency, are anomalies which, though true individually, are as false generally as the accidental deformities which vary the average outline of the human figure. They would be as much out of place in a fictitious narrative, as a wen in an academic model. But any *direct* attempt at moral teaching, and any attempt whatever to give scientific information will, we fear, unless managed with the utmost discretion, interfere with what, after all, is the immediate and peculiar object of the novelist, as of the poet, *to please*. If instruction do not join as a volunteer, she will do no good service. Miss Edgeworth's novels put us in mind of those clocks and watches which are condemned 'a double or a treble debt to pay:' which, besides their legitimate object, to show the hour, tell you the day of the month or the week, give you a landscape for a dial-plate, with a second hand forming the sails of a windmill, or have a barrel to play a tune, or an alarum to remind you of an engagement: all very good things in their way; but so it is that these watches never tell the time so well as those in which that is the exclusive object of the maker. Every additional movement is an obstacle to the original design. We do not deny that we have learned much physic, and much law, from *Patronage*, particularly the latter, for Miss Edgeworth's law is of a very original kind; but it was not to learn law and physic that we took up the book, and we suspect we should have been more pleased if we had been less taught. With regard to the influence of religion, which is scarcely, if at all, alluded to in Miss Edgeworth's novels, we would abstain from pronouncing any decision which should apply to her personally. She may, for aught we know, entertain opinions which would not permit her, with consistency, to attribute more to it than she has done; in that case she stands acquitted, in foro conscientiæ, of wilfully suppressing any thing which she acknowledges to be true and important; but, as a writer, it must still be considered as a blemish, in the eyes at least of those who think differently, that virtue should be studiously inculcated with scarcely any reference to what they regard as the main spring of it; that vice should be traced to every other source except the want of religious principle; that the most radical change from worthlessness to excellence should be represented as wholly independent of that agent which they consider as the only one that can accomplish it; and that consolation under affliction should be represented as derived from every source except the one which they look to as the only true and sure one: 'is it not because there is no God in Israel that ye have sent to inquire of Baalzebub the God of Ekron?'

Miss Austin has the merit (in our judgment most essential) of being evidently a Christian writer: a merit which is much enhanced, both on the score of good taste, and of practical utility, by her religion being not at all obtrusive. She might defy the most fastidious critic to call any of her novels, (as Cœlebs was designated, we will not say altogether without reason,) a 'dramatic sermon.' The subject is rather alluded to, and that incidentally, than studiously brought forward and dwelt upon. In fact she is more sparing of it than would be thought desirable by some persons; perhaps even by herself, had she consulted merely her own sentiments; but she probably introduced it as far as she thought would be generally acceptable and profitable: for when the purpose of inculcating a religious principle is made too palpably prominent, many readers, if they do not throw aside the book with disgust, are apt to fortify themselves with that respectful kind of apathy with which they undergo a regular sermon, and prepare themselves as they do to swallow a dose of medicine, endeavouring to *get it down* in large gulps, without tasting it more than is necessary.

The moral lessons also of this lady's novels, though clearly and impressively conveyed, are not offensively put forward, but spring incidentally from the circumstances of the story; they are not forced upon the reader, but he is left to collect them (though without any difficulty) for himself: her's is that unpretending kind of instruction which is furnished by real life; and certainly no author has ever conformed more closely to real life, as well in the incidents, as in the characters and descriptions. Her fables appear to us to be, in their own way, nearly faultless; they do not consist (like those of some of the writers who have attempted this kind of common-life novel writing) of a string of unconnected events which have little or no bearing on one main plot, and are introduced evidently for the sole purpose of bringing in characters and conversations; but have all that compactness of plan and unity of action which is generally produced by a sacrifice of probability: yet they have little or nothing that is not probable; the story proceeds without the aid of extraordinary accidents; the events which take place are the necessary or natural consequences of what has preceded;

and yet (which is a very rare merit indeed) the final catastrophe is scarcely ever clearly foreseen from the beginning, and very often comes, upon the generality of readers at least, quite unexpected. We know not whether Miss Austin ever had access to the precepts of Aristotle; but there are few, if any, writers of fiction who have illustrated them more successfully.

The vivid distinctness of description, the minute fidelity of detail, and air of unstudied ease in the scenes represented, which are no less necessary than probability of incident, to carry the reader's imagination along with the story, and give fiction the perfect appearance of reality, she possesses in a high degree; and the object is accomplished without resorting to those deviations from the ordinary plan of narrative in the third person, which have been patronized by some eminent masters. We allude to the two other methods of conducting a fictitious story, viz. either by narrative in the first person, when the hero is made to tell his own tale, or by a series of letters; both of which we conceive have been adopted with a view of heightening the resemblance of the fiction to reality. At first sight, indeed, there might appear no reason why a story told in the first person should have more the air of a real history than in the third; especially as the majority of real histories actually are in the third person; nevertheless, experience seems to show that such is the case: provided there be no want of skill in the writer, the resemblance to real life, of a fiction thus conducted, will approach much the nearest (other points being equal) to a deception, and the interest felt in it, to that which we feel in real transactions. We need only instance Defoe's Novels, which, in spite of much improbability, we believe have been oftener mistaken for true narratives, than any fictions that ever were composed. Colonel Newport is well known to have been cited as an historical authority; and we have ourselves found great difficulty in convincing many of our friends that Defoe was not himself the citizen, who relates the plague of London. The reason probably is, that in the ordinary form of narrative, the writer is not content to exhibit, like a real historian, a bare detail of such circumstances as might actually have come under his knowledge; but presents us with a description of what is passing in the minds of the parties, and gives an account of their feelings and motives, as well as their most private conversations in various places at once. All this is very amusing, but perfectly unnatural: the merest simpleton could hardly mistake a fiction of *this* kind for a true history, unless he believed the writer to be endued with omniscience and omnipresence, or to be aided by familiar spirits, doing the office of Homer's Muses, whom he invokes to tell him all that could not otherwise be known;

'Υμεις γαζ Θεοι εσε, ωαρεσε τε, ιοε τε ωανλα'.[1]

Let the events, therefore, which are detailed, and the characters described, be ever so natural, the way in which they are presented to us is of a supernatural cast, perfectly unlike any real history that ever was or can be written, and thus requiring a greater stretch of imagination in the reader. On the other hand, the supposed narrator of his own history never pretends to dive into the thoughts and feelings of the other parties; he merely describes his own, and gives his conjectures as to those of the rest, just as a real autobiographer might do; and thus an author is enabled to assimilate his fiction to reality, without withholding that delineation of the inward workings of the human heart, which is so much coveted. Nevertheless novels in the first person have not succeeded so well as to make that mode of writing become very general. It is objected to them, not without reason, that they want a *hero*: the person intended to occupy that post being the narrator himself, who of course cannot so describe his own conduct and character as to make the reader thoroughly acquainted with him; though the attempt frequently produces an offensive appearance of egotism.

The plan of a fictitious correspondence seems calculated in some measure to combine the advantages of the other two; since, by allowing each personage to be the speaker in turn, the feelings of each may be described by himself, and his character and conduct by another. But these novels are apt to become excessively tedious; since, to give the letters the appearance of reality, (without which the main object proposed would be defeated,) they must contain a very large proportion of matter which has no bearing at all upon the story. There is also generally a sort of awkward disjointed appearance in a novel which proceeds entirely in letters, and holds together, as it were, by continual spicing.

Miss Austin, though she has in a few places introduced letters with great effect, has on the whole conducted her novels on the ordinary plan, describing, without scruple, private conversations and uncommunicated feelings: but she has not been forgetful of the important maxim, so long ago illustrated by Homer, and afterwards enforced by Aristotle, of saying as little as possible in her own person, and giving a

---

[1] 'For you are divine and are everywhere and know everything' (Homer, *Iliad*, i).

dramatic air to the narrative, by introducing frequent conversations; which she conducts with a regard to character hardly exceeded even by Shakspeare himself. Like him, she shows as admirable a discrimination in the characters of fools as of people of sense; a merit which is far from common. To invent, indeed, a conversation full of wisdom or of wit, requires that the writer should himself possess ability; but the converse does not hold good: it is no fool that can describe fools well; and many who have succeeded pretty well in painting superior characters, have failed in giving individuality to those weaker ones, which it is necessary to introduce in order to give a faithful representation of real life: they exhibit to us mere folly in the abstract, forgetting that to the eye of a skilful naturalist the insects on a leaf present as wide differences as exist between the elephant and the lion. Slender, and Shallow, and Ague-cheek, as Shakspeare has painted them, though equally fools, resemble one another no more than Richard, and Macbeth, and Julius Cæsar; and Miss Austin's Mrs. Bennet, Mr. Rushworth, and Miss Bates, are no more alike than her Darcy, Knightley, and Edmund Bertram. Some have complained, indeed, of finding her fools too much like nature, and consequently tiresome; there is no disputing about tastes; all we can say is, that such critics must (whatever deference they may out-wardly pay to received opinions) find the *Merry Wives of Windsor* and *Twelfth Night* very tiresome; and that those who look with pleasure at Wilkie's pictures, or those of the Dutch school, must admit that excellence of imitation may confer attraction on that which would be insipid or disagreeable in the reality.

Her minuteness of detail has also been found fault with; but even where it produces, at the time, a degree of tediousness, we know not whether that can justly be reckoned a blemish, which is absolutely essential to a very high excellence. Now, it is absolutely impossible, without this, to produce that thorough acquaintance with the characters, which is necessary to make the reader heartily interested in them. Let any one cut out from the Iliad or from Shakspeare's plays every thing (we are far from saying that either might not lose some parts with advantage, but let him reject every thing) which is absolutely devoid of importance and of interest *in itself;* and he will find that what is left will have lost more than half its charms. We are convinced that some writers have diminished the effect of their works by being scrupulous to admit nothing into them which had not some absolute, intrinsic, and indepen-dent merit. They have acted like those who strip off the leaves of a fruit tree, as being of themselves good for nothing, with the view of securing more nourishment to the fruit, which in fact cannot attain its full maturity and flavour without them.

Mansfield Park contains some of Miss Austin's best moral lessons, as well as her most humorous descriptions. The following specimen unites both: it is a sketch of the mode of education adopted for the two Miss Bertrams, by their aunt Norris, whose father, Sir Thomas, has just admitted into his family a poor niece, Fanny Price, (the heroine) a little younger, and much less accomplished than his daughters.

[quotes ch. 2 ' "Dear Mamma" ' to ' "be a difference".']

The character of Sir Thomas is admirably drawn; one of those men who always judge rightly, and act wisely, when a case is fairly put before them; but who are quite destitute of acuteness of discernment and adroitness of conduct. The Miss Bertrams, without any peculiarly bad natural disposition, and merely with that selfishness, self-importance, and want of moral training, which are the natural result of their education, are conducted, by a train of probable circumstances, to a catastrophe which involves their father in the deepest affliction. It is melancholy to reflect how many young ladies in the same sphere, with what is ordinarily called every advantage in point of education, are so precisely in the same situation, that if they avoid a similar fate, it must be rather from good luck than any thing else. The care that is taken to keep from them every thing in the shape of affliction, prevents their best feelings from being exercised; and the pains bestowed on their accomplishment, raises their idea of their own consequence: the heart becomes hard, and is engrossed by vanity with all its concomitant vices. Mere moral and religious *instruction* are not adequate to correct all this. But it is a shame to give in our own language sentiments which are so much better expressed by Miss Austin.

[quotes ch. 48 'Too late' to 'character and temper.']

Edmund Bertram, the second son, a sensible and worthy young man, is captivated by a Miss Crawford, who, with her brother, is on a visit at the Parsonage with her half-sister, Mrs. Grant: the progress of his passion is very happily depicted:

[quotes ch. 8 'Miss Crawford' to 'and sentiment.']

He is, however, put in doubt as to her character, by the occasional levity of her sentiments, and her aversion to his intended profession, the church, and to a retired life. Both she and her brother are very clever, agreeable, and good-humoured, and not without moral taste, (for Miss Austin does not deal in fiends and angels,) but brought up without strict principles, and destitute of real self-denying benevolence. The latter falls in love with Fanny Price, whom he had been originally intending to flirt with for his own amusement. She, however, objects to his principles; being not satisfied with religious belief and practice in herself, and careless about them in her husband. In this respect she presents a useful example to a good many modern females, whose apparent regard for religion in themselves, and indifference about it in their partners for life, make one sometimes inclined to think that they hold the opposite extreme to the Turk's opinion, and believe men to have no souls. Her uncle, Sir Thomas, however, who sees nothing of her objection, is displeased at her refusal; and thinking that she may not sufficiently prize the comforts of wealth to which she has been so long accustomed, without the aid of contrast, encourages her paying a visit to her father, a Captain Price, of the Marines, settled with a large family at Portsmouth. She goes, accompanied by her favourite brother William, with all the fond recollections, and bright anticipations, of a visit after eight years' absence.

With a candour very rare in a novelist, Miss Austin describes the remedy as producing its effect. After she has spent a month in the noise, privations, and vulgarities of home, Mr. Crawford pays her a visit of a couple of days; after he was gone,

[quotes ch. 43 'Fanny was out' to 'distressing to her?']

Fanny is, however, armed against Mr. Crawford by a stronger feeling than even her disapprobation; by a vehement attachment to Edmund. The silence in which this passion is cherished—the slender hopes and enjoyments by which it is fed—the restlessness and jealousy with which it fills a mind naturally active, contented and unsuspicious—the manner in which it tinges every event and every reflection, are painted with a vividness and a detail of which we can scarcely conceive any one but a female, and we should almost add, a female writing from recollection, capable.

To say the truth, we suspect one of Miss Austin's great merits in our eyes to be, the insight she gives us into the peculiarities of female character. Authoresses can scarcely ever forget the esprit de corps—can scarcely ever forget that they *are authoresses*. They seem to feel a sympathetic shudder at exposing naked a female mind. Elles se peignent en buste, and leave the mysteries of womanhood to be described by some interloping male, like Richardson or Marivaux, who is turned out before he has seen half the rites, and is forced to spin from his own conjectures the rest. Now from this fault Miss Austin is free. Her heroines are what one knows women must be, though one never can get them to acknowledge it. As liable to 'fall in love first,' as anxious to attract the attention of agreeable men, as much taken with a striking manner, or a handsome face, as unequally gifted with constancy and firmness, as liable to have their affections biassed by convenience or fashion, as we, on our part, will admit men to be. As some illustration of what we mean, we refer our readers to the conversation between Miss Crawford and Fanny, vol. iii. p. 102,[1] Fanny's meeting with her father, p. 199,[2] her reflections after reading Edmund's letter, 246,[3] her happiness (good, and heroine though she be) in the midst of the misery of all her friends, when she finds that Edmund has decidedly broken with her rival; feelings, all of them, which, under the influence of strong passion, must alloy the purest mind, but with which scarcely any *authoress* but Miss Austin would have ventured to temper the ætheriel materials of a heroine.

But we must proceed to the publication of which the title is prefixed to this article. It contains, it seems, the earliest and the latest productions of the author; the first of them having been purchased, we are told, many years back by a bookseller, who, for some reason unexplained, thought proper to alter his mind and withhold it. We do not much applaud his taste; for though it is decidedly inferior to her other works, having less plot, and what there is, less artificially wrought up, and also less exquisite nicety of moral painting; yet the same kind of excellences which characterise the other novels may be perceived in this, in a degree which would have been highly creditable to most other writers of the same school, and which would have entitled the author to considerable praise, had she written nothing better.

We already begin to fear, that we have indulged too much in extracts, and we must save some room for *Persuasion*, or we could not resist giving a specimen of John Thorpe, with his horse that *cannot* go less than 10 miles an hour, his refusal to drive his sister 'because she has such thick ankles,' and his sober consumption of five pints of port a day; altogether the best portrait of a species, which, though almost extinct cannot yet be quite classed among the Palæotheria, the Bang-up Oxonian. Miss Thorpe, the jilt of middling life, is, in her way, quite as good, though she has not the advantage of being the representative of a rare or

[1] Ch. 36.   [2] Ch. 38.   [3] Ch. 46.

a diminishing species. We fear few of our readers, however they may admire the naiveté, will admit the truth of poor John Morland's postscript, 'I can never expect to know such another woman.'

The latter of these novels, however, *Persuasion*, which is more strictly to be considered as a posthumous work, possesses that superiority which might be expected from the more mature age at which it was written, and is second, we think, to none of the former ones, if not superior to all. In the humorous delineation of character it does not abound quite so much as some of the others, though it has great merit even on that score; but it has more of that tender and yet elevated kind of interest which is aimed at by the generality of novels, and in pursuit of which they seldom fail of running into romantic extravagance: on the whole, it is one of the most elegant fictions of common life we ever remember to have met with.

Sir Walter Elliot, a silly and conceited baronet, has three daughters, the eldest two, unmarried, and the third, Mary, the wife of a neighbouring gentleman, Mr. Charles Musgrove, heir to a considerable fortune, and living in a genteel cottage in the neighbourhood of the Great house which he is hereafter to inherit. The second daughter, Anne, who is the heroine, and the only one of the family possessed of good sense, (a quality which Miss Austin is as sparing of in her novels, as we fear her great mistress, Nature, has been in real life,) when on a visit to her sister, is, by that sort of instinct which generally points out to all parties the person on whose judgment and temper they may rely, appealed to in all the little family differences which arise, and which are described with infinite spirit and detail.

The following touch reminds us, in its minute fidelity to nature, of some of the happiest strokes in the subordinate parts of Hogarth's prints: Mr. C. Musgrove has an aunt whom he wishes to treat with becoming attention, but who, from being of a somewhat inferior class in point of family and fashion, is studiously shunned by his wife, who has all the family pride of her father and eldest sister: he takes the opportunity of a walk with a large party on a fine day, to visit this despised relation, but cannot persuade his wife to accompany him; she pleads fatigue, and remains with the rest to await his return; and he walks home with her, not much pleased at the incivility she has shown.

[quotes ch. 10 'She joined Charles' to 'along at all'.]

But the principal interest arises from a combination of events which cannot be better explained than by a part of the prefatory narrative, which forms, in general, an Euripidean prologue to Miss Austin's novels.

[quotes ch. 4 'He was not' to 'unnatural beginning'.]

After an absence of eight years, he returns to her neighbourhood, and circumstances throw them frequently in contact. Nothing can be more exquisitely painted than her feelings on such occasions. First, dread of the meeting,—then, as that is removed by custom, renewed regret for the happiness she has thrown away, and the constantly recurring contrast, though known only to herself, between the distance of their intercourse and her involuntary sympathy with all his feelings, and instant comprehension of all his thoughts, of the meaning of every glance of his eye, and curl of his lip, and intonation of his voice. In him her mild good sense and elegance gradually re-awake long-forgotten attachment: but with it return the usual accompaniments of undeclared love, distrust of her sentiments towards him, and suspicions of their being favourable to another. In this state of regretful jealousy he overhears, while writing a letter, a conversation she is holding with his friend Captain Harville, respecting another naval friend, Captain Benwick, who had been engaged to the sister of the former, and very speedily after her death had formed a fresh engagement: we cannot refrain from inserting an extract from this conversation, which is exquisitely beautiful.

[quotes ch. 23 ' "Your feelings" ' to ' "too much oppressed." ']

While this conversation has been going on, he has been replying to it on paper, under the appearance of finishing his letter: he puts the paper into her hand, and hurries away.

[quotes ch. 23 the letter from Wentworth.]

We ventured, in a former article, to remonstrate against the dethronement of the once powerful God of Love, in his own most especial domain, the novel; and to suggest that, in shunning the ordinary fault of recommending by examples a romantic and uncalculating extravagance of passion, Miss Austin had rather fallen into the opposite extreme of exclusively patronizing what are called prudent matches, and too much disparaging sentimental enthusiasm. We urged, that, mischievous as is the extreme on this side, it is not the one into which the young folks of the present day are the most likely to run: the prevailing fault is not now, whatever it may have been, to sacrifice all for love:

Venit enim magnum donandi parca juventus,
Nec tantum Veneris quantum studiosa culinæ.[1]

We may now, without retracting our opinion, bestow unqualified
approbation; for the distresses of the present heroine all arise from her
prudent refusal to listen to the suggestions of her heart. The catastrophe
however is happy, and we are left in doubt whether it would have been
better for her or not, to accept the first proposal; and this we conceive
is precisely the proper medium; for, though we would not have prudential calculations the sole principle to be regarded in marriage, we are
far from advocating their exclusion. To disregard the advice of sober-
minded friends on an important point of conduct, is an imprudence we
would by no means recommend; indeed, it is a species of selfishness, if,
in listening only to the dictates of passion, a man sacrifices to its gratification the happiness of those most dear to him as well as his own;
though it is not now-a-days the most prevalent form of selfishness. But
it is no condemnation of a sentiment to say, that it becomes blameable
when it interferes with duty, and is uncontrouled by conscience: the
desire of riches, power, or distinction,—the taste for ease and comfort,
—are to be condemned when they transgress these bounds; and love, if
it keep within them, even though it be somewhat tinged with enthusiasm, and a little at variance with what the worldly call prudence, i.e.
regard for pecuniary advantage, may afford a better moral discipline to
the mind than most other passions. It will not at least be denied, that it
has often proved a powerful stimulus to exertion where others have
failed, and has called forth talents unknown before even to the possessor.
What, though the pursuit may be fruitless, and the hopes visionary?
The result may be a real and substantial benefit, though of another kind;
the vineyard may have been cultivated by digging in it for the treasure
which is never to be found. What, though the perfections with which
imagination has decorated the beloved object, may, in fact, exist but in
a slender degree? still they are believed in and admired as real; if not,
the love is such as does not merit the name; and it is proverbially true
that men become assimilated to the character (i.e. what they *think* the
character) of the being they fervently adore: thus, as in the noblest
exhibitions of the stage, though that which is contemplated be but a
fiction, it may be realized in the mind of the beholder; and, though
grasping at a cloud, he may become worthy of possessing a real goddess.
Many a generous sentiment, and many a virtuous resolution, have been

[1] 'For she came unwilling to give much to young men, wanting food rather than love.'

called forth and matured by admiration of one, who may herself perhaps have been incapable of either. It matters not what the object is that a man aspires to be worthy of, and proposes as a model for imitation, if he does but *believe* it to be excellent. Moreover, all doubts of success (and they are seldom, if ever, entirely wanting) must either produce or exercise humility; and the endeavour to study another's interests and inclinations, and prefer them to one's own, may outlast the present occasion. Every thing, in short, which tends to abstract a man in any degree, or in any way, from self,—from self-admiration and self-interest, has, so far at least, a beneficial influence in forming the character.

On the whole, Miss Austin's works may safely be recommended, not only as among the most unexceptionable of their class, but as combining, in an eminent degree, instruction with amusement, though without the direct effort at the former, of which we have complained, as sometimes defeating its object. For those who cannot, or will not, *learn* any thing from productions of this kind, she has provided entertainment which entitles her to thanks; for mere innocent amusement is in itself a good, when it interferes with no greater; especially as it may occupy the place of some other that may *not* be innocent. The Eastern monarch who proclaimed a reward to him who should discover a new pleasure, would have deserved well of mankind had he stipulated that it should be blameless. Those, again, who delight in the study of human nature, may improve in the knowledge of it, and in the profitable application of that knowledge, by the perusal of such fictions as those before us.

17. Scott on Jane Austen

1822, 1826, 1827

(a) Extract from letter, 10 February 1822, to Joanna Baillie: 'By the way did you know Miss Austen Authoress of some novels which have a great deal of nature in them—nature in ordinary and middle life to be sure but valuable from its strong resemblance and correct drawing.' (*Letters of Scott 1821-23* (1934), ed., H. J. C. Grierson, vii, 60).

(b) Extract from Journal entry, 14 March 1826: 'Also read again and for the third time at least Miss Austen's very finely written novel of *Pride and Prejudice*. That young lady had a talent for describing the involvement and feelings and characters of ordinary life which is to me the most wonderful I ever met with. The Big Bow-wow strain I can do myself like any now going, but the exquisite touch which renders ordinary commonplace things and characters interesting from the truth of the description and the sentiment is denied to me. What a pity such a gifted creature died so early!' (*Journal of Walter Scott 1825-26* (1939), ed. J. G. Tait, p. 135).

(c) Extract from Journal entry for 28 March 1826: 'The women do this better—Edgeworth, Ferrier, Austen have all had their portraits of real society, far superior to any thing Man, vain Man, has produced of the like nature.' (p. 144.)

(d) Extract from Journal entry for 18 September 1827: '. . . whiled away the evening over one of Miss Austen's novels. There is a truth of painting in her writings which always delights me. They do not, it is true, get above the middle classes of society, but there she is inimitable.' (*Journal 1827-28* (1941) p. 103.)

(e) 'There's a finishing-off in some of her scenes that is really quite above every body else.' (A remark quoted in *Life of Scott* (1837), J. G. Lockhart, vii, 338.)

18. A Novelist of the Age
1823

Extract from an unsigned review of the *Life and Adventures of Peter Wilkins, Retrospective Review* (no month, 1823), vii, 131–35.

The reviewer is writing in the spirit of Scott and Whately. He remarks that the present age is tired of the extravagance and articiality of sentimental melodrama. 'We require nothing but good sense and good morals, exhibited in a succession of events, flowing from natural causes, and arriving at a probable conclusion.' He cites Fanny Burney and Jane Austen as two novelists typifying successive ages in the history of fiction. (See Introduction, p. 22).

But two female writers there are, each the favourite of her generation, whom we would particularly specify, as illustrating in their works the opposite tastes of two successive ages; one still, we believe, in existence, but belonging, as a writer, to the last century; and the other, though coeval with ourselves, now no more, cut short by that early doom, which Heaven has ordained for all of the porcelain clay of human kind. In the lively and spirited caricatures of the author of *Evelina* and *Cecilia*, we may see the style of portrait-painting relished by our fathers. Turning from them to the soberly coloured and faithful likenesses of Jane Austen, we may behold that approved by ourselves.

Over the works of the first, we laugh abundantly; but this is an expression which an author should be least anxious to extort. Do we ever experience that agreeable serenity and complacency, which is diffused over the mind by the sensible and pleasant conversation of persons with whose feelings we sympathise? There are a great many turns and changes in the eventful course of the narrative; but do we see, are we at the trouble to see, what produced them? and if we are so happy as to discern the cause, does it always appear a probable or a sufficiently important one? The hero and the heroine—the lover and the beloved—fall out and in, and out again, through the whole five volumes —do *they* always know, or *even* care to understand why? The heroine is constantly in distress—poor lady! does the hard-hearted reader ever take his share of the burden? The hero is always a very respectable young man—we have no fault to find with his moral qualities—but do we ever take a jot more interest in him, than in any well-behaved, insipid young gentleman, with whom it may be our hard lot to ride fifty miles or so on a rainy day? Then there are your villains—marvellous, shrewd, calculating villains—but do they ever plot with the least probability of success? And gay deceivers, too, there are, with whom no woman can be safe in heart or reputation. But are they your men, 'to love, fight, banter, in a breath,' and stay by a torrent of wit the angry speech just kindling in the blushing cheek, and glancing eye, and half-opened lip? O no!—mere conquerors they of hearts that beat against the shop-board. Whatever a man's cue is, that he never forgets for an instant. The miser is always most miserly, and always showing it. The proud man has the pride of Lucifer, and that in perpetuity. The bookworm, again, has a trick of absence of mind, and he forgets his dinner till it is clear he ought to die of starvation. The vulgar man is broad, irredeemably, intensely vulgar. The gay, dissipated man rides down hill to the devil, with unlocked wheels, and never spends a thought as to whither he is speeding. But is there not, in this medley of all the vices, follies, and absurdities personified, some intermixture of tenderness and sentiment? Yes; two persons are set apart to talk it—two soft-sighing sentimental souls, who whine and cry through the drama; and then, heart-broken for the loss of the objects of their separate affection, at the end of the play, club together each other's fragments, and become heart-whole again.

We ask the reader's pardon for speaking with so much levity of works, which, after all that can be said in detraction, are monuments of genius. The exaggeration of nature—the everlasting sameness of character—the perpetual acting—the want of truth in the incidents—of simplicity in the structure, and above all, of moral beauty in the tone and sentiments of the story, are the faults of that bad taste which she derived from her contemporaries. Great talents seldom or never err, but in compliance with the fashion or feeling of the age; and what a mist these can spread before the eagle vision of high-soaring genius, may be abundantly seen in the memorable example of Dryden. But the cleverness and spirit, the humour and acuteness, the observation, at once discriminating and deep, which has given its admirable possessor more experience of the world and knowledge of man at nineteen, than most have at ninety, belong solely to their author; and, in an age of female excellence, justly entitled her to the friendship of Johnson, and the gallant admiration of Burke—'Miss Burney *die* to-night!' She has, doubtless, in the course of a long life, heard and read her praises, till she can repeat them by rote; but this deep and emphatic expression of admiration will be found written in legible characters on her heart. She has, however, lived to see herself superseded in the public favour by writers, perhaps, then unborn; and the absolute failure of her latest production, must have brought home the sorrowful conviction of having outlived the admiration of her countrymen.

Born in the same rank of life, familiar with the same description of people, equally precocious, and equally possessed of a lively fancy, and an acute perception of character, with the single advantage of belonging to a later generation, the author of *Persuasion* and *Mansfield Park* has produced works of much fresher verdure, much sweeter flavour, and much purer spirit. Without any wish to surprise us into attention, by strangeness of incident, or complication of adventure,—with no great ambition of being amazingly facetious, or remarkably brilliant,—laboriously witty, or profoundly sentimental,—of dealing out wise saws and deep reflections, or keeping us on the broad grin, and killing us with laughter;—the stream of her Tale flows on in an easy, natural, but spring tide, which carries us out of ourselves, and bears our feelings, affections, and deepest interest, irresistably along with it. She has not been at the trouble to look out for subjects for her pencil of a peculiar and eccentric cast, nor cared to outstep the modesty of nature, by spicing with a too rich vein of humour, such as fell in her way in the ordinary intercourse of life. The people with whom her works bring us acquainted were, we feel certain, like those among whom she herself shared the good and ill of life,—with whom she thought and talked—danced and sung—laughed and wept—joked and reasoned. They are not the productions of an ingenious fancy, but beings instinct with life;—they breathe and move, and think and speak, and act, before our mind's eye, with a distinctness, that rivals the pictures we see in memory of scenes we ourselves have beheld, and upon the recollections of which we love to dwell. They mingle in our remembrances with those, whom we ourselves have known and loved, but whom accident, or coldness, or death, have separated from us before the end of our pilgrimage.

Into those of her characters in particular, who engage our best affections, and with whom we sympathise most deeply, she seems to have transfused the very essence of life. These are, doubtless, the finest of her compositions, and with reason; for she had only, on any supposed interesting occurrence of life, to set her own kind and amiable feelings in motion, and the tide sprang up from the heart to the pen, and flowed in a rich stream of nature and truth over the page. Into one particular character, indeed, she has breathed her whole soul and being; and in this we please ourselves with thinking, we see and know herself.

And what is this character?—A mind beautifully framed, graceful, imaginative, and feminine, but penetrating, sagacious, and profound.— A soul harmonious, gentle, and most sweetly attuned,—susceptible of all that is beautiful in nature, pure in morals, sublime in religion;—a soul—on which, if, by any accidental contact with the vulgar, or the vicious, the slightest shade of impurity was ever thrown, it vanished instantaneously, like man's breath from the polished mirror; and, retreating, left it in undiminished lustre.—A heart large and expansive, the seat of deep, kind, honest, and benevolent feelings.—A bosom capacious of universal love, but through which there flowed a deeper stream of domestic and holy affections,—as a river through the lake's broad expanse, whose basin it supplies with its overflowing waters, and through which its course is marked only by a stronger current.—A temper even, cheerful, gladdening, and serene as the mild evening of summer's loveliest day, in which the very insect that lives but an hour, doth desport and enjoy existence.—Feelings generous and candid,— quick, but not irritable,—sensitive to the slightest degree of coolness in friend or lover, but not easily damped;—or, if overwhelmed by any heart-rending affliction, rallying, collecting, settling into repose again, like some still and deep waters disturbed by the fall of an impending rock.—Modest in hope, sober in joy, gay in innocence,—sweet soother of others' affliction,—most resigned and patient bearer of her own. With a sunny eye to reflect the glad smiles of happy friends,—dim and cloudy at the sight of others' grief; but not revealing the deep seated woes of the remote chambers of her own breast, by aught but that wild, pensive, regardful, profound expression, which tells nothing to a stranger or acquaintance, but, if a parent or friend, might break your heart but to look upon.—The beloved confidante of the young and infantine—at once playmate and preceptress;—the patient nurser of their little fretful ailments;—the more patient bearer of their rude and noisy mirth, in her own moments of illness or dejection;—exchanging smiles, that would arrest an angel on his winged way, for obstreperous laughs;—and sweet low accents, for shrill treble screams. The friend of the humble, lowly, and indigent; respecting in them, as much as in those of highest degree and lordliest bearing, the image of their common Maker. Easy, pleasant, amusing, playful, and kind in the intercourse of equals—an attentive hearer, considerate, patient, cheerfully sedate, and affectionate in that of elders. In scenes of distress or difficulty, self-dependent, collected, deliberate, and provident,—the one to whom all instinctively turned for counsel, sympathy, and consolation. Strong in innocence as a tower, with a face of serenity, and a collectedness of demeanour, from which danger and misery—the very tawny lion in his rage—might flee discomfited,—a fragile, delicate, feeble, and most feminine woman!

Whether, in this enumeration of female excellencies, one of those deeply attached friends, of whom she was sure to have had many, might recognize some, or most of the admirable qualities of JANE AUSTEN, we cannot say;—but sure we are, if our memory have not failed us, or our fancy deceived us, or our hearts betrayed us, such, or nearly such, are those, of which she has herself compounded one of the most beautiful female characters ever drawn;—we mean, the heroine of *Persuasion*.

But we have digressed farther than we intended.—Indeed, so fast and thick do recollections of what is beautiful and good in the works of this admirable woman, throng into our mind, that we are borne away involuntarily and irresistibly. They stole into the world without noise, —they circulated in quiet,—they were far from being much extolled,— and very seldom noticed in the journals of the day,—they came into our hands, as nothing different from ordinary novels,—and they have enshrined themselves in the heart, and live for ever in the thoughts,— along with the recollections of all that is best and purest in our own experience of life. Their author we, ourselves, had not the happiness of knowing,—a scanty and insufficient memoir, prefixed to her posthumous work, not written in the best taste, is all the history of her life, that we or the world have before us; but, perhaps, that history is not wanted,— her own works furnish that history. Those imaginary people, to whom she gave their most beautiful ideal existence, survive to speak for her, now that she herself is gone.

The mention of her works happened to fall in our way as the noblest illustration we could give of that improvement in this department of literature, which we are fond to believe in; but we frankly confess, we would, at any time, have travelled far out of it to pay our humble tribute of respect to the memory of Jane Austen. Nor is it so foreign to our regular speculations, as the reader may be apt to imagine. Our conversation, as one of our own number has well observed, is among the tombs; and *there* dwells all that once enshrined in a form of beauty a soul of exceeding and surpassing brightness.—O lost too soon to us!— but our loss has been thy immortal gain.

19. Sober Sketches

1824

Extract from an unsigned review of Susan Ferrier's *The Inheritance, Blackwood's Edinburgh Magazine* (June 1824), xv, 659.

The writer is commending the then-anonymous authoress of the novel under review, a story of Scottish life; 'the great novelist of Ireland', mentioned at the close, is Maria Edgeworth.

. . . it is impossible for us to deny her a place considerably above any other female who has come before the British public in these days, as a writer of works of imagination. She has *all* that Miss Austin had—but she is not merely a Scotch Miss Austin. Her mind is naturally one of a more firm, vigorous, and so to speak, masculine tone; and besides, while nothing can be better than Miss Austin's sketches of that sober, orderly, small-town parsonage, sort of society in which she herself had spent her life, and nothing more feeble than Miss Austin's pen, whenever she steps beyond that walk, either up the hill or downwards—this lady, on the contrary, can paint the inmates of the cottage, the farmhouse, the manse, the mansion-house, and the castle; aye, and most difficult, or at least most rare of all, my lady's saloon too—all with equal truth, ease, and effect. In this particular respect she is far above not only Miss Austin, but Miss Burney, and confesses equality with no female author our country has as yet produced, except only the great novelist of Ireland.

20. The Superior Novelist

1830

Extract from an unsigned review by Thomas Henry Lister of *Women as they are* by Mrs. Catherine Gore, *Edinburgh Review* (July 1830), liii, 448–51.

Lister (1800–42) was a prolific writer, best known for his society novels.

Miss Austen has never been so popular as she deserved to be. Intent on fidelity of delineation, and averse to the commonplace tricks of her art, she has not, in this age of literary quackery, received her reward. Ordinary readers have been apt to judge of her as Partridge, in Fielding's novel, judged of Garrick's acting. He could not see the merit of a man who merely behaved on the stage as any body might be expected to behave under similar circumstances in real life. He infinitely preferred the 'robustious periwig-pated fellow,' who flourished his arms like a windmill, and ranted with the voice of three. It was even so with many of the readers of Miss Austen. She was too natural for them. It seemed to them as if there could be very little merit in making characters act and talk so exactly like the people whom they saw around them every day. They did not consider that the highest triumph of art consists in its concealment; and here the art was so little perceptible, that they believed there was none. Her works, like well-proportioned rooms, are rendered less apparently grand and imposing by the very excellence of their adjustment. It must perhaps be confessed, that she availed herself too little of the ordinary means of attracting attention and exciting interest. Her plots are very simple, formed upon the most rigid view of probabilities, excluding every thing romantic or surprising, or calculated to produce a very powerful emotion, and including only such events as occur in every-day life. Her characters are, for the most part, commonplace people, little distinguished by their mental qualities from the mass of their fellow-creatures, of secondary station, and hardly ever exhibited through that halo of rank and wealth which makes many an ill-drawn sketch pass current with a credulous public. '*Materiam superabat opus*,'[1] may be said of her works. No novelist perhaps ever employed more unpromising materials, and by none have those materials been more admirably treated. Her forte lay not so much in describing events, as in drawing characters; and in this she stands almost alone. She possessed the rare and difficult art of making her readers intimately acquainted with the characters of all whom she describes. We feel as if we had lived among them; and yet she employs no elaborate description—no metaphysical analysis—no antithetical balance of their good and bad qualities. She scarcely does more than make them act and talk, and we know them directly. In dialogue she also excelled. Her conversations are never *bookish*—they are just what might have been said; and they are eminently characteristic. We have seen a good deal of spirited dialogue, in which the parts might be transposed and given to other interlocutors, with very little injury to the effect of the whole. This is never the case in the conversations introduced by Miss Austen. Every thing that is said, however short and simple, belongs peculiarly to the person by whom it is uttered, and is indicative of their situation, or turn of mind. And yet they do not seem to talk for effect; they merely say just what it seems most natural that they should have said. In the ridicule of human foibles, she showed great delicacy and address. She never railed in set terms, and seldom launched the shafts of direct satire; but she made us equally sensible of the absurdity or unreasonableness which she wished to expose,—perhaps without even having recourse to one single condemnatory expression. A nicely-regulated vein of humour runs through her writings, never breaking out into broad mirth, but ever ready to communicate a pleasing vivacity to the current of her story. To the above merits may be added those of the purest morality, and most undeviating good sense. Few, if any, fictitious writings have a more decided tendency to improve the hearts of those who read them; and this end is gained without any thing that could be called sermonizing even by the most impatient. . . The authoress[2] of *Marriage*, and *The Inheritance*, has received the public commendation of the Author of Waverley, and she is not unworthy of that flattering distinction. She combines much of Miss Austen's skill in pourtraying character, and her nice perception of its more delicate shades, with a far greater knowledge of picturesque effect, and what may be called the poetry of her art, and a power to excite a deep interest, and to cope with difficult situations and violent emotions, and to display them successfully. She is not, however, very attentive to probabilities. . . .

[1] 'The art masters the material' (Ovid, *Metamorphoses*, xxv). [2] Susan Ferrier.

21. The Novels

1833

Unsigned entry in a series of notes on the English novelists, Allan
Cunningham, *The Athenaeum* (16 November 1833), p. 777.

Dumbiedykes is Jock Dumbie in Scott's *The Heart of Midlothian*.
The *Quarterly Review* quotation is taken from Whately (No. 16).

The works of JANE AUSTEN have quietly won their way to the public
heart, as all works of genius will. She is a prudent writer; there is good
sense in all she says, a propriety in all her actions; and she sets her face
zealously against romantic attachments and sentimental associations.
She lived and died a spinster; yet she seems to have had a large experience in the perfidy of all attachments which belonged not to prudence
and calculation. When Dumbiedykes fell in love, it was with a lady who
sat next him in the kirk, and that put it into his head; in like manner
Miss Austen's heroes and heroines are touched most sensibly when the
object of their contemplation stands on a fair estate, or is endowed with
bonds and bills, and other convertible commodities. 'On the whole,'
says the *Quarterly Review*, 'Miss Austen's works may safely be recommended, not only as among the most unexceptionable of their class, but
as combining, in an eminent degree, instruction and amusement.' Her
works are, *Sense and Sensibility, Pride and Prejudice, Mansfield Park,
Emma,* and *Northanger Abbey,* and *Persuasion.*

22. Some Views of the 1830s

(a) Sir James Mackintosh (1765–1832) wrote on philosophical and historical topics. His particular interest in French affairs brought him into contact with Madame de Staël. The novel he recommended may have been *Pride and Prejudice*, published in January 1813; he met her in London that year: 'Something recalled to his mind the traits of character which are so delicately touched in Miss Austen's novels. 'There was a genius in the sketching out that new kind of novel.' He was vexed for the credit of the *Edinburgh Review*, that it had left her unnoticed; the *Quarterly* had done her more justice. It was impossible for a foreigner to understand fully the merit of her works. Madame de Staël to whom he had recommended one of her novels, found no interest in it, and in her note to him in reply said it was "*vulgaire*", and yet he said nothing could be more true than what he wrote in answer,—"there is no book which that word would suit so little. . . . Every village could furnish matter for a novel to Jane Austen. She did not need the common materials for a novel—strong passion, or strong incident." ' (*Memoirs of Sir James Mackintosh* (1835), R. J. Mackintosh, ii, 471; this recollection is dated about 1830.)

(b) The poet Robert Southey (1774–1843), extract from letter 8 April 1830: 'You mention Miss Austen; her novels are more true to nature, and have (for my sympathies) passages of finer feeling than any others of this age.' (*Autobiography* (1834), Samuel Egerton Brydges, ii, 269).

(c) The novelist Edward Bulwer-Lytton (1803–73), extract from letter 23 October 1834, to his mother: 'You surprise me greatly by what you say of *Emma* and the other books. They enjoy the highest reputation, and I own, for my part, I was delighted with them. I fear they must have been badly read aloud to you. At all events, they are generally much admired, and I was quite serious in my praise of them.' (*Life of Edward Bulwer* (1913), Earl of Lytton, i, 457.)

(d) Coleridge, Southey and Wordsworth, views reported by Sara Coleridge (1802–52), the poet's daughter.

Extract from letter, August 1834, to Emily Trevenen: 'Jane Austen, who, if not the greatest, is surely the most faultless of female novelists. My uncle Southey and my father had an equally high opinion of her merits, but Mr. Wordsworth used to say that though he admitted that her novels were an admirable copy of life, he could not be interested in productions of that kind; unless the truth of nature were presented to him clarified, as it were, by the pervading light of imagination, it had scarce any attractions in his eyes . . .' (*Memoirs and Letters of Sara Coleridge* (1873), ed. E. Coleridge, i, 75.)

(e) John Newman (1801–90), Cardinal and poet. This comment dates from before his entry to the Roman Catholic church in 1845.

Extract from letter, 10 January 1837, to Mrs. John Mozley: 'I have been reading *Emma*. Everything Miss Austen writes is clever, but I desiderate something. There is a want of *body* to the story. The action is frittered away in over-little things. There are some beautiful things in it. Emma herself is the most interesting to me of all her heroines. I feel kind to her whenever I think of her. But Miss Austen has no romance— none at all. What vile creatures her parsons are! she has not a dream of the high Catholic ethos. That other woman, Fairfax, is a dolt—but I like Emma.' (*Letters* (1891), ed. A. Mozley, ii, 223.)

(f) Henry Wadsworth Longfellow (1807–82), the American prose writer and poet.

Extract from journal entry, 23 May 1839: 'I am amusing myself with Miss Austin's novels. She has great power and discrimination in delineating common-place people; and her writings are a capital picture of real life, with all the little wheels and machinery laid bare like a patent clock. But she explains and fills out too much. Those who have not power to fill up gaps and bridge over chasms as they read, must therefore take particular delight in such minuteness of detail. It is a kind of Bowditch's Laplace[1] in the romantic astronomy. But readers of lively imagination naturally prefer the original with its unexplained steps, which they so readily supply.' (*Life of Longfellow* (1886), S. L. Longfellow, i, 323.)

[1] Longfellow is referring to the enormous edition of Laplace's *Mécanique Celeste* (1799–1805) translated, noted and painstakingly elucidated by the astronomer Nathaniel Bowditch, published 1829–39.

23. Macready on Jane Austen
1834, 1836

William Charles Macready (1793-1873), the famous Shake-spearian actor and actor-manager.

(a) Diary entry, 15 February 1834: 'Finished Miss Austen's *Emma*, which amused me very much, impressing me with a high opinion of her powers of drawing and sustaining character, though not satisfying me always with the end and aim of her labours. She is successful in painting the ridiculous to the life, and while she makes demands on our patience for the almost intolerable absurdities and tediousness of her well-meaning gossips, she does not recompense us for what we suffer from her conceited and arrogant nuisances by making their vices their punishments. We are not much better, but perhaps a little more prudent for her writings. She does not probe the vices, but lays bare the weaknesses of character; the blemish on the skin, and not the corruption at the heart, is what she examines. Mrs. Brunton's books have a far higher aim; they try to make us better, and it is an addition to previous faults if they do not. The necessity, the comfort, and the elevating influence of piety is continually inculcated throughout her works—which never appear in Miss Austen's.' (*Macready's Reminiscences* (1875), ed. Frederick Pollock, i, 412.)

(b) Diary entry, 8 July 1836: 'After dinner read a part of *Northanger Abbey*, which I do not much like. Heavy, and too long a strain of irony on one topic.' (ii, 39.)

(c) Diary entry, 9 July 1836: 'Lay down on the sofa, reading Miss Austen's *Mansfield Park* . . . The novel, I think, has the prevailing fault of the pleasant authoress's books; it deals too much in descriptions of the various states of mind, into which her characters are thrown, and amplifies into a page a search for motives which a stroke of the pen might give with greater power and interest. Is Richardson her model? She is an excellent portrait painter, she catches a man near to the life.' (ii, 39.)

(d) Diary entry, 10 July 1836: 'Finished *Mansfield Park*, which hurried with a very inartificial and disagreeable rapidity to its conclusion, leaving some opportunities for most interesting and beautiful scenes particularly the detailed expression of the "how and the when" Edward's love was turned from Miss Crawford to Fanny Price. The great merit of Miss Austen is in the finishing of her characters; the action and conduct of her stories I think frequently defective.' (ii, 40.)

24. A Poetic Tribute

1835

This poem was contributed by George Howard, 6th Earl of Carlisle (1773–1848) to *The Keepsake for MDCCCXXXV*, p. 27. It was accompanied by an illustration of a woman reading a book, the two entitled 'The Lady and the Novel'.

The sister referred to in the penultimate line is probably the sister-novelist Susan Ferrier, author of *The Inheritance* (see head-note to No. 19).

Beats thy quick pulse o'er Inchbald's thrilling leaf,
Brunton's high moral, Opies's deep wrought grief?
Has the mild chaperon claimed thy yielding heart,
Carroll's dark page, Trevelyan's gentle art?
Or is it thou, all perfect Austen? Here
Let one poor wreath adorn thy early bier,
That scarce allowed thy modest youth to claim
Its living portion of thy certain fame!
Oh! Mrs Bennet! Mrs. Norris too!
While memory survives we'll dream of you.
And Mr. Woodhouse, whose abstemious lip
Must thin, but not too thin, his gruel sip.
Miss Bates, our idol, though the village bore;
And Mrs. Elton, ardent to explore.
While the clear style flows on without pretence,
With unstained purity, and unmatched sense:
Or, if a sister e'er approached the throne,
She called the rich 'inheritance' her own.

25. Jane Austen and Harriet Martineau
1839

Extract from an unsigned review of *Deerbrook* (1839) by Harriet Martineau, *Edinburgh Review* (July 1839), lxix, 495–6.

The Wellesley Index suggests that this review may be by T. H. Lister.

This work reminds us, in some respects, of the writings of an authoress, who, though eventually much esteemed, did not immediately receive her due meed of popularity—we mean the late Miss Austin. There is the same microscopic observation of foibles—the same quick sense of the ridiculous, especially as displayed in affectation and pretension; both avoid the leaven of romance; and both draw their scenes among country society of the middle classes. Both have displayed a very uncommon knowledge of human nature; but Miss Austin is like one who plays by ear, while Miss Martineau understands the science. Miss Austin has the air of being led to right conclusions by an intuitive tact—Miss Martineau unfolds her knowledge of the principles on which her correct judgment is founded. Each also has advantages which the other does not possess. Miss Martineau has more eloquence, more poetry, more masculine vigour of style; Miss Austin had more grace, more ease, more playful humour, and a more subtle and lively power of ridicule— more skill in making her personages speak characteristically—and a more exquisite completeness of design and strict attention to probability.

26. Macaulay on Jane Austen

1843

Extract from an unsigned article, 'The Diary and Letters of Mme D'Arblay', *Edinburgh Review* (January 1843), lxxvi, 561–2.

Thomas Babington Macaulay (1800–59), politician, essayist and historian, was rather unkindly described by Henry James as Jane Austen's 'first slightly ponderous *amorosa*', presumably on account of his praise for her character-portrayal and the association of her name with Shakespeare. Consciously or unconsciously Macaulay is developing points already suggested by Whately (No. 16). In the section immediately preceding this extract Macaulay distinguishes between caricature and the true representation of human nature, found supremely in the characters of Shakespeare.

Shakspeare has had neither equal nor second. But among the writers who, in the point which we have noticed, have approached nearest to the manner of the great master, we have no hesitation in placing Jane Austen, a woman of whom England is justly proud. She has given us a multitude of characters, all in a certain sense, common-place, all such as we meet every day. Yet they are all as perfectly discriminated from each other as if they were the most eccentric of human beings. There are, for example, four clergymen, none of whom we should be surprised to find in any parsonage in the kingdom, Mr Edward Ferrars, Mr Henry Tilney, Mr Edmund Bertram, and Mr Elton. They are all specimens of the upper part of the middle class. They have all been liberally educated. They all lie under the restraints of the same sacred profession. They are all young. They are all in love. Not one of them has any hobbyhorse, to use the phrase of Sterne. Not one has a ruling passion, such as we read of in Pope. Who would not have expected them to be insipid likenesses of each other? No such thing. Harpagon is not more unlike to Jourdain, Joseph Surface is not more unlike to Sir Lucius O'Trigger, than every one of Miss Austen's young divines to all his reverend brethren. And almost all this is done by touches so delicate, that they elude analysis, that they defy the powers of description, and that we know them to exist only by the general effect to which they have contributed.

A line must be drawn, we conceive, between artists of this class, and those poets and novelists whose skill lies in the exhibiting of what Ben Jonson called humours. The words of Ben are so much to the purpose, that we will quote them:—

> When some one peculiar quality
> Doth so possess a man, that it doth draw
> All his affects, his spirits, and his powers,
> In their confluxions all to run one way,
> This may be truly said to be a humour.

There are undoubtedly persons, in whom humours such as Ben describes have attained a complete ascendency. The avarice of Elwes, the insane desire of Sir Egerton Brydges for a barony to which he had no more right than to the crown of Spain, the malevolence which long meditation on imaginary wrongs generated in the gloomy mind of Bellingham, are instances. The feeling which animated Clarkson and other virtuous men against the slave-trade and slavery, is an instance of a more honourable kind.

Seeing that such humours exist, we cannot deny that they are proper subjects for the imitations of art. But we conceive that the imitation of such humours, however skilful and amusing, is not an achievement of the highest order; and, as such humours are rare in real life, they ought, we conceive, to be sparingly introduced into works which profess to be pictures of real life. Nevertheless, a writer may show so much genius in the exhibition of these humours, as to be fairly entitled to a distinguished and permanent rank among classics. The chief seats of all, however, the places on the dais and under the canopy, are reserved for the few who have excelled in the difficult art of portraying characters in which no single feature is extravagantly overcharged.

27. G. H. Lewes on Jane Austen

1847

Extract from an unsigned review, 'Recent Novels: French and English', *Fraser's Magazine* (December 1847), xxxvi, 687.

George Henry Lewes (1817–78) was an accomplished and scholarly journalist with a great interest in fiction. His championing of Jane Austen dates from this review, although in the *New Quarterly Review* for October 1845 he mentioned her alongside Goethe, Fielding and Cervantes as the only authors to have depicted character with the profundity, subtlety and consistency of Shakespeare and Molière. In this *Fraser's* review he is prefacing his remarks on individual novels with a statement of his conviction that the novel is in 'the first rank of literature' and a confession, for the benefit of the reader, of his own 'peculiar tastes'. Clearly, he judged that his recommendation of Jane Austen would be read with surprise, as indeed it was, by Charlotte Brontë (see No. 28 a, b).

What we most heartily enjoy and applaud, is truth in the delineation of life and character: incidents however wonderful, adventures however perilous, are almost as naught when compared with the deep and lasting interest excited by any thing like a correct representation of life. That, indeed, seems to us to be Art, and the only Art we care to applaud. To make our meaning precise, we should say that Fielding and Miss Austen are the greatest novelists in our language. Scott has greater invention, more varied powers, a more poetical and pictorial imagination; but although his delineation of character is generally true, as far as it goes, it is never deep; and his deficiencies are singularly apparent, when, as in *St. Ronan's Well*, he ventures into the perilous sphere of contemporary life. We bid no one adopt our opinions on this point. If Scott is preferred to all others, we have no quarrel on that score; we have merely to record an individual opinion, that great—

indeed, astonishing as Scott's powers of attraction are, we would rather have written *Pride and Prejudice*, or *Tom Jones*, than any of the Waverley Novels. Scott was the Ariosto of prose romance. Let no word savouring of depreciation fall from our lips; but if he was an Ariosto, he was not a Shakspeare: he had not that singular faculty of penetrating into the most secret recesses of the heart, and of shewing us a character in its inward and outward workings, in its involuntary self-betrayals and subtle self-sophistications; he had not, above all, those two Shakspearian qualities —tenderness and passion. We can never hear him likened to Shakspeare without a strange sense of the incongruity. The two minds had certainly some peculiarities in common, but they belonged altogether to a different species. Now Miss Austen has been called a prose Shakspeare; and, among others, by Macaulay[1]. In spite of the sense of incongruity which besets us in the words *prose* Shakspeare, we confess the greatness of Miss Austen, her marvellous dramatic power, seems more than any thing in Scott akin to the greatest quality in Shakspeare.

Not to pursue this point further, we may repeat our confession of decided preference for true and artistic delineation of life and character to all the other ingredients supposed to be necessary for the success of a novel. Adventure will not replace it; eloquence will not atone for its absence; wit or humour will not conceal the deficiency. A novel may by the dashing brilliancy of its style create a momentary sensation; by some well-kept-up mystery, some rapid incidents, or some subject of horror dragged from the reeking shambles of civilisation, it may hurry the reader onward through its three volumes; but to produce a pleasant, satisfactory, and lasting impression, it must be true to nature. It will then live. It will bear reading and re-reading. It will create towards the author a feeling of regard in all his readers, to whom it will be a pleasant and thought-suggesting reminiscence. It will have fulfilled the real purpose of literature.

[1] Lewes seems to be putting the phrase 'prose Shakspeare' into Macaulay's mouth. These very words do not, in fact, appear in Macaulay's only known comments (No. 26); nor do we know of the mysterious 'others' to whom Lewes also credits the phrase.

28. Charlotte Brontë on Jane Austen

1848, 1850

Extracts from letters, *The Brontës: Their Friendships Lives, and Correspondence* (1932), edd. T. J. Wise and J. A. Symington.

Charlotte Brontë (1816–55) wrote to G. H. Lewes after reading his review (No. 27) in *Fraser's*. She was gratified at his praise for her first novel, *Jane Eyre* (1847), but puzzled, and perhaps even a little piqued, at the extent of his praise for Jane Austen.

(a) Extract from letter, 12 January 1848, to G. H. Lewes: 'Why do you like Miss Austen so very much? I am puzzled on that point. What induced you to say that you would have rather written *Pride and Prejudice* or *Tom Jones*, than any of the Waverley Novels?

I had not seen *Pride and Prejudice* till I read that sentence of yours, and then I got the book. And what did I find? An accurate daguerreotyped portrait of a commonplace face;[1] a carefully fenced, highly cultivated garden, with neat borders and delicate flowers; but no glance of a bright, vivid physiognomy, no open country, no fresh air, no blue hill, no bonny beck. I should hardly like to live with her ladies and gentlemen, in their elegant but confined houses. These observations will probably irritate you, but I shall run the risk.

Now I can understand admiration of George Sand; for though I never saw any of her works which I admired throughout (even *Consuelo*, which is the best, or the best that I have read, appears to me to couple strange extravagance with wondrous excellence), yet she has a grasp of mind which, if I cannot fully comprehend, I can very deeply respect: she is sagacious and profound; Miss Austen is only shrewd and observant.

Am I wrong; or were you hasty in what you said? If you have time I should be glad to hear further on this subject; if not, or if you think the question frivolous, do not trouble yourself to reply.' (ii, 178–9.)

---

[1] Indisputably 'commonplace' engraved portraits of Elizabeth Bennet face the reader on the title-pages of Bentley's 1833 edition of *Pride and Prejudice*.

(b) Extract from letter, 18 January 1848, to G. H. Lewes. She is answering his reply to her first letter (a); unfortunately, Lewes's reply is not extant, although there is no difficulty in reconstructing the tenor of his remarks: 'What a strange lecture comes next in your letter! You say I must familiarise my mind with the fact that "Miss Austen is not a poetess, has no 'sentiment' " (you scornfully enclose the word in inverted commas), "no eloquence, none of the ravishing enthusiasm of poetry"; and then you add, I *must* "learn to acknowledge her as *one of the greatest artists, of the greatest painters of human character,* and one of the writers with the nicest sense of means to an end that ever lived."

The last point only will I ever acknowledge.

Can there be a great artist without poetry?

What I call—what I will bend to, as a great artist, then—cannot be destitute of the divine gift. But by *poetry*, I am sure, you understand something different to what I do, as you do by "sentiment." It is *poetry*, as I comprehend the word, which elevates that masculine George Sand, and makes out of something coarse something godlike. It is "sentiment," in my sense of the term—sentiment jealously hidden, but genuine, which extracts the venom from that formidable Thackeray, and converts what might be corrosive poison into purifying elixir.

If Thackeray did not cherish in his large heart deep feeling for his kind, he would delight to exterminate; as it is, I believe, he wishes only to reform. Miss Austen being, as you say, without "sentiment," without *poetry*, maybe *is* sensible, real (more *real* than *true*), but she cannot be great.

I submit to your anger, which I have now excited (for have I not questioned the perfection of your darling?); the storm may pass over me. Nevertheless I will, when I can (I do not know when that will be, as I have no access to a circulating library), diligently peruse all Miss Austen's works, as you recommend.' (ii, 180-1.)

(c) Extract from letter, 12 April 1850, to W. S. Williams. Williams was the publisher's reader instrumental in the acceptance and publication of *Jane Eyre* by Smith and Elder. She corresponded with him very extensively. In this letter she has just reported on her reading of the life of Southey: 'I have likewise read one of Miss Austen's works *Emma*—read it with interest and with just the degree of admiration which Miss Austen herself would have thought sensible and suitable—anything like warmth or enthusiasm; anything energetic, poignant, heartfelt, is utterly out of place in commending these works: all such demonstration the authoress would have met with a well-bred sneer, would have calmly scorned as outré and extravagant. She does her business of delineating the surface of the lives of genteel English people curiously well; there is a Chinese fidelity, a miniature delicacy in the painting: she ruffles her reader by nothing vehement, disturbs him by nothing profound: the Passions are perfectly unknown to her; she rejects even a speaking acquaintance with that stormy Sisterhood; even to the Feelings she vouchsafes no more than an occasional graceful but distant recognition; too frequent converse with them would ruffle the smooth elegance of her progress. Her business is not half so much with the human heart as with the human eyes, mouth, hands and feet; what sees keenly, speaks aptly, moves flexibly, it suits her to study, but what throbs fast and full, though hidden, what the blood rushes through, what is the unseen seat of Life and the sentient target of death—*this* Miss Austen ignores; she no more, with her mind's eye, beholds the heart of her race than each man, with bodily vision sees the heart in his heaving breast. Jane Austen was a complete and most sensible lady, but a very incomplete, and rather insensible (*not senseless*) woman, if this is heresy— I cannot help it. If I said it to some people (Lewes for instance) they would directly accuse me of advocating exaggerated heroics, but I am not afraid of your falling into any such vulgar error.' (iii, 99.)

29. An American View
1849

Extract from an American handbook, *Outlines of General Literature* (1849), T. B. Shaw, 479–80.

The entry for Jane Austen comes in the section for *Fashionable Novels*, immediately following an account of the novelists of high-life, of whom only Dis'raeli is remembered today.

Descending the social scale, we come to a very large and characteristic department of works—the department which undoubtedly possesses not only the greatest degree of value for the English reader, but will have the most powerful attraction for foreign students of our literature. This is that class of fictions which depicts the manners of the middle and lower classes: and here again we shall encounter a singular amount of female names. The first in point of time, and perhaps almost the first in point of merit, in this class, especially among the ladies, is Miss Austen, whose novels may be considered as models of perfection in a new and very difficult species of writing. She depends for her effect upon no surprising adventures, upon no artfully involved plot, upon no scenes deeply pathetic or extravagantly humorous. She paints a society which, though virtuous, intelligent, and enviable above all others, presents the fewest salient points of interest and singularity to the novelist—we mean the society of English country gentlemen. Whoever desires to know the interior life of that vast and admirable body the rural gentry of England —a body which absolutely exists in no other country on earth, and to which the nation owes many of its most valuable characteristics—must read the novels of Miss Austen. In these works the reader will find very little variety and no picturesqueness of persons, little to inspire strong emotion, nothing to excite wonder or laughter; but he will find admirable good sense, exquisite discrimination, and an unrivalled power of easy and natural dialogue. Miss Ferrier has also written a number of novels, generally depicting with great vivacity and truth the oddities and affectations of semi-vulgar life, but her works are far inferior, as artistic productions, to the elegant sketches of Miss Austen.

30. Lewes: Jane Austen as a 'Prose Shakespeare'
1851

Extracts from an unsigned review of the anonymous *The Fair Carew*, *The Leader* (22 November 1851), p. 115.

Lewes takes this opportunity to qualify further the implications of Macaulay's association of Jane Austen with Shakespeare (No. 26), although it was Lewes himself who had coined the phrase 'prose Shakespeare' (No. 27). Immediately before the opening of this extract, Lewes conjectures that the author of the novel under review had been using Jane Austen 'consciously or unconsciously' as a model.

May we suggest to all novelists that Miss Austen, incomparable as an artist, is the most dangerous of models. It is only plenitude of power that restrains her from the perils of the form she has chosen—the perils, namely, of tedium and commonplace. Dealing as she does with every day people and every day life, avoiding all the grander tragic emotions and more impassioned aspects of Life, her art consists in charming us by the fidelity of the picture while relieving it of all the tedium of reality. One degree less felicitous, and failure begins! She makes her people speak and act as they speak and act in every day life; and she is the only artist who has done this with success and pleasant effect. Macaulay styled her a Prose Shakespeare. We cannot, for our parts, conceive Shakespeare under prosaic conditions, poetry being so essentially involved in the whole structure of his works; but if we divest him, in thought, of his winged attributes—if we set aside his passion, imagination, fancy, and rhythm, there will remain a central power of dramatic creation, the power of constructing and animating character, which may truly be said to find a younger sister in Miss Austen. Observe, however, that in place of his poetry we must put her daring prose—daring from its humble truthfulness. Here again is a serious danger: into it all Miss Austen's imitators fall, they cannot keep to the severe level of prose; they rise above it, and the result is incongruity; or they sink below it, and the result is tediousness.

31. The mid-century view

1852

Unsigned article, the first in a series on the 'Female Novelists',
New Monthly Magazine (May 1852), xcv, 17–23.

Historic as the first considerable 'middle-brow' piece on Jane
Austen, this article is aimed at introducing a relatively unknown
and undervalued author to the reading-public at large (see Introduction, p. 25).

Given a subject of composition like the novel, it is reasonable to expect
a goodly proportion of what Monkbarns[1] called 'womankind' among
the compositors. The subject is attractive to those tastes, and within the
scope of those faculties, which are, generally speaking, characteristic of
the fairer sex. Perhaps, indeed—and some critics would substitute 'un-
questionably' for 'perhaps'—none but a man, of first-rate powers
withal, can produce a first-rate novel; and, if so, it may be alleged that
a woman of corresponding genius (*quâ* woman) can only produce one
of a second-rate order. However *that* may be—and leaving the definition
of what is first-rate and what second-rate to critics of a subtler vein and
weightier calibre than we shall ever attain to—proofs there are, enough
and to spare, in the literature of our land, that clever women can write,
and have written, very clever novels; that this is a department where
they feel and show themselves at home; that, in the symmetry of a
complicated plot, the elaboration of varied character, and the filling-in
of artistic touches and imaginative details, they can design and accomplish works which go down to posterity not very far behind those of
certain Titanic lords of creation. As it was reasonable to predicate an
abundance of female novelists, so is it evident, by every circulating
library and every advertising journal, that such abundance exists.
Almost the earliest pieces of prose fictions in our language are from the
pen of a woman—not the most exemplary of her sex—Mistress Aphra
Behn, the 'Astræa' of Charles the Second's days. After the novel, more
properly so called, had acquired a local habitation and a name amongst

[1] The principal character in Scott's *The Antiquary*.

131

us, by the performances of Richardson, Fielding, and Smollett, we find, during the past century, an imposing array of 'womankind' successfully cultivating these 'pastures new.' Clara Reeve wrote several tales of the *Otranto* type, all marked, in the judgment of Sir Walter Scott, by excellent good sense, pure morality, and a competent command of those qualities which constitute a good romance. If the Minerva Press deluged the town with its spring-tide of fluent nonsense, much of it the billowy froth of feminine as well as effeminate *Persons of Quality*, there soon uprose to stem the current a succession of ladies who could cope better with its surges than Mrs. Partington with those of the Atlantic. Mrs. Radcliffe is by no means the *beau-ideal* of a novelist; yet even *her* atrocities were an improvement upon, and instrumentally fatal to, the squeamish woes of that maudlin clique. Then, too, came Charlotte Smith, of *Old Manor House* celebrity; and little Fanny Burney, with her Evelinas and Cecilias and Camillas; and the sisters Lee, with their *Canterbury Tales*; and the sisters Porter, of whom Anna Maria alone published half a century of volumes; and Mrs. Brunton, the still popular authoress of *Self-Control*; and Miss Edgeworth, whose gift it was to dispense common sense to her readers, and to bring them within the 'precincts of real life and natural feeling.' As we approach more closely to our own times, the name of the fair company becomes legion. Mrs. Shelley appears:

> And Shelley, four-famed—for her parents, her lord,
> And the poor, lone, impossible monster abhorred—[1]

Frankenstein, to wit—a romance classed by Moore with those original conceptions that take hold of the public mind at once and for ever. Miss Ferrier is a foremost reaper of what Scott called the large harvest of Scottish characters and fiction, a harvest in which recent labourers (witness 'Mrs. Margaret Maitland,' &c.) have found new sheaves for their sickle. Lady Morgan presents us with a *Wild Irish Girl* and *Florence Macarthy*. Mrs Trollope is seen in the plethora of exhaustless authorship, surpassed therein only by Mrs. Gore, with her

> Heaps of 'Polite Conversation,' so true
> That one cannot but wish the three volumes were two;
> But not when she dwells upon daughters or mothers—
> Oh, then the three make us quite long for three others.

[1] This couplet and the four lines quoted later are from Leigh Hunt's satirical poem 'Blue-Stocking Revels' (1837); Jane Austen does not win a place in the catalogue of female novelists.

And who will not be ready to name Mary Russell Mitford, one of England's truest *autochthonai*?[1] and Mrs. S. C. Hall, that kindly and wise-hearted limner of the lights and shadows of Irish life? and Mrs. Bray, of Tavistock, the accomplished delineator of Devonshire characters and characteristics? and Lady Blessington, whose writings often beam, like her face in the golden age of Gore House (before the *entrée* of Soyer and the Symposium), with 'enjoyment, and judgment, and wit, and good-nature?' and Mrs. Marsh, the powerful as well as industrious authoress of many an impressive fiction? and Currer Bell, one of the few who have lately excited a real 'sensation?' and Mrs. Crowe, with her melodramatic points and supernatural adjuncts, some of which make even utilitarians and materialists look transcendental for the nonce? and Mrs. Gaskill, whose 'mission' is as benevolent and practical as her manner is clear and forcible? The catalogue might be lengthened out with many other well-known titles, such as Landon, Martineau, Hoffland, Pardoe, Bowles, Pickering, Norton, Howitt, Johnstone, Ellis, Kavanagh, &c., &c.

In her own line of things, Jane Austen is surpassed, perhaps equalled, by none of this pleasant and numerous family. She is perfect mistress of all she touches, and certainly *nil tetigit quod non ornavit*[2]—if not with the embellishments of idealism and romance, at least with the fresh strokes of nature. She fascinates you with common-place people. She effectually interests you in the 'small-beer chronicles' of every-day household life. She secures your attention to a group of 'walking gentlemen,' who have not even the

> Start theatric practised at the glass

to attract admiration, and of unremarkable ladies, who, shocking as it may seem to seasoned novel-readers, are

> Not too bright or good
> For human nature's daily food.

You have actually met all her heroes and heroines before—not in novels, but in most unromantic and prosaic circumstances; you have talked with them, and never seen anything in them—anything, at least, worthy of three volumes, at half-a-guinea a volume. How *could* such folks find their way into a printed book? That is a marvel, a paradox, a practical solecism. But a greater marvel remains behind, and that is, how comes it that such folks, having got into the book, make it so interesting?

[1] Natives.
[2] Touches nothing without embellishing it.

Take, reader, that quiet, unassuming gentleman with whom you exchanged a few mercurial trivialities in the omnibus this morning, touching the weather and the adjourned debate; take that elderly burgess who called on you about some railway shares, and left you without having said (never mind whether he heard) one smart thing in the course of twenty minutes' unbroken conversation—at which absence of piquancy and Attic salt neither you were surprised nor he a whit ashamed; take that semi-sleepy clergyman, whose homily you listened to yesterday morning with such phlegmatic politeness, and who (it is your infallible conviction) is guiltless of the power to say or do anything clever, original, or even unusual; take that provincial attorney, who bores you so with his pedantries and platitudes whenever you are vegetating in a midland county with your country cousins; take, also, that well-intentioned, loquacious old maid with whom you walked home yesterday from morning service, and who discoursed so glibly and so illogically about an infinity of very finite things; and take those good-natured, unexceptionable misses with whom and their mamma you drink tea this evening, without any fear of the consequences:— take these, and as many more as you please of a similar fabric—people who never astonished you, never electrified you with revelations of strange experience, never made your each particular hair to stand on end by unfolding a tale of personal mystery, never affected the *rôle* of Wandering Jews, or Sorrowing Werters, or Justifiable Homicides, or Mysterious Strangers, or Black-veiled Nuns; take, we say, a *quantum suff.* of these worthy prosaists, and set up in type their words and actions of this current day, and you have a fair specimen of the sort of figures and scenes pictured on Miss Austen's canvas. The charm is, that they are so exquisitely real; they are transcripts of actual life; their features, gestures, gossip, sympathies, antipathies, virtues, foibles, are all true, unexaggerated, uncoloured, yet singularly entertaining. We do not mean that we, or you, reader, or even that professed and successful novelists now living, could produce the same result with the same means, or elicit from the given terms an equivalent remainder. Herein, on the contrary, lies the unique power of Jane Austen, that where every one else is nearly sure of failing, she invariably and unequivocally triumphs. What, in other hands, would be a flat, insipid, intolerable piece of impertinent dulness, becomes, at her bidding, a sprightly, versatile, never-flagging chapter of realities. She knows how far to go in describing a character, and where to stop, never allowing that character to soar into romance or to sink into mere twaddle. She is a thorough artist

in the management of nature. Her sketches from nature are not pro-
fusely huddled together in crude and ill-assorted heaps—the indiscriminate riches of a crowded portfolio, into which genius has recklessly
tossed its manifold essays, all clever, but not all in place; but they are
selected and arranged with the practised skill of a disciplined judgment,
and challenge the scrutiny of tasteful students of design.

Miss Austen has not even yet, we submit, reaped her rightful share of
public homage. Both Sir Walter Scott and Archbishop Whately—the
one in 1815, the other in 1821—saw and proclaimed her distinguished
merits in the pages of the *Quarterly Review*. Sir Walter observes, that,
keeping close to common incidents, and to such characters as occupy
the ordinary walks of life, she has produced sketches of such spirit and
originality that we never miss the excitation which depends upon a
narrative of uncommon events, arising from the consideration of minds,
manners, and sentiments greatly above our own. She 'confines herself
chiefly to the middling classes of society. Her most distinguished
characters do not rise greatly above well-bred country gentlemen and
ladies; and those which are sketched with most originality and precision
belong to a class rather below that standard. The narrative of all her
novels is composed of such common occurrences as may have fallen
under the observation of most folks, and her *dramatis personæ* conduct
themselves upon the motives and principles which the readers may
recognise as ruling their own and that of most of their acquaintances.'
So wrote the unknown novelist who had just given to the world
Waverley and *Guy Mannering*. Eleven years of personal and unparalleled
triumph found Sir Walter confirmed in his admiration of Jane Austen;
for, in 1826—that is, after he had composed *Rob Roy*, and the *Tales of
my Landlord*, and *Ivanhoe*, and *Quentin Durward*, and while he was busy
at *Woodstock*—we find the following characteristic entry in his diary,
or 'gurnal,' as he loved to style it: 'Read again, and for the third time at
least, Miss Austen's very finely-written novel of *Pride and Prejudice*.
That young lady had a talent for describing the involvments, and feelings, and characters of ordinary life which is to me the most wonderful
I ever met with. The big bow-wow strain I can do myself, like any
now going; but the exquisite touch which renders ordinary commonplace things and characters interesting, from the truth of the description
and the sentiment, is denied to me. What a pity such a gifted creature
died so early!' An Edinburgh Reviewer justly remarks, that ordinary
readers have been apt to judge of her as Partridge judged of Garrick's
acting. He could not see the merit of a man behaving on the stage as

anybody might be expected to behave under similar circumstances in real life. He infinitely preferred the 'robustious, periwigpated fellow,' who flourished his arms like a windmill, and ranted with the voice of three. Even thus is Miss Austen too natural for superficial readers. 'It seems to them as if there can be very little merit in making characters talk and act so exactly like the people whom they see around them every day. They do not consider that the highest triumph of art consists in its concealment; and here the art is so little perceptible that they believe there is none.'[1] Meanwhile, readers of more refined taste and critical acumen feel something like dissatisfaction with almost every other domestic novelist, after they have once appreciated Miss Austen. After her unaffected good-sense, her shrewd insight, her felicitous irony, and the fruitful harvest of her quiet eye, they are palled by the laboured unrealities of her competitors. Certainly, the consummate ease with which this gifted lady filled up her designs and harmonised her colours is of a kind vouchsafed unto the fewest, and, we apprehend, to no one else in an equal degree. She is never at a loss—never has occasion for the 'big bow-wow style' to which others have such frequent recourse

To point their moral and adorn their tale.

She walks without irons to keep her in shape, or stilts to exalt her. Her diction is innocent of *sesquipedalia verba*;[2] her manners and deportment were learnt under no Gallic dancing-master. If she occasionally dons a piece of *bijouterie*, be assured that it is no paste jewellery, and that Birmingham was not its birthplace. The fresh bloom upon her cheek comes from fresh air and sound health, not from the rouge-pot or any cognate source. Between this novel-writer and the conventional novel-wright, what a gulf profound! Alike, but oh, *how* different!

Fault has been found with Miss Austen, and with considerable show of justice, on account of the prodigious amount of love-making in her tales. Love is the beginning, middle, and end of each and all. Page the first and page the last are occupied with the conjugation of the verb *amo*. Every new chapter is like a new tense, every volume a mood, of that all-absorbing verb. She plunges at once *in medias res* (see, for example, the first sentence in *Pride and Prejudice*), and confines herself to the working out the proposed equation with wonderful singleness of purpose. Now, where this topic is so uniformly and protractedly debated—where this one string is so incessantly harped on, it becomes a

---

[1] With slight change, quotes Lister, see above p. 113.
[2] Long words.

question whether, with all her admirable qualities freely recognised, Miss Austen's writings are of that healthy type which is calculated to benefit the world. We may well admit, with one of the authors of *Guesses at Truth*, that ordinary novels, which string a number of incidents and a few commonplace pasteboard characters around a love-story, teaching people to fancy that the main business of life is to make love, and to be made love to, and that, when it is made, all is over, are little or nothing else than mischievous; since it is most hurtful to be wishing to act a romance of this kind in real life—most hurtful to fancy that the interest of life lies in its pleasures and passions, not in its duties. But then Miss Austen's are *not* ordinary novels; her's are *not* pasteboard characters; and, with all her devotion to the task of delineating this master-principle, she, too, teaches that it is *not* the main business of life— she, too, contends that duty is before pleasure and passion, sense before sensibility. If languishing demoiselles appear in her works, whose pan-theism is made up of wedding-prophecies, marriage-bells, and bride-cake, it is only that they may be roundly ridiculed—tarred and feathered, as a warning to their sisterhood—nailed up as scarecrows, with every attendant circumstance of derision. Miss Austen's estimate of love in its true form is as far as can be from that of sickly sentimentalism or flighty schoolgirlishness. She honours it only when invested with the dignity, intensity, and equable constancy of its higher manifestations— where it comprehends and fulfils its wide circle of duties, and is as self-denying as it is self-respecting. There is a righteous intolerance of the mawkish trash which constitutes the staple of so many love-tales; and one cannot but admire Horace Walpole, for once, when he stops impatiently at the fourth volume of *Sir Charles Grandison*, and confesses: 'I am *so* tired of sets of people getting together, and saying, "Pray, miss, with whom are you in love," &c., &c.' And we grant that Miss Austen is a little too prodigal of scenes of love-making and preparations for match-making; but let us at the same time insist upon the marked difference between her descriptions and those of the common herd of novelists, with whom she is unjustly confounded; the fact being, that her most caustic passages, and the hardest hits and keenest thrusts of her satire, are directed against them and their miss-in-her-teens ex-travaganzas. Mr. Thackeray himself is not more sarcastic against snob-bism, than is Miss Austen against whatever is affected or perverted, or merely sentimental, in the province of love.

Plot she has little or none. If you only enjoy a labyrinthine *nexus* of events, an imbroglio of accidents, an atmosphere of mystery, you will probably toss aside her volumes as 'desperately slow.' Yet, in the careful, artist-like management of her story, in the skilful evolution of its processes, in the tactics of a gradually-wrought *dénouement*, in the truthful and natural adaptation of means to ends, she is almost, if not quite, unrivalled. Nothing can be more judicious than her use of suggestions and intimations of what is to follow. And all is conducted with a quiet grace that is, or seems to be, inimitable.

Writing, as she invariably does, 'with a purpose,' she yet avoids with peculiar success the manner of a sententious teacher, which very frequently ruffles and disgusts those who are to be taught. She spares us the infliction of sage aphorisms and doctrinal appeals; compassing her end by the simple narration of her stories, and the natural intercourse of her characters. The variety of those characters is another remarkable point. But we become intimate with, and interested in, them all. It has been said that the effect of reading Richardson's novels is, to acquire a vast accession of near relations. The same holds good of Miss Austen's. In the earliest of her works, *Northanger Abbey*—which, however, did not appear until after her death, in 1817—we have a capital illustration of a girl who designs to be very romantic, and to find a Castle of Udolpho in every possible locality, but whose natural good-sense and excellent heart work a speedy and radical cure. Another lifelike figure is that of General Tilney, so painfully polite, so distressingly punctilious, so uncivilly attentive, so despotically selfish; and then there are the motley visitors at Bath, all hit off *à merveille*, especially the Thorpe family. *Persuasion*, also published after the writer's decease, teems with individuality: Sir Walter Elliot, whose one book is the *Baronetage*, where he finds occupation for his idle hours, and consolation in his distressed ones; Mrs. Clay, clever, manœuvring, and unprincipled; Captain Wentworth, so intelligent, spirited, and generously high-minded; Anne Elliot, the self-sacrificing and noble-hearted victim of undue *persuasion*; her sister Mary, so prone to add to every other trouble that of fancying herself neglected and ill-used; Admiral and Mrs. Croft, a naval couple of the 'first water,' so frank, hearty, and constitutionally good-natured. Then again, in *Mansfield Park*, what a bewitching 'little body' is Fanny Price—what finish in the portraits of Crawford and his sister—what Dutch-school accuracy of detail in the home-pictures at Portsmouth, and what fine truth in the moral of the tale! In *Pride and Prejudice* we are introduced to five sisters, each possessing a marked idiosyncrasy: Jane, tender, confiding, and mildly contemplative; Lizzy, acute, impulsive, enthusiastic, and strong-minded; Mary, who, being the only plain one in the family, has worked hard for knowledge and accomplishments, and is always impatient for display; and the two youngest, Lydia and Kitty, who are mad after red coats and balls, both vulgar hoydens, the one leading and the other led, active and passive voices of the same irregular verb. Their mother, Mrs. Bennet, is done to the life—a sort of Mrs. Nickleby, without the caricature. Mr. Collins, the prim, soft-headed, tuft-hunting clergyman (by the way, excepting Edmund Bertram, what a goodly fellowship Miss Austen's clergymen are!); Lady de Bourgh, his insolent, coarse-mannered patroness; Mr. Darcy, the heart-sound representative of pride and prejudice; the Bingley sisters, shallow, purse-proud, intriguing; Wickham, the artful, double-faced adventurer—profligate, impudent, and perennially smiling; and Mr. Bennet himself, that strange compound of the amiable and disagreeable, with that supreme talent of his for ironical humour: all these are models of drawing. In *Sense and Sensibility* there are exact representatives of vulgar good-temper and vulgar selfishness, in Mrs. Jennings and Lucy Steele respectively; and of good sense and sensitiveness, in the sisters Elinor and Marianne. But if we must give the precedence to any one of Miss Austen's novels, we incline to name *Emma*, notwithstanding a little inconsistency in the character of the delightful heroine. The people we there consort with, please us mightily. It were hard to excel the humour with which Miss Bates is portrayed—that irresistible spinster, and eternal but most inoffensive gossip; or nervous, invalid, coddling Mr. Woodhouse; or that intolerably silly piece of egotism, Mr. Elton; and equally rare are the observation and delicacy employed in characterising Jane Fairfax and Mr. Knightley. The tale abounds in high feeling, sterling wisdom, and exquisite touches of art.

If this paper has something of the *rechauffé* odour of a 'retrospective' review, it is written not without a 'prospective' purpose; the writer being persuaded that Jane Austen needs but to be more widely known, to be more justly appreciated, and accordingly using this opportunity 'by way of remembrance.' If the Wizard of the North felt her

Weave a circle round him *thrice*,

and acknowledged at the 'third reading' a yet more potent spell than at the first, surely, to know that so many living novel readers by wholesale are uninitiated in her doctrine, is a thing to be classed under Pepys's favourite comment—'which did vex me.'

32. Lewes: Jane Austen the 'artist'

1852

Extract from an unsigned article, 'The Lady Novelists', *Westminster Review* (July 1852), lviii, 134–5.

Lewes takes up yet again (see Nos. 27, 30) the concept of Jane Austen as a 'prose Shakespeare', and the view of her artistic economy which he had communicated to Charlotte Brontë (No. 28b). His sympathy for what he identifies as 'her special quality of womanliness' may owe something to his friendship with George Eliot, which dates from 1851, as may his tribute to George Sand (continued in the body of the article), which could have been influenced by Charlotte Brontë's view (No. 28a).

First and foremost let Jane Austen be named, the greatest artist that has ever written, using the term to signify the most perfect mastery over the means to her end. There are heights and depths in human nature Miss Austen has never scaled nor fathomed, there are worlds of passionate existence into which she has never set foot; but although this is obvious to every reader, it is equally obvious that she has risked no failures by attempting to delineate that which she had not seen. Her circle may be restricted, but it is complete. Her world is a perfect orb, and vital. Life, as it presents itself to an English gentlewoman peacefully yet actively engaged in her quiet village, is mirrored in her works with a purity and fidelity that must endow them with interest for all time. To read one of her books is like an actual experience of life: you know the people as if you had lived with them, and you feel something of personal affection towards them. The marvellous reality and subtle distinctive traits noticeable in her portraits has led Macaulay to call her a prose Shakspeare. If the whole force of the distinction which lies in that epithet *prose* be fairly appreciated, no one, we think, will dispute the compliment; for out of Shakspeare it would be difficult to find characters so typical yet so nicely demarcated within the limits of their kind. We do not find such profound psychological insight as may be found in George Sand (not to mention male writers), but taking the type to which the characters belong, we see the most intimate and accurate knowledge in all Miss Austen's creations.

Only cultivated minds fairly appreciate the exquisite art of Miss Austen. Those who demand the stimulus of 'effects;' those who can only see by strong lights and shadows, will find her tame and uninteresting. We may illustrate this by one detail. Lucy Steele's bad English, so delicately and truthfully indicated, would in the hands of another have been more obvious, more 'effective' in its exaggeration, but the loss of this comic effect is more than replaced to the cultivated reader by his relish of the nice discrimination visible in its truthfulness. And so of the rest. *Strong* lights are unnecessary, *true* lights being at command. The incidents, the characters, the dialogue—all are of every day life, and so truthfully presented, that to appreciate the art we must try to imitate it, or carefully compare it with that of others.

We are but echoing an universal note of praise in speaking thus highly of her works, and it is from no desire of simply swelling that chorus of praise that we name her here, but to call attention to the peculiar excellence at once womanly and literary which has earned this reputation. Of all imaginative writers she is the most *real*. Never does she transcend her own actual experience, never does her pen trace a line that does not touch the experience of others. Herein we recognise the first quality of literature. We recognise the second and more special quality of womanliness in the tone and point of view: they are novels written by a woman, an Englishwoman, a gentlewoman; no signature could disguise that fact; and because she has so faithfully (although unconsciously) kept to her own womanly point of view, her works are durable. There is nothing of the *doctrinaire* in Jane Austen; not a trace of woman's 'mission;' but as the most truthful, charming, humorous, pure-minded, quick-witted, and unexaggerated of writers, female literature has reason to be proud of her.

Of greater genius, and incomparably deeper experience, George Sand represents woman's literature more illustriously and more obviously. In her, quite apart from the magnificent gifts of Nature, we see the influence of Sorrow, as a determining impulse to write, and the abiding consciousness of the womanly point of view as the subject matter of her writings.

33. Jane Austen in America
1853

Extract from an unsigned article by J. F. Kirk, 'Thackeray as a Novelist', *North American Review* (July 1853), lxxvii, 200–3.

Kirk (1824–1904), a writer on historical and literary subjects and periodical editor. By British standards, an unremarkable view, but of some interest as one of the very few early items of American origin.

There are few novelists who combine creative powers and a knowledge of the human heart with the faculty of delineating actual life and manners. The pathos and sublimity of Richardson, wellnigh smothered as they are by pompous sentiment and a cumbrous phraseology, are among the miracles of literature; but for any picture that he has left us of English life in the eighteenth century, he might have been destitute of eyes and ears. Scott was doubtless a keen observer of manners as well as of men; but poetry and romance-writing spoiled him for depicting the tamer features of modern society; and he was fain to acknowledge that the 'bow-wow' style was that which he managed best. Smollet's characters, admirable as they are, are mostly oddities; and his scenes, with all their humor, are the extravagances of nature, not its ordinary displays. The creations of Godwin, like the conceptions of the transcendental philosopher, are all evolved from his own *ich*; they are possibilities, deduced by *à priori* reasoning from the first principles of metaphysics. Miss Burney, on the other hand, gives us clever sketches of society, but she never penetrates below the surface; she makes us familiar with the company at Ranelagh and Vauxhall, but not with the more secret motives of conduct. In short, there are, as it seems to us, but three English novelists,—Fielding, Jane Austen, and Thackeray,—who both reveal the springs of action, and exhibit its outward aspects and local peculiarities; whose characters are types of classes, and in whose works we find reflected various phases of human nature as well as of English life. . . .

In placing Jane Austen in the same rank with Fielding and Thackeray, we do not expect to meet with general assent. In this country, at least, her writings have not acquired popularity. This may, perhaps, be owing to the narrow limits and almost unbroken level of the society which she paints. She has none of those bold conceptions which stamp themselves indelibly on the mind. There is no Parson Adams or Squire Western, no Becky Sharp or Major Pendennis, in any of her novels; no characters whose strongly marked features stand out in full relief, and whose names have become as familiar in men's mouths as those of celebrated men. If you speak of Sir Thomas Bertram, of Fanny Price, or of Mr. Collins, the allusion will require explanation. But this is owing, not to any deficiency of skill, but to the perfection of her art. She passed her life in the sphere of a respectable, but not high-born Englishwoman—familiar with the better classes of society in country towns; with the *beau monde* she seems to have been altogether unacquainted. She gives us only such characters and scenes as faithfully represent the manners of the society in which she lived. To have admitted incidents and persons, which, however real in themselves, did not belong to the ordinary features of the life which she portrays, would have destroyed the harmony of the picture. Nothing more commonplace can be imagined than the routine of action which forms the groundwork of each of her tales. But neither is it possible to imagine a more faithful delineation of any phase of society, or a more admirable constructive genius than that with which, from these materials, she forms a work of art. Her plots are so skilfully framed, that, while the interest of the story is always preserved, she never oversteps the bounds of probability. She never has recourse to the clumsy expedients of common novelists, who involve themselves in labyrinths from which they can only escape by a *coup-de-main*—who win the game by moving their knight diagonally, or making their bishop leap over a pawn. The *dénouement* of her plots is as simple as the development; the difficulty is solved by natural, yet unforeseen methods. Her talent is essentially dramatic. The authoress herself is never visible, never even peeps from behind the curtain. The characters are not described; they exhibit themselves in action and in speech; and there are no prose works of fiction in which the individuality of all the actors is so well maintained. Miss Austen's humor is rich and suggestive. She is not, however, a *humorist*, who sees that every object may be viewed in a sportive light. She never satirizes a class. She finds a theme for comedy only in those peculiarities which are laughed at by all the world; but she exposes these traits with a bold, yet delicate touch. *Mansfield Park* has more variety of incident than any of her other works, and is, on this account perhaps, a more general favorite. *Pride and Prejudice*, however, is superior in wit and humor; while the plot of *Emma* is equal to that of any of Ben Jonson's comedies. *Sense and Sensibility*, the earliest of her stories, is the least pleasing of them all; yet in none does she exhibit so profound an insight into human nature; and we have never read the work without astonishment that the most subtle play of motives, and the most delicate traits of character should have been thus faithfully portrayed by a woman at the age of twenty-five.

34. Unelevating Jane Austen
1853

Extract from an unsigned article, 'The Progress of Fiction as an Art', *Westminster Review* (October 1853), lx, 358–9.

Professor Gordon S. Haight has suggested, on internal evidence, that the author may be George Eliot. Immediately before the opening of this extract the essayist has been mentioning the tricks of the gothic and the Victorian sentimental novelists.

. . . the high reputation which Miss Austin's novels gained, and still retain, is a proof of the ready appreciation which is always felt when an author dares to be natural. Without brilliancy of any kind—without imagination, depth of thought, or wide experience, Miss Austin, by simply describing what she knew and had seen, and making accurate portraits of very tiresome and uninteresting people, is recognised as a true artist, and will continue to be admired, when many authors more ambitious, and believing themselves filled with a much higher inspiration, will be neglected and forgotten. There is an instinct in every unwarped mind which prefers truth to extravagance, and a photographic picture, if it be only of a kitten or a hay-stack, is a pleasanter subject in the eyes of most persons (were they brave enough to admit it), than many a glaring piece of mythology, which those who profess to worship High Art find themselves called upon to pronounce divine. People will persist in admiring what they can appreciate and understand, and Wilkie will keep his place among national favourites when poor Haydon's Dentatus is turned to the wall. But Miss Austin's accurate scenes from dull life, and Miss Burney's long histories of amiable and persecuted heroines, though belonging to the modern and reformed school of novels, must still be classed in the lower division. As pictures of manners, they are interesting and amusing, but they want the broader foundation, the firm granite substratum, which the great masters who have followed them have taught us to expect. They show us too much of the littlenesses and trivialities of life, and limit themselves so scrupulously to the sayings and doings of dull, ignorant, and disagreeable people, that their very truthfulness makes us yawn. They fall short of fulfilling the objects, and satisfying the necessities of Fiction in its highest aspect—as the art whose office it is 'to interest, to please, and sportively to elevate—to take man from the low passions and miserable troubles of life into a higher region, to beguile weary and selfish pain, to excite a generous sorrow at vicissitudes not his own, to raise the passions into sympathy with heroic troubles, and to admit the soul into that serener atmosphere from which it rarely returns to ordinary existence without some memory or association which ought to enlarge the domain of thought, and exalt the motives of action.'[1]

[1] Bulwer Lytton, Preface to *Night and Morning* (1841).

35. Unelevating Jane Austen again
1854

Extract from an unsigned review of the anonymous *Heartease, Fraser's Magazine* (November 1854), 1, 490.

That we English dearly love truth be it great or small (for small truths are very different from half-truths), is clearly evidenced by the reception which Miss Austin's novels met with on their first appearance, and the reputation they have continued to sustain. She confined herself, however, to the narrow sphere of the petty interests, the loves, jealousies, and intrigues of small country towns; and whilst we are interested and amused with her faithful, Teniers-like pictures of the domestic interiors of provincial homes, we receive but little improvement from them, excepting in so far as it is impossible to contemplate truth of any kind without finding in it something from which we may derive benefit— some lesson which we may take to ourselves. In these novels it is the lower class of feelings which is principally appealed to; the nature sketched with such inimitable skill is not nature of a very exalted kind, improved, strengthened, and refined by the discipline of sorrow and trial; and now that we have been taught to love and admire excellence of a nobler description we almost wonder how we could ever have been so strongly interested in characters which have nothing high or ideal about them. Although it be an essential part of the duty of an artist to give us a faithful likeness, he will not have performed his highest function, or produced a work of genius, unless he present us with that likeness idealized by his having imparted to it the sum total of the noblest characteristics of the spiritual as well as the material life.

36. Lewes: The great appraisal
1859

Unsigned article, 'The Novels of Jane Austen', *Blackwood's Edinburgh Magazine* (July 1859), lxxxvi, 99–113.

Lewes's last and most important appraisal of Jane Austen (see Introduction, pp. 25, 28–9).

For nearly half a century England has possessed an artist of the highest rank, whose works have been extensively circulated, whose merits have been keenly relished, and whose name is still unfamiliar in men's mouths. One would suppose that great excellence and real success would inevitably produce a loud reputation. Yet in this particular case such a supposition would be singularly mistaken. So far from the name of Miss Austen being constantly cited among the glories of our literature, there are many well-informed persons who will be surprised to hear it mentioned among the best writers. If we look at Hazlitt's account of the English novelists, in his *Lectures on the Comic Writers*, we find Mrs Radcliff, Mrs Inchbald, Mrs Opie, Miss Burney, and Miss Edgeworth receiving due honour, and more than is due; but no hint that Miss Austen has written a line. If we cast a glance over the list of English authors republished by Baudry, Galignani, and Tauchnitz, we find there writers of the very smallest pretensions, but not the author of *Emma*, and *Mansfield Park*. Mention the name of Miss Austen to a cultivated reader, and it is probable that the sparkle in his eye will at once flash forth sympathetic admiration, and he will perhaps relate how Scott, Whately, and Macaulay prize this gifted woman, and how the English public has bought her works; but beyond the literary circle we find the name almost entirely unknown; and not simply unknown in the sense of having no acknowledged place among the remarkable writers, but unremembered even in connection with the very works which are themselves remembered. We have met with many persons who remembered to have read *Pride and Prejudice*, or *Mansfield Park*, but who had altogether forgotten by whom they were written. 'Miss Austen? Oh, yes; she translates from the German, doesn't she?' is a not uncommon question—a vague familiarity with the name of Mrs Austin being uppermost. From time to time also the tiresome twaddle of lady novelists is praised by certain critics, as exhibiting the 'quiet truthfulness of Miss Austin.'

That Miss Austen is an artist of high rank, in the most rigorous sense of the word, is an opinion which in the present article we shall endeavour to substantiate. That her novels are very extensively read, is not an opinion, but a demonstrated fact; and with this fact we couple the paradoxical fact, of a fine artist, whose works are widely known and enjoyed, being all but unknown to the English public, and quite unknown abroad. The causes which have kept her name in comparative obscurity all the time that her works have been extensively read, and her reputation every year has been settling itself more firmly in the minds of the better critics, may well be worth an inquiry. It is intelligible how the blaze of Scott should have thrown her into the shade, at first: beside his frescoes her works are but miniatures; exquisite as miniatures, yet incapable of ever filling that space in the public eye which was filled by his massive and masterly pictures. But although it is intelligible why Scott should have eclipsed her, it is not at first so easy to understand why Miss Edgeworth should have done so. Miss Austen, indeed, has taken her revenge with posterity. She will doubtless be read as long as English novels find readers; whereas Miss Edgeworth is already little more than a name, and only finds a public for her children's books. But contemporaries, for the most part, judged otherwise; and in consequence Miss Edgeworth's name has become familiar all over the three kingdoms. Scott, indeed, and Archbishop Whately, at once perceived the superiority of Miss Austen to her more fortunate rival; but the *Quarterly* tells us that 'her fame has grown fastest since she died: there was no *éclat* about her first appearance: the public took time to make up its mind; and she, not having staked her hopes of happiness on success or failure, was content to wait for the decision of her claims. Those claims have been long established beyond a question; but the merit of *first* recognising them belongs less to reviewers than to general readers.' There is comfort in this for authors who see the applause of reviewers lavished on works of garish effect. Nothing that is really good can fail, at last, in securing its audience; and it is evident that Miss Austen's works must possess elements of indestructible excellence, since, although never 'popular,' she survives writers who were very popular; and forty years after her death, gains more recognition than she gained when alive. Those who, like ourselves, have read and re-read her works several times, can understand this duration, and this increase of her fame. But the fact that her name is not even now a household word proves that her excellence must be of an unobtrusive kind, shunning the glare of popularity, not appealing to temporary tastes and vulgar sympathies, but demanding culture in its admirers. Johnson wittily says of somebody, 'Sir, he managed to make himself public without making himself known.' Miss Austen has made herself known without making herself public. There is no portrait of her in the shop windows; indeed, no portrait of her at all. But she is cherished in the memories of those whose memory is fame.

As one symptom of neglect we have to notice the scantiness of all biographical details about her. Of Miss Burney, who is no longer read, nor much worth reading, we have biography, and to spare. Of Miss Brontë, who, we fear, will soon cease to find readers, there is also ample biography; but of Miss Austen we have little information. In the first volume of the edition published by Mr Bentley (five charming volumes, to be had for fifteen shillings) there is a meagre notice, from which we draw the following details.

Jane Austen was born on the 16th December 1775, at Steventon in Hampshire. Her father was rector of the parish during forty years, and then quitted it for Bath. He was a scholar, and fond of general literature, and probably paid special attention to his daughter's culture. In Bath, Jane only lived four years; but that was enough, and more than enough, for her observing humour, as we see in *Northanger Abbey*. After the death of her father, she removed with her mother and sister to Southampton; and finally, in 1809, settled in the pleasant village of Chawton, in Hampshire, from whence she issued her novels. Some of these had been written long before, but were withheld, probably because of her great diffidence. She had a high standard of excellence, and knew how prone self-love is to sophisticate. So great was this distrust, that the charming novel, *Northanger Abbey*, although the first in point of time, did not appear in print until after her death; and this work, which the *Quarterly Review* pronounces the weakest of the series (a verdict only, intelligible to us because in the same breath *Persuasion* is called the best!) is not only written with unflagging vivacity, but contains two characters no one else could have equalled—Henry Tilney and John Thorpe. *Sense and Sensibility* was the first to appear, and that was in 1811. She had laid aside a sum of money to meet what she expected would be her loss on that publication, and 'could scarcely believe her great good fortune when it produced a clear profit of £150.' Between 1811 and

1816 appeared her three *chefs-d'œuvre—Pride and Prejudice, Mansfield Park*, and *Emma*. The applause these met with, gratified her, of course; but she steadily resisted every attempt to 'make a lion of her,' and never publicly avowed her authorship, although she spoke freely of it in private. Soon after the publication of *Emma*, symptoms of an incurable decline appeared. In the month of May 1817 she was removed to Winchester, in order that constant medical advice might be secured. She seems to have suffered much, but suffered it with resignation. Her last words were, 'I want nothing but death.' This was on Friday the 18th July 1817; presently after she expired in the arms of her sister. Her body lies in Winchester Cathedral.

One might gather from her works that she was personally attractive, and we are told in the memoir that this was the case. 'Her stature rather exceeded the middle height; her carriage and deportment were quiet but graceful; her features were separately good; their assemblage produced an unrivalled expression of that cheerfulness, sensibility, and benevolence which were her real characteristics; her complexion was of the finest texture—it might with truth be said that her eloquent blood spoke through her modest cheek; her voice was sweet; she delivered herself with fluency and precision; indeed, she was formed for elegant and rational society, excelling in conversation as much as in composition.' We may picture her as something like her own sprightly, natural, but by no means perfect Elizabeth Bennet, in *Pride and Prejudice*, one of the few heroines one would seriously like to marry.

We have no means of ascertaining how many copies of these exquisite pictures of English life have been circulated, but we know that the number is very large. Twice or thrice have the railway editions been out of print; and Mr Bentley's edition is stereotyped. This success implies a hold on the Public, all the more certainly because the popularity is 'not loud but deep.' We have re-read them all four times; or rather, to speak more accurately, they have been read aloud to us, one after the other; and when it is considered what a severe test that is, how the reading aloud permits no skipping, no evasion of weariness, but brings both merits and defects into stronger relief by forcing the mind to dwell on them, there is surely something significant of genuine excellence when both reader and listener finish their fourth reading with increase of admiration. The test of reading aloud applied to *Jane Eyre*, which had only been read once before, very considerably modified our opinion of that remarkable work; and, to confess the truth, modified it so far that we feel as if we should never open the book again. The same test applied to such an old favourite as *Tom Jones*, was also much more damaging than we should have anticipated—bringing the defects and shortcomings of that much overrated work into very distinct prominence, and lessening our pleasure in its effective, but, on the whole, coarse painting. Fielding has greater vigour of mind, greater experience, greater attainments, and a more effective *mise en scène*, than Miss Austen; but he is not only immeasurably inferior to her in the highest department of art—the representation of character—he is also inferior to her, we think, in real humour; and in spite of his 'construction,' of which the critics justly speak in praise, he is inferior to her in the construction and conduct of his story, being more commonplace and less artistic. He has more invention of situation and more vigour, but less truth and subtlety. This is at any rate our individual judgment, which the reader is at liberty to modify as he pleases. In the course of the fifteen years which have elapsed since we first read *Emma*, and *Mansfield Park*, we have outlived many admirations, but have only learned to admire Miss Austen more; and as we are perfectly aware of *why* we so much admire her, we may endeavour to communicate these reasons to the reader.

If, as probably few will dispute, the art of the novelist be the representation of human life by means of a story; and if the *truest* representation, effected by the *least expenditure* of means, constitutes the highest claim of art, then we say that Miss Austen has carried the art to a point of excellence surpassing that reached by any of her rivals. Observe we say 'the art;' we do not say that she equals many of them in the *interest* excited by the art; that is a separate question. It is probable, nay certain, that the interest excited by the *Antigone* is very inferior to that excited by *Black-eyed Susan*. It is probable that *Uncle Tom* and *Dred* surpassed in interest the *Antiquary* or *Ivanhoe*. It is probable that *Jane Eyre* produced a far greater excitement than the *Vicar of Wakefield*. But the critic justly disregards these fervid elements of immediate success, and fixes his attention mainly on the art which is of eternal substance. Miss Austen has nothing fervid in her works. She is not capable of producing a profound agitation in the mind. In many respects this is a limitation of her powers, a deduction from her claims. But while other writers have had more power over the emotions, more vivid imaginations, deeper sensibilities, deeper insight, and more of what is properly called invention, no novelist has approached her in what we may style the 'economy of art,' by which is meant the easy adaptation of means to ends, with no aid from extraneous or superfluous elements. Indeed, paradoxical as the juxtaposition of the names may perhaps appear to those who have not reflected much on this subject, we venture to say that the only names we can place above Miss Austen, in respect of this economy of art, are Sophocles and Molière (in *Le Misanthrope*). And if any one will examine the terms of the definition, he will perceive that almost all defects in works of art arise from neglect of this economy. When the *end* is the representation of human nature in its familiar aspects, moving amid every-day scenes, the *means* must likewise be furnished from every-day life: romance and improbabilities must be banished as rigorously as the grotesque exaggeration of peculiar characteristics, or the presentation of abstract types. It is easy for the artist to choose a subject from every-day life, but it is *not* easy for him so to represent the characters and their actions that they shall be at once lifelike and interesting; accordingly, whenever ordinary people are introduced, they are either made to speak a language never spoken out of books, and to pursue conduct never observed in life; or else they are intolerably wearisome. But Miss Austen is like Shakespeare: she makes her very noodles inexhaustibly amusing, yet accurately real. We never tire of her characters. They become equal to actual experiences. They live with us, and form perpetual topics of comment. We have so personal a dislike to Mrs Elton and Mrs Norris, that it would gratify our savage feeling to hear of some calamity befalling them. We think of Mr Collins and John Thorpe with such a mixture of ludicrous enjoyment and angry contempt, that we alternately long and dread to make their personal acquaintance. The heroines—at least Elizabeth, Emma, and Catherine Morland—are truly *lovable*, flesh-and-blood young women; and the good people are all really good, without being goody. Her reverend critic in the *Quarterly* truly says, 'She herself compares her productions to a little bit of ivory, two inches wide, worked upon with a brush so fine that little effect is produced with much labour. It is so: her portraits are perfect likenesses, admirably finished, many of them gems; but it is all miniature-painting; and having satisfied herself with being inimitable in one line, she never essayed canvass and oils; never tried her hand at a majestic daub.' This is very true: it at once defines her position and lowers her claims. When we said that in the highest department of the novelist's art—namely, the truthful representation of character—Miss Austen was without a superior, we ought to have added that in this department she did not choose the highest range; the truth and felicity of her delineation are exquisite, but the characters delineated are not of a high rank. She belongs to the great dramatists;

but her dramas are of homely common quality. It is obvious that the nature of the thing represented will determine degrees in art. Raphael will always rank higher than Teniers; Sophocles and Shakespeare will never be lowered to the rank of Lope de Vega and Scribe. It is a greater effort of genius to produce a fine epic than a fine pastoral; a great drama, than a perfect lyric. There is far greater strain on the intellectual effort to create a Brutus or an Othello, than to create a Vicar of Wakefield or a Squire Western. The higher the aims, the greater is the strain, and the nobler is success.

These, it may be said, are truisms; and so they are. Yet they need restatement from time to time, because men constantly forget that the dignity of a high aim cannot shed lustre on an imperfect execution, though to *some* extent it may lessen the contempt which follows upon failure. It is only success which can claim applause. Any fool can select a great subject; and in general it is the tendency of fools to choose subjects which the strong feel to be too great. If a man can leap a five-barred gate, we applaud his agility; but if he attempt it, without a chance of success, the mud receives him, and we applaud the mud. This is too often forgotten by critics and artists, in their grandiloquence about 'high art.' No art can be high that is not good. A grand subject ceases to be grand when its treatment is feeble. It is a great mistake, as has been wittily said, 'to fancy yourself a great painter because you paint with a big brush;' and there are unhappily too many big brushes in the hands of incompetence. Poor Haydon was a type of the big-brush school; he could not paint a small picture because he could not paint at all; and he believed that in covering a vast area of canvass he was working in the grand style. In every estimate of an artist's rank we necessarily take into account the nature of the subject and the excellence of the execution. It is twenty times more difficult to write a fine tragedy than a fine lyric; but it is more difficult to write a perfect lyric than a tolerable tragedy; and there was as much sense as sarcasm in Beranger's reply when the tragic poet Viennet visited him in prison, and suggested that of course there would be a volume of songs as the product of this leisure. 'Do you suppose,' said Beranger, 'that chansons are written as easily as tragedies?'

To return to Miss Austen: her delineation is unsurpassed, but the characters delineated are never of a lofty or impassioned order, and therefore make no demand on the highest faculties of the intellect. Such genius as hers is excessively rare; but it is not the highest kind of genius. Murillo's peasant boys are assuredly of far greater excellence than the infant Christs painted by all other painters, except Raphael; but the divine children of the *Madonna di San Sisto* are immeasurably beyond anything Murillo has painted. Miss Austen's two-inch bit of ivory is worth a gallery of canvass by eminent R.A.'s, but it is only a bit of ivory after all. 'Her two inches of ivory,' continues the critic recently quoted, 'just describes her preparations for a tale in three volumes. A village— two families connected together—three or four interlopers, out of whom are to spring a little *tracasserie;* and by means of village or country-town visiting and gossiping, a real plot shall thicken, and its "rear of darkness" never be scattered till six pages off *finis.* . . . . . The work is all done by half-a-dozen people; no person, scene, or sentence is ever introduced needless to the matter in hand: no catastrophes, or discoveries, or surprises of a grand nature are allowed—neither children nor fortunes are found or lost by accident—the mind is never taken off the level surface of life—the reader breakfasts, dines, walks, and gossips with the various worthies, till a process of transmutation takes place in him, and he absolutely fancies himself one of the company. . . . The secret is, Miss Austen was a thorough mistress in the knowledge of human character; how it is acted upon by education and circumstance, and how, when once formed, it shows itself through every hour of every day, and in every speech of every person. Her conversations would be tiresome but for this; and her personages, the fellows to whom may be met in the streets, or drank tea with at half an hour's notice, would excite no interest; but in Miss Austen's hands we see into their hearts and hopes, their motives, their struggles within themselves; and a sympathy is induced which, if extended to daily life and the world at large, would make the reader a more amiable person; and we must think it that reader's own fault who does not close her pages with more charity in his heart towards unpretending, if prosing worth; with a higher estimation of simple kindness and sincere good-will; with a quickened sense of the duty of bearing and forbearing in domestic inter-course, and of the pleasure of adding to the little comforts even of per-sons who are neither wits nor beauties.' It is worth remembering that this is the deliberate judgment of the present Archbishop of Dublin, and not a careless verdict dropping from the pen of a facile reviewer. There are two points in it to which especial attention may be given: *first,* The indication of Miss Austen's power of representing life; and, *secondly,* The indication of the effect which her sympathy with ordinary life produces. We shall touch on the latter point first; and we do so for the sake of introducing a striking passage from one of the works of Mr George Eliot, a writer who seems to us inferior to Miss Austen in the art of telling a story, and generally in what we have called the 'economy of art;' but equal in truthfulness, dramatic ventriloquism, and humour, and greatly superior in culture, reach of mind, and depth of emotional sensibility. In the first of the *Scenes of Clerical Life* there occurs this apology to the reader:—

'The Rev. Amos Barton, whose sad fortunes I have undertaken to relate, was, you perceive, in no respect an ideal or exceptional character, and perhaps I am doing a bold thing to bespeak your sympathy on behalf of a man who was so very far from remarkable,—a man whose virtues were not heroic, and who had no undetected crime within his breast; who had not the slightest mystery hanging about him, but was palpably and unmistakably commonplace; who was not even in love, but had had that complaint favourably many years ago. "An utterly uninteresting character!" I think I hear a lady reader exclaim—Mrs Farthingale, for example, who prefers the ideal in fiction; to whom tragedy means ermine tippets, adultery, and murder; and comedy, the adventures of some personage who is quite a "character."

'But, my dear madam, it is so very large a majority of your fellow-countrymen that are of this insignificant stamp. At least eighty out of a hundred of your adult male fellow-Britons returned in the last census, are neither extraordinarily silly, nor extraordinarily wicked, nor extraordinarily wise; their eyes are neither deep and liquid with sentiment, nor sparkling with suppressed witticisms; they have probably had no hairbreadth escapes or thrilling adventures; their brains are certainly not pregnant with genius, and their passions have not manifested themselves at all after the fashion of a volcano. They are simply men of complexions more or less muddy, whose conversation is more or less bald and disjointed. Yet these commonplace people—many of them—bear a conscience, and have felt the sublime prompting to do the painful right; they have their unspoken sorrows, and their sacred joys; their hearts have perhaps gone out towards their first-born, and they have mourned over the irreclaimable dead. Nay, is there not a pathos in their very insignificance,—in our comparison of their dim and narrow existence with the glorious possibilities of that human nature which they share?

'Depend upon it, you would gain unspeakably if you would learn with me to see some of the poetry and the pathos, the tragedy and the comedy, lying in the experience of a human soul that looks out through dull grey eyes, and that speaks in a voice of quite ordinary tones.'

But the real secret of Miss Austen's success lies in her having the exquisite and rare gift of dramatic creation of character. Scott says of her, 'She had a talent for describing the involvements, and feelings, and characters of ordinary life, which is to me the most wonderful I ever met with. The big bow-wow strain I can do myself like any now going; but the exquisite touch, which renders ordinary commonplace things and characters interesting, from the truth of the description and the sentiment, is denied me. What a pity such a gifted creature died so early!' Generously said; but high as the praise is, it is as much below the real excellence of Miss Austen, as the 'big bow-wow strain' is below the incomparable power of the Waverley Novels. Scott felt, but did not define, the excellence of Miss Austen. The very word 'describing' is altogether misplaced and misleading. She seldom describes anything, and is not felicitous when she attempts it. But instead of *description*, the common and easy resource of novelists, she has the rare and difficult art of *dramatic presentation:* instead of telling us what her characters are, and what they feel, she presents the people, and they reveal themselves. In this she has never perhaps been surpassed, not even by Shakespeare himself. If ever living beings can be said to have moved across the page of fiction, as they lived, speaking as they spoke, and feeling as they felt, they do so in *Pride and Prejudice, Emma*, and *Mansfield Park*. What incomparable noodles she exhibits for our astonishment and laughter! What silly, good-natured women! What softly-selfish men! What lively-amiable, honest men and women, whom one would rejoice to have known!

But all her power is dramatic power; she loses her hold on us directly she ceases to speak through the *personæ;* she is then like a great actor *off* the stage. When she is making men and women her mouthpieces, she is exquisitely and inexhaustibly humorous; but when she speaks in her own person, she is apt to be commonplace, and even prosing. Her dramatic ventriloquism is such that, amid our tears of laughter and sympathetic exasperation at folly, we feel it almost impossible that she did not hear those very people utter those very words. In many cases this was doubtless the fact. The best invention does not consist in finding *new* language for characters, but in finding the *true* language for them. It is easy to invent a language never spoken by any one out of books; but it is so far from easy to invent—that is, to find out—the language which certain characters would speak and did speak, that in all the thousands of volumes written since Richardson and Fielding, every difficulty is more frequently overcome than *that*. If the reader fails to perceive the extraordinary merit of Miss Austen's representation of character, let him try himself to paint a portrait which shall be at once many-sided and interesting, without employing any but the commonest colours, without calling in the aid of eccentricity, exaggeration, or literary 'effects;' or let him carefully compare the writings of Miss Austen with those of any other novelist, from Fielding to Thackeray.

It is probably this same dramatic instinct which makes the construction of her stories so admirable. And by construction, we mean the art which, selecting what is useful and rejecting what is superfluous, renders our interest unflagging, because one chapter evolves the next, one character is necessary to the elucidation of another. In what is commonly called 'plot' she does not excel. Her invention is wholly in character and motive, not in situation. Her materials are of the commonest every-day occurrence. Neither the emotions of tragedy, nor the exaggerations of farce, seem to have the slightest attraction for her. The reader's pulse never throbs, his curiosity is never intense; but his interest never wanes for a moment. The action begins; the people speak, feel, and act; everything that is said, felt, or done tends towards the entanglement or disentanglement of the plot; and we are almost made actors as well as spectators of the little drama. One of the most difficult things in dramatic writing is so to construct the story that every scene shall advance the denouement by easy evolution, yet at the same time give scope to the full exhibition of the characters. In dramas, as in novels, we almost always see that the action stands still while the characters are being exhibited, and the characters are in abeyance while the action is being unfolded. For perfect specimens of this higher construction demanded by art, we would refer to the jealousy-scenes of *Othello*, and the great scene between Célimène and Arsinoé in *Le Misanthrope;* there is not in these two marvels of art a verse which does not exhibit some *nuance* of character, and thereby, at the same time, tends towards the full development of the action.

So entirely dramatic, and so little descriptive, is the genius of Miss Austen, that she seems to rely upon what her people say and do for the whole effect they are to produce on our imaginations. She no more thinks of describing the physical appearance of her people than the dramatist does who knows that his persons are to be represented by living actors. This is a defect and a mistake in art: a defect, because, although every reader must necessarily conjure up to himself a vivid image of people whose characters are so vividly presented; yet each reader has to do this for himself without aid from the author, thereby missing many of the subtle connections between physical and mental organisation. It is not enough to be told that a young gentleman had a fine countenance and an air of fashion; or that a young gentlewoman was handsome and elegant. As far as any direct information can be derived from the authoress, we might imagine that this was a purblind world, wherein nobody ever saw anybody, except in a dim vagueness which obscured all peculiarities. It is impossible that Mr Collins should not have been endowed by nature with an appearance in some way heralding the delicious folly of the inward man. Yet *all* we hear of this fatuous curate is, that 'he was a tall heavy-looking young man of five-and-twenty. His air was grave and stately, and his manners were very formal.' Balzac or Dickens would not have been content without making the reader *see* this Mr Collins. Miss Austen is content to make us *know* him, even to the very intricacies of his inward man. It is not stated whether she was shortsighted, but the absence of all sense of outward world—either scenery or personal appearance—is more remarkable in her than in any writer we remember.

We are touching here on one of her defects which help to an explanation of her limited popularity, especially when coupled with her deficiencies in poetry and passion. She has little or no sympathy with what is picturesque and passionate. This prevents her from painting what the popular eye can see, and the popular heart can feel. The struggles, the ambitions, the errors, and the sins of energetic life are left untouched by her; and these form the subjects most stirring to the general sympathy. Other writers have wanted this element of popularity, but they have compensated for it by a keen sympathy with, and power of representing, the adventurous, the romantic, and the picturesque. Passion and adventure are the sources of certain success with the mass of mankind. The passion may be coarsely felt, the romance may be ridiculous, but there will always be found a large majority whose sympathies will be awakened by even the coarsest daubs. Emotion is in its nature sympathetic and uncritical: a spark will ignite it. Types of villany never seen or heard of out of books, or off the stage, types of heroism and virtue not less hyperbolical, are eagerly welcomed and *believed* in by a public which would pass over without notice the subtlest creations of genius, and which would even *resent* the more truthful painting as disturbing its emotional enjoyment of hating the bad, and loving the good. The nicer art which mingles goodness with villany, and weakness with virtue, as in life they are always mingled, causes positive distress to young and uncultivated minds. The mass of men never ask whether a character is true, or the event probable; it is enough for them that they are moved; and to move them strongly, black must be very black, and white without a shade. Hence it is that caricature and exaggeration of all kinds—inflated diction and daubing delineation—are, and always will be, popular: a certain breadth and massiveness of effect being necessary to produce a strong impression on all but a refined audience. In the works of the highest genius we sometimes find a breadth and massiveness of effect which make even these works popular, although the qualities most highly prized by the cultivated reader are little appreciated by the public. The *Iliad,* Shakespeare and Molière, *Don Quixote* and *Faust,* affect the mass powerfully; but how many admirers of Homer would prefer the *naïveté* of the original to the epigrammatic splendour of Pope?

The novelist who has no power of broad and massive effect can never expect to be successful with the great public. He may gain the suffrages of the highest minds, and in course of time become a classic; but we all know what the *popularity* of a classic means. Miss Austen is such a novelist. Her subjects have little intrinsic interest; it is only in their treatment that they become attractive; but treatment and art are not likely to captivate any except critical and refined tastes. Every reader will be amused by her pictures, because their very truth carries them home to ordinary experience and sympathy; but this amusement is of a tepid nature, and the effect is quickly forgotten. Partridge expressed the general sentiment of the public when he spoke slightingly of Garrick's *Hamlet,* because Garrick did just what he, Partridge, would have done in presence of a ghost; whereas the actor who performed the king powerfully impressed him by sonorous elocution and emphatic gesticulation: *that* was acting, and required art; the other was natural, and not worth alluding to.

The absence of breadth, picturesqueness, and passion, will also limit the appreciating audience of Miss Austen to the small circle of cultivated minds; and even these minds are not always capable of greatly relishing her works. We have known very remarkable people who cared little for her pictures of every-day life; and indeed it may be anticipated that those who have little sense of humour, or whose passionate and insurgent activities demand in art a reflection of their own emotions and struggles, will find little pleasure in such homely comedies. Currer Bell may be taken as a type of these. She was utterly without a sense of humour, and was by nature fervid and impetuous. In a letter published in her memoirs she writes,—'Why do you like Miss Austen so very much? I am puzzled on that point. . . . I had not read *Pride and Prejudice* till I read that sentence of yours, and then I got the book. And what did I find? An accurate daguerreotyped portrait of a commonplace face; a carefully-fenced, highly-cultivated garden, with neat borders and delicate flowers; but no glance of a bright, vivid physiognomy, no open country, no fresh air, no blue hill, no bonny beck. I should hardly like to live with her elegant ladies and gentlemen, in their elegant but confined houses.' The critical reader will not fail to remark the almost contemptuous indifference to the art of truthful portrait-painting which this passage indicates; and he will understand, perhaps, how the writer of such a passage was herself incapable of drawing more than characteristics, even in her most successful efforts. Jane Eyre, Rochester, and Paul Emmanuel, are very vigorous sketches, but the reader observes them from the *outside*, he does not penetrate their souls, he does not know them. What is said respecting the want of open country, blue hill, and bonny beck, is perfectly true; but the same point has been more felicitously touched by Scott, in his review of *Emma:* 'Upon the whole,' he says, 'the turn of this author's novels bears the same relation to that of the sentimental and romantic cast, that cornfields and cottages and meadows bear to the highly-adorned grounds of a show mansion, or the rugged sublimities of a mountain landscape. It is neither so captivating as the one, nor so grand as the other; but it affords those who frequent it a pleasure nearly allied with the experience of their own social habits.' Scott would also have loudly repudiated the notion of Miss Austen's characters being 'mere daguerreotypes.' Having himself drawn both ideal and real characters, he knew the difficulties of both; and he well says, 'He who paints from *le beau idéal*, if his scenes and sentiments are striking and interesting, is in a great measure exempted from the difficult task of reconciling them with the ordinary probabilities of life; but he who paints a scene of common occurrence, places his composition within that extensive range of criticism which general experience offers to every reader. . . . Something more than a mere sign-post likeness is also demanded. The portrait must have spirit and character as well as resemblance; and being deprived of all that, according to Bayes, goes to "elevate and surprise," it must make amends by displaying depth of knowledge and dexterity of execution.'

While defending our favourite, and giving critical reasons for our liking, we are far from wishing to impose that preference on others. If any one frankly says, 'I do not care about these pictures of ordinary life: I want something poetical or romantic, something to stimulate my imagination, and to carry me beyond the circle of my daily thoughts,'—there is nothing to be answered. Many persons do not admire Wordsworth, and cannot feel their poetical sympathies aroused by waggoners and potters. There are many who find no enjoyment in the Flemish pictures, but are rapturous over the frescoes at Munich and Berlin. Individual tastes do not admit of dispute. The imagination is an imperious faculty, and demands gratification; and if a man be content to have this faculty stimulated, to the exclusion of all other faculties, or if only peculiar works are capable of stimulating it, we have no right to object. Only when a question of Art comes to be discussed, it must not be confounded with a matter of individual feeling; and it requires a distinct reference to absolute standards. The art of novel-writing, like the art of painting, is founded on general principles, which, because they have their psychological justification, because they are derived from tendencies of the human mind, and not, as absurdly supposed, derived from 'models of composition,' are of universal application. The law of colour, for instance, is derived from the observed relation between certain colours and the sensitive retina. The laws of construction, likewise, are derived from the invariable relation between a certain order and succession of events, and the amount of interest excited by that order. In novel-writing, as in mechanics, every obstruction is a loss of power; every superfluous page diminishes the artistic pleasure of the whole. Individual tastes will always differ; but the laws of the human mind are universal. One man will prefer the humorous, another the pathetic; one will delight in the adventurous, another in the simple and homely; but the principles of Art remain the same for each. To tell a story well, is quite another thing from having a good story to tell. The construction of a good drama is the same in principle whether the subject be Antigone, the Misanthrope, or Othello; and the real critic detects this principle at work under these various forms. It is the same with the delineation of character: however various the types, whether a Jonathan Oldbuck, a Dr Primrose, a Blifil, or a Falstaff—ideal, or real, the principles of composition are the same.

Miss Austen has generally but an indifferent story to tell, but her art of telling it is incomparable. Her characters, never ideal, are not of an eminently attractive order; but her dramatic ventriloquism and power of presentation is little less than marvellous. Macaulay declares his opinion that in this respect she is second only to Shakespeare. 'Among the writers,' he says, 'who, in the point we have noticed, have approached nearest the manner of the great master, we have no hesitation in placing Jane Austen, a woman of whom England is justly proud. She has given us a multitude of characters, all, in a certain sense, commonplace—all such as we meet every day. Yet they are all as perfectly discriminated from each other as if they were the most eccentric of human beings. . . . And all this is done by touches so delicate that they elude analysis, that they defy powers of description, and that we only know them to exist by the general effect to which they have contributed.'

The art of the novelist consists in telling the story and representing the characters; but besides these, there are other powerful though extraneous sources of attraction often possessed by novels, which are due to the literary talent and culture of the writer. There is, for example, the power of description, both of scenery and of character. Many novels depend almost entirely on this for their effect. It is a lower kind of power, and consequently much more frequent than what we have styled the *art* of the novelist; yet it may be very puissant in the hands of a fine writer, gifted with a real sense of the picturesque. Being very easy, it has of late become the resource of weak writers; and the prominent position it has usurped has tended in two ways to produce weariness—first, by encouraging incompetent writers to do what is easily done; and, secondly, by seducing writers from the higher and better method of dramatic exposition.

Another source of attraction is the general vigour of mind exhibited by the author, in his comments on the incidents and characters of his story: these comments, when proceeding from a fine insight or a large experience, give additional charm to the story, and make the delightful novel a delightful book. It is almost superfluous to add, that this also has its obverse: the comments too often painfully exhibit a general weakness of mind. Dr Johnson refused to take tea with some one because, as he said, 'Sir, there is no vigour in his talk.' This is the complaint which must be urged against the majority of novelists: they put too much water in their ink. And even when the talk is good, we must remember that it is, after all, only one of the side-dishes of the feast. All the literary and philosophic culture which an author can bring to bear upon his work will *tend* to give that work a higher value, but it will not really make it a better novel. To suppose that culture can replace invention, or literature do instead of character, is as erroneous as to suppose that archæological learning and scenical splendour can raise poor acting to the level of fine acting. Yet this is the common mistake of literary men. They are apt to believe that mere writing will weigh in the scale against artistic presentation; that comment will do duty for dramatic revelation; that analysing motives with philosophic skill will answer all the purpose of creation. But whoever looks closely into this matter will see that literature—that is, the writing of thinking and accomplished men—is excessively cheap, compared with the smallest amount of invention or creation; and it is cheap because more easy of production, and less potent in effect. This is apparently by no means the opinion of some recent critics, who evidently consider their own *writing* of more merit than *humour* and *invention*, and who are annoyed at the notion of 'mere serialists', without 'solid acquirements', being regarded all over Europe as our most distinguished authors. Yet it may be suggested that writing such as that or the critics in question can be purchased in abundance, whereas humour and invention are among the rarest of products. If it is a painful reflection that genius should be esteemed more highly than solid acquirements, it should be remembered that learning is only the diffused form of what was *once* invention. 'Solid acquirement' is the genius of wits, which has become the wisdom of reviewers.

Be this as it may, we acknowledge the great attractions which a novel may receive from the general vigour and culture of the author; and acknowledge that such attractions form but a very small element in Miss Austen's success. Her pages have no sudden illuminations. There are neither epigrams nor aphorisms, neither subtle analyses nor eloquent descriptions. She is without grace or felicity of expression; she has neither fervid nor philosophic comment. Her charm lies solely in the art of representing life and character, and that is exquisite.

We have thus endeavoured to characterise, in general terms, the qualities which her works display. It is less easy to speak with sufficient distinctness of the particular works, since, unless our readers have these vividly present to memory (in which case our remarks would be super-fluous), we cannot hope to be perfectly intelligible; no adequate idea of them can be given by a review of one, because the 'specimen brick' which the noodle in Hierocles thought sufficient, and which really does suffice in the case of many a modern novel, would prove no specimen at all. Her characters are so gradually unfolded, their individuality reveals itself so naturally and easily in the course of what they say and do, that we learn to know them as if we had lived with them, but cannot by any single speech or act make them known to others. Aunt Norris, for instance, in *Mansfield Park*, is a character profoundly and variously delineated; yet there is no scene in which she exhibits herself to those who have not the pleasurable disgust of her acquaintance; while to those who have, there is no scene in which she does not exhibit herself. Mr Collins, making an offer to Elizabeth Bennet, formally stating the reasons which induced him to marry, and the prudential motives which have induced him to select her, and then adding, 'Nothing now remains for me but to assure you, in the most animated language, of the violence of my affection. To fortune I am perfectly indifferent, and shall make no demand of that nature on your father, since I am well aware that it could not be complied with; and that one thousand pounds in the Four-per-Cents, which will not be yours till after your mother's decease, is all that you may ever be entitled to. On that head, therefore, I shall be uniformly silent; and you may assure yourself that no ungenerous reproach shall ever pass my lips when we are married;' and after her refusal, persisting in accepting this refusal as only what is usual with young ladies, who reject the addresses of the man they secretly mean to accept, 'I am therefore by no means discouraged by what you have just said, and shall hope to lead you to the altar ere long;'—this scene, ludicrous as it is throughout, receives its exquisite flavour from what has gone before. We feel morally persuaded that so Mr Collins would speak and act. The man who, on taking leave of his host, formally assures him that he will not fail to send a 'letter of thanks' on his return, and does send it, is just the man to have made this declaration. Mrs Elton, in *Emma*, is the very best portrait of a vulgar woman we ever saw: she is vulgar in soul, and the vulgarity is indicated by subtle yet unmistakable touches, never by coarse language, or by caricature of any kind. We will quote here a bit of her conversation in the first interview she has with Emma Woodhouse, in which she endeavours to be very fascinating. It should be premised that she is only just married, and this is the wedding-visit. She indulges in 'raptures' about Hartfield (the seat of Emma's father), and Emma quietly replies:—

[quotes ch. 32 ' "When you have seen" ' to ' "we shall see".']

Our limits force us to break off in the middle of this conversation, but the continuation is equally humorous. Quite as good in another way is Miss Bates with her affectionate twaddle. But, as we said before, the characters reveal themselves; and in general reveal themselves only in the course of several scenes, so that extracts would give no idea of them.

The reader who has yet to make acquaintance with these novels, is advised to begin with *Pride and Prejudice* or *Mansfield Park*; and if these do not captivate him, he may fairly leave the others unread. In *Pride and Prejudice* there is the best story, and the greatest variety of character: the whole Bennet family is inimitable: Mr Bennet, caustic, quietly, indolently selfish, but honourable, and in some respects amiable; his wife, the perfect type of a gossiping, weak-headed, fussy mother; Jane a sweet creature; Elizabeth a sprightly and fascinating flesh-and-blood heroine; Lydia a pretty, but vain and giddy girl; and Mary, plain and pedantic, studying 'thorough bass and human nature.' Then there is Mr

Collins, and Sir William Lucas, and the proud foolish old lady Catherine de Bough, and Darcy, Bingley, and Wickham, all admirable. From the first chapter to the last there is a succession of scenes of high comedy, and the interest is unflagging. *Mansfield Park* is also singularly fascinating, though the heroine is less of a favourite with us than Miss Austen's heroines usually are; but aunt Norris and Lady Bertram are perfect; and the scenes at Portsmouth, when Fanny Price visits her home after some years' residence at the Park, are wonderfully truthful and vivid. The private theatricals, too, are very amusing; and the day spent at the Rushworths' is a masterpiece of art. If the reader has really tasted the flavour of these works, he will need no other recommendation to read and re-read the others. Even *Persuasion*, which we cannot help regarding as the weakest, contains exquisite touches, and some characters no one else could have surpassed.

We have endeavoured to express the delight which Miss Austen's works have always given us, and to explain the sources of her success by indicating the qualities which make her a model worthy of the study of all who desire to understand the art of the novelist. But we have also indicated what seems to be the limitations of her genius, and to explain why it is that this genius, moving only amid the quiet scenes of every-day life, with no power over the more stormy and energetic activities which find vent even in every-day life, can never give her a high rank among great artists. Her place is among great artists, but it is not high among them. She sits in the House of Peers, but it is as a simple Baron. The delight derived from her pictures arises from our sympathy with ordinary characters, our relish of humour, and our intellectual pleasure in art for art's sake. But when it is admitted that she never stirs the deeper emotions, that she never fills the soul with a noble aspiration, or brightens it with a fine idea, but, at the utmost, only teaches us charity for the ordinary failings of ordinary people, and sympathy with their goodness, we have admitted an objection which lowers her claims to rank among the great benefactors of the race; and this sufficiently explains why, with all her excellence, her name has not become a household word. Her fame, as we think, must endure. Such art as hers can never grow old, never be superseded. But, after all, miniatures are not frescoes, and her works are miniatures. Her place is among the Immortals; but the pedestal is erected in a quiet niche of the great temple.

37. W. F. Pollock on Jane Austen
1860

Extract from 'British Novelists—Richardson, Miss Austen, Scott', *Fraser's Magazine* (January 1860), lxi, 30–35.

Sir William Frederick Pollock (1815–88), barrister, legal officer and man of letters.

Miss Austen is, of all his successors, the one who most nearly resembles Richardson in the power of impressing reality upon her characters. There is a perfection in the exhibition of Miss Austen's characters which no one else has approached; and truth is never for an instant sacrificed in that delicate atmosphere of satire which pervades her works. Like Richardson's, her people are made to develope themselves in the progress of the story through which the reader accompanies them; and except when at the beginning of each novel she may give a short account of the situation of its leading personages, the machinery of representation is almost wholly concealed from observation. The whole thoughts of the reader are abstracted from the world of outer life, and are confined to the mimic world contained within the covers of the book in his hand. No allusion or reference is ever made to real events or persons; the figures never step out of their frame, and the frame itself is unseen. The persons and events of this lesser world are, indeed, not heroical: they belong not to the heights or depths or romantic regions of existence, but to the level and ordinary passages of comfortable English upper life. The extremes of manners are avoided; the characters are ladies and gentlemen belonging to the same class as that of their painter—the daughter of a country clergyman who mixed in society at Bath, Southampton, and the village in which she ended her too short life. Hardly ever is a person of greater rank than a baronet of easy means introduced, nor does any fall below the professional and commercial classes.

The plots are simple but well constructed, sufficiently involved to excite interest, and they are brought round at the end by means neither too obvious nor unnatural. The field of view may be in some sense a small one; but like that of a good microscope in able hands, there is abundance of light, and the minutest markings of character are beautifully shown in it.

Miss Austen never attempts to describe a scene or a class of society with which she was not herself thoroughly acquainted. The conversations of ladies with ladies, or of ladies and gentlemen together, are given, but no instance occurs of a scene in which men only are present. The uniform quality of her work is one most remarkable point to be observed in it. Let a volume be opened at any place: there is the same good English, the same refined style, the same simplicity and truth. There is never any deviation into the unnatural or exaggerated; and how worthy of all love and respect is the finely-disciplined genius which rejects the forcible but transient modes of stimulating interest which can so easily be employed when desired, and which knows how to trust to the never-failing principles of human nature! This very trust has sometimes been made an objection to Miss Austen, and she has been accused of writing dull stories about ordinary people. But her supposed ordinary people are really not such very ordinary people. Let any one who is inclined to criticize on this score, endeavour to construct one character from among the ordinary people of his own acquaintance that shall be capable of interesting any reader for ten minutes. It will then be found how great has been the discrimination of Miss Austen in the selection of her characters, and how skilful is her treatment in the management of them. It is true that the events are for the most part those of daily life, and the feelings are those connected with the usual joys and griefs of familiar existence; but these are the very events and feelings upon which the happiness or misery of most of us depends; and the field which embraces them, to the exclusion of the wonderful, the sentimental, and the historical, is surely large enough, as it is certainly the one which admits of the most profitable cultivation. In the end, too, the novel of daily real life is that of which we are least apt to weary: a round of fancy balls would tire the most vigorous admirers of variety in costume, and the return to plain clothes would be hailed with greater delight than their occasional relinquishment ever gives. Miss Austen's personages are always in plain clothes, but no two suits are alike: all are worn with their appropriate differences, and under all human thoughts and feelings are at work.

It is in the dramatic power with which her characters are exhibited that Miss Austen is unapproachable. Every one says the right thing in the right place and in the right way. The conservation of character is complete. We can never exactly predict what a particular person will say; there are no catch words or phrases perpetually recurring from the same person; yet we recognise as soon as spoken the truthful individuality of everything that is made to fall from each speaker. In this kind of genius she is without a rival, unless we look for one in the very highest name of our literature. Sometimes, in the admiration expressed for her greatest excellence, her claim to qualities exercised more in common with others has been overlooked; yet whenever accurate description is wanted, either of places or persons, it is supplied with ease and skill. Take, for instance, from *Sense and Sensibility* the account of Mrs. Dashwood's new residence in Devonshire.

[quotes ch. 6 'As a house' to 'steepest of them'.]

Or take, as an example of personal portraiture, from the same novel, the description of Elinor Dashwood and her sister.

[quotes ch. 10 'Miss Dashwood' to 'without delight'.]

Sense and Sensibility was the first published of Miss Austen's novels. It has perhaps more of movement than its successors, and in no other is there a character of so much passionate tenderness as belongs to Marianne. It is not, however, as a whole, equal to her later works; yet it may be as often resorted to with advantage as any of them, and it is full of its author's genius. How well the littleness and respectable selfishness of Mr. John Dashwood are brought out. How naturally his generous intentions to provide for his sisters dwindle down from a splendid three thousand pounds to half that amount—then to an annuity—then to an occasional present of fifty pounds—and lastly to vague promises of kindness and assistance. The charming but not too judicious mother of Elinor and Marianne Dashwood has always been one of our greatest favourites among Miss Austen's ladies. The sensible, considerate, and self-denying Elinor is a beautiful character, and is well contrasted with the enthusiastic and delightful, but somewhat unreasonable, Marianne. So is the delicate, well-informed, and high-minded Edward Ferrars, with his coxcomb brother Robert, and the agreeable but selfish Willoughby. The youngest sister, Margaret, must not be forgotten, though she seldom appears; for the object of her existence is amply justified by her utterance of the famous wish 'that somebody would give us all a large fortune a-piece,' even if she were not wanted to live with Mrs. Dashwood after her sisters are married. Then there is the good-humoured and friendly Sir John Middleton, who never came to the cottage without either inviting them to dine at the Park the next day, or to drink tea that evening. We like Mrs. Jennings, with her good nature and gossip, and her notion that poor Marianne, in the first agonies of disappointed love, could be consoled by sweetmeats, constantia, and playing at her favourite round game. Mr. Palmer, a gentleman when he pleases, but spoiled by living with people inferior to himself, and discontented, even to rudeness, with his silly wife, is brought out with much humour. We properly feel how objectionable are the Miss Steeles, with their vulgar cunning and admiration for smart beaux. We despise and shrink from the elder Mrs. Ferrars, with her pride, ill-nature, and narrow mind. We cordially respect and like the excellent Colonel Brandon, who though suffering under the advanced age and infirmities of thirty-six, is at length accepted by the youthful and once scornful Marianne. We are personally glad when Edward is released from his odious engagement to the artful Lucy Steele, and when his marriage with Elinor is rendered possible. Finally, we acquiesce in the sober and natural sentences with which the characters are dismissed from appearance. No poetical justice dogs those who have behaved wrongly and foolishly, to make them miserable to the end of time. We are invited to think of Willoughby as enjoying some share of domestic felicity with the wife whom he married for money and without love. Robert Ferrars, who actually marries the very woman for refusing to give up whom his brother was disinherited in his favour, regains his mother's goodwill—the two low natures suiting each other too well to be long separated—and is tolerably happy with his underbred wife. This is as it all would be in real life, and so Miss Austen, abjuring her undoubted right to inflict retribution, chooses it to be in that transcript of an imagined portion of it which she has selected for consideration in the tale called *Sense and Sensibility*.

In *Pride and Prejudice*, the characters are more complex, and those upon which the greatest elaboration has been bestowed are not of the kind which can be described by an epithet or two. Mr. Bennet, in this respect like Mr. Palmer, derives many of his peculiarities from being united to a woman of mean understanding and no cultivation; but he has the additional misfortune to contend with, of uncertain temper and a more active amount of foolishness. Driven back on his own reserve, caprice, and love of sarcasm, he takes refuge with his books, and renounces the duties of domestic and parental life. Jane Bennet is one of those attractive and gentle persons whom everybody must like, but without the interest of peculiarity. This is reserved for Elizabeth, whose occasional forwardness and want of perfect good breeding, with her powers of amusement, love of the ridiculous, and her real excellence and ability, make her alternately a person to like or be provoked with. As admirers of Miss Elizabeth, and in common we suppose with the rest of her friends, we must regret that the vivacity of her manners should ever degenerate into pertness. Her enemies, too, will always remark on the course of coincidence by which her dislike to Darcy begins to disappear after seeing his fine place in Derbyshire, and how she begins to comprehend that he is exactly the man who in disposition and talents would most suit her, precisely when the folly of Lydia has brought disgrace on her own family. It is true, however, that at Pemberley she first learns Darcy's real character, and the worthlessness of Wickham, who had prejudiced her mind against him; and it was the elopement of her sister which gave occasion for Darcy's generous and delicate assistance. Miss Austen, indeed, herself has anticipated and disarmed this sort of objection, by a stroke of conscious power, equal to that of Richardson in the allusion to Sir Charles Grandison and the ass between two bundles of hay. For in answer to her sister's inquiries, 'How long she had loved Mr. Darcy?' Elizabeth is herself made to say, playfully, 'I believe I must date it from my first seeing his beautiful grounds at Pemberley.' Mary with her books, and Lydia and Catherine with their officers, are very unworthy of their elder sisters; and we might be almost inclined to hold Jane and Elizabeth to some extent responsible for the faults and follies of the younger ones. But with such parents, and with so little difference of age to give authority, it would be unfair upon them to do so.

The pair of friends by whose visit to Hertfordshire the fortunes of the Bennet family are so much affected, are admirably drawn. The popular, good-looking, and gentlemanly Bingley, with his easy temper and manners, is one of those people whom every one is always glad to meet, but whose absence can be supported with equanimity. Darcy is perhaps the highest pitched of all Miss Austen's male characters. Externally haughty, reserved, refined to a fault, and making enemies in general society because he will not take the trouble to make himself agreeable, he has a noble mind and a generous temper.

Sir William Lucas (probably one of Peg Nicholson's knights) and his lady are specimens of not very wise but inoffensive and friendly people. It is a capital touch (and distinguishes him from the common herd of pompous civic knights), that though elated by his dignity, Sir William's presentation at St. James's, acting on a kindly nature, had made him courteous, and anxious to occupy himself in being civil to all the world. The servile and self-important Mr. Collins is a special delineation. It is wonderful how so much absurdity can be so well kept together and handled without producing weariness or disgust. He is always good, but is perhaps to be seen at his greatest perfection in his letters to Mr. Bennet, written on the occasion of Lydia's going off with Wickham, and on Elizabeth's intended marriage to Darcy. Mr. Collins' patroness, Lady Catherine de Bourgh, is of a commoner type. Pride, love of management, and vulgarity still maintain themselves in the world, in spite of Miss Austen and other teachers. She is however allowed to get over her discomfiture by the young lady who dares to engage herself to her nephew against her commands, and she has sense enough to make the best of what she cannot help. Wickham is, after all, not much more than a walking gentleman. Of pleasing manners, but without principle or more than ordinary ability, he is capable of making a superficial impression in his favour. Intensely self-indulgent, he fortunately is without the necessary qualities to be more than a second-rate villain. He can be bought with money, and his price is not high. Contempt for him is complete when the necessary pecuniary arrangements are made for his marriage with the wretched Lydia. The moral of Miss Austen's tales does not lie in the consideration of the final fortunes of her personages, but in the general opportunity afforded of regarding character and manners; but if any deduction is to be drawn from *Pride and Prejudice*, it is to the effect that handsome and agreeable girls need not despair of making good matches, although they may have bad connexions, and foolish or odd parents. Here, as in the rest, the level of excellence is not high: we should prefer to live among a very different set of people. Darcy, however, suggests loftier aspirations; and if we could continue our acquaintance with the characters in this novel after closing the volume, we should like to be often at Pemberley, and as seldom as possible at Hunsford or Longbourn.

In *Mansfield Park* the characters are still more like such as may be encountered every day. They are not, however, the less distinct and well marked as individual specimens; and this novel shows an advance in the construction and conduct of the story. It contains also more of those passages of fine observation on life and manners which deserve to be remembered and extracted for the commonplace book.

Emma will generally be recognised by the admirers of Miss Austen as the best of her works. In delicate investigation of the nicer peculiarities of character, and in its perfectly finished execution, it cannot be surpassed. It is a pleasure even to write down the names of the persons composing the little circle at Highbury. Emma, handsome, clever, and charming, too fond only of management, and thinking perhaps a little too much of herself; Mr. Woodhouse, as finely drawn as one of Shakspeare's fools; Mr. and Mrs. Weston, some time Miss Taylor; Mr. Knightley; the John Knightleys; Mr. and Mrs. Elton; Frank Churchill; Jane Fairfax; Harriet Smith, whose patronage by Emma was for the time so unfortunate for her; Perry, whose name has become a household word for the family medical attendant; Mrs. and Miss Bates. What a wonderful amount of reality and individualization do they suggest to those who are already acquainted with them! What new pleasures are untasted by those who have yet to visit at Hartfield and Rardalls, or to spend the day at Donwell Abbey! No other novels but Miss Austen's have ever excited so much minute as well as general interest. In *Emma*, for instance, a passage occurs (vol. ii., end of chap 16) which has led to frequent and anxious research into the manners of polite society at the time. It is at the first dinner given at Hartfield to the Eltons after their marriage. The party consisted of eight persons—Mr. Woodhouse and Emma, Mr. and Mrs. Elton, Mr. Knightley, Mrs. Weston, Mr. John Knightley (the husband of the one and the wife of the other not being present), and Jane Fairfax. They are assembled before dinner; Mr. Woodhouse hands the bride into the dining-room, leaving to follow three ladies and three gentlemen. These, however, did not pair off together, as would be the case at present, but the ladies seem to have gone out together, Emma and Jane Fairfax, arm in arm; and the gentlemen, it must be presumed, followed them; and such appears to have been the custom of the period. In another place in the same novel Miss Austen's accuracy may be impeached with more probability of success; for, 'in the middle of June,' or rather 'at almost Mid-summer,' strawberries are described as being eaten from the beds in the gardens of Donwell Abbey, while the orchard is in blossom at the neighbouring Abbey-Mill Farm—an anachronism—which we have never met with any horticulturist able to explain by bringing together even the earliest and latest varieties of apple and strawberry.

Northanger Abbey, the first written but latest published of the series, is not unworthy of its companions, although it was not thought deserving of publication until after its writer's reputation was made. *Persuasion* is memorable for containing Anne Elliot, the most perfect in character and disposition of all Miss Austen's women. Through it also Lyme Regis and its Cobb are made as much classic ground in prose fiction by Louisa Musgrove's accident, as they were before famous in English history as the landing-place of the luckless Monmouth.

To Miss Austen all subsequent novelists have been infinitely indebted. She led the way in the return to nature; she again described individuals instead of classes or nationalities; she re-indicated and worked the inexhaustible mines of wealth for the writer of fiction which everywhere lie beneath the surface of ordinary life. None, however, have worked them like her. The aluminium is all around us in the clay of our fields and in the common bricks of our houses. It is one of the most plentifully distributed elements on earth. Its abundance, however, in no way increases the facility of obtaining it: only the subtle chemist can extract the coy metal for our use.

Note

An interesting reaction to Pollock's article is found in the correspondence of the poet and translator Edward Fitzgerald (1809–83), who wrote to the critic soon after its publication, and mentioned the article again eleven years later.

Extract from letter, 23 February 1860: 'I laid out half a crown on your Fraser: and liked much of it very much: especially the Beginning about the Advantage the Novelist has over the Playwriter. A little too much always about Miss Austen, whom yet I think quite unendurable to walk in. . . . I have been very glad to find I could take to a Novel again, in Trollope's *Barchester Towers*, etc.: not perfect, like Miss Austen: but then so much wider Scope: and perfect enough to make me feel I know the People though caricatured or carelessly drawn.' (*Letters of Edward Fitzgerald* (1894), i, 13–14.)

Fitzgerald wrote again, 24 December 1871, requesting a copy of the article and complaining lightly that in so praising Jane Austen Pollock was 'rather driven away by a fashion. . . . She is capital as far as she goes: but she never goes out of the Parlour.' (ii, 131.)

38. Lewes: a note on Jane Austen's artistic economy

1860

Extract from an unsigned article, 'A Word about *Tom Jones*', *Blackwood's Edinburgh Magazine* (March 1860), lxxxvii, 335.

Pride and Prejudice is a finely-constructed work, and shows what a fine artistic sense Miss Austen had. The ease and naturalness of the evolution of the story are so perfect, that only very critical readers are aware of its skill in selection. Take it to pieces, examine the characters, scenes and dialogue, in relation to each other and to the story, and you will find that there is nothing superfluous—that all this variety is secretly tending to one centre; that all this ease of nature, which looks so like the ordinary life of everyday, is subordinate to principles of Economy and Selection; and nothing is dragged in, nothing is superfluous. Then turn to *Tom Jones,* and remember that while scarcely any one has insisted on Miss Austen's construction, everyone insists on the excellence of Fielding.

39. Julia Kavanagh on Jane Austen

1862

Chapter 18, 'Miss Austen's Six Novels', in *English Women of Letters* (1862), pp. 251-74.

Julia Kavanagh (1824-77), a prolific novelist and literary biographer, wrote an unwarrantably ignored critical and historical study of the women novelists in *English Women of Letters*. The chapter on the novels of Jane Austen is the first satisfactory attempt to divine the nature of the reader's experience. The previous chapter is a brief biographical sketch. (See Introduction, pp. 29-30.)

The writings of women are betrayed by their merits as well as by their faults. If weakness and vagueness often characterize them, they also possess when excellent, or simply good, three great redeeming qualities, which have frequently betrayed anonymous female writers. These qualities are: Delicacy, Tenderness, and Sympathy. We do not know if there exists, for instance, a novel of any merit written by a woman, which fails in one of these three attributes. Delicacy is the most common —delicacy in its broadest sense, not in its conventional meaning. Where that fails, which is a rare case, one of the other qualities assuredly steps in. Aphra Behn had no delicacy of intellect or of heart, but she had sympathy. Perhaps only a woman could have written *Oroonoko*, as only another woman could have written *Uncle Tom's Cabin* two hundred years later. Man has the sense of injustice, but woman has essentially pity for suffering and sorrow. Her side is the vanquished side, amongst men or nations, and when she violates that law of her nature she rarely fails to exceed man in cruelty and revenge.

Delicacy was the great attribute of the writer under our notice. Mademoiselle de Scudéry alone equalled Miss Austen in delicacy, with this difference, however, that one applied hers to thought, feeling, and intellectual speculation, and that the other turned hers to the broader and more living field of character and human nature. The method, too, was as different as the application. One analyzed, the other painted.

Miss Austen, however, though she adopted the pictorial method, is not an effective writer. Her stories are moderately interesting—her heroes and heroines are not such as to charm away our hearts, or to fascinate our judgment; but never has character been displayed in such delicate variety as in her tales; never have commonplace men and women been invested with so much reality. She cannot be said to have created or invented; Jane Austen had an infinitely rarer gift—she saw.

Not without cause did the faith and superstition of our forefathers invest with veneration and awe that mysterious word—a seer. The poet, the painter, are no more—they see. To see well is one of the greatest, and strange, too, of the rarest attributes of the mind. Commonplace people see little or nothing. Beauty and truth escape their dull perceptions. Character does not exist for them; for them life is no story—Nature no wonderful poem.

That great gift Miss Austen possessed, not in its fulness, for her range of vision was limited, but in all its keenness. The grand, the heroic, the generous, the devoted, escaped her, or, at least, were beyond her power; but the simply good, the dull, the lively, the mean, the coarse, the selfish, the frivolous, she saw and painted with a touch so fine that we often do not preceive its severity. Yet inexorable it is, for it is true. To this rare power Miss Austen added another equally rare—she knew where to stop. Two qualities are required to write a good book: to know what to say and what to withhold. She had the latter gift, one which is rarely appreciated: it seems so natural not to say more than is needed! In this respect she must have exercised great judgment, or possessed great tact, since her very qualities are those that lead to minuteness. Mademoiselle de Scudéry's prolixity was the result of a delicate and subtle mind, and that prolixity ruined her, for it made her well-nigh unreadable. Her fame decreased with time; steady progress has marked that of Jane Austen. In vain every year sees the birth of works of fiction that prove her deficiencies. She has remained unequalled in her own region—a wide one, the region of commonplace.

Persons who care to think on literary subjects, as well as to enjoy literature, must often be struck with the want of truth which tragedy and comedy display, whether on the stage or in fiction. There is nothing so unlike life as either. Life as we see it around us is not cast in sorrow or in mirth—it is not all stately or ridiculous—but a strange compound in which commonplace acts a far more striking part than heroic events or comic incidents. This middle region Jane Austen painted with a master-hand. Great calamities, heroic sorrows, adventures, and all that hangs upon them, she left to more gifted or to more ambitious painters. Neither did she trench on that other world of fiction where satire, ridicule, and exaggerated character are needed. She was satisfied with life and society, as she saw them around her, without endless sorrows, without great passions or unbecoming follies, and especially without exaggeration. Her men and women are neither very good nor very bad; nothing singular or very dramatic falls to their lot; they move in the circle of friends and home, and the slight incidents of their life are not worked up to gloomy interest, in order to suit the purposes of a tale. Indeed, if Miss Austen's merit, and it is a great one, is to have painted simply and naturally such people as we meet with daily, her fault is to have subdued life and its feelings into even more than their own tameness. The stillness of her books is not natural, and never, whilst love and death endure, will human lives flow so calmly as in her pages.

The impression life produced on Miss Austen was peculiar. She seems to have been struck especially with its small vanities and small falsehoods, equally remote from the ridiculous or the tragic. She refused to build herself, or to help to build for others, any romantic ideal of love, virtue, or sorrow. She laughed at her first heroine, Catherine Morland, in *Northanger Abbey*, and described her by negatives. Her irony, though gentle, was a fault, and the parent of much coldness. She learned to check it, but she never conquered it entirely. Catherine, though she makes us smile, is amiable and innocent, and she contrasts pleasantly with Isabella Thorpe. The selfish enthusiasm, the foolish ardour, of this girl were fit food for satire—for such satire especially as Miss Austen loved; for to deceit, assumption, and mere simple silliness she was inexorable. Isabella introduces Catherine to Mrs. Radcliffe's romances, and she promises her plenty more.

'But are you sure they are all horrid?' anxiously asks Catherine.

'Yes, quite sure; for a particular friend of mine, a Miss Andrews, a sweet girl, one of the sweetest creatures in the world, has read every one of them. I wish you knew Miss Andrews; you would be delighted with her. She is netting herself the sweetest cloak you can conceive.'

The connexion between the Radcliffe school of fiction and one of the sweetest creatures in the world, and between being delighted with her and the sweet cloak she is netting, are irresistibly absurd. Over such instances of folly Miss Austen exulted—not ill-naturedly, but with the keen enjoyment of humour and sense, and, to complete her triumph over the hollow Isabella, she makes her conclude her praise of 'the sweetest girl' by the acknowledgment that 'there is something amazingly insipid about her.'

Isabella's brother, Mr. Thorpe, is a masculine variety of the same species of hollow, selfish talkers. But he is a boaster, which partly redeems him, for boasters have a sort of breadth and imagination—and he, for one, has talked himself into a half belief of his horse's spirit and vivacity. There is really an air of good faith about him which cannot be all assumed. We really do think that he believes in the speed and wickedness of that slow horse of his, and that, when he entreats Catherine not to be frightened if she sees him dance and plunge a little at first setting off, he expects that exhibition of liveliness and vigour. There is a sort of tenderness, too, in his declaration—'He will soon know his master. He is full of spirits, playful as can be, but there is no vice in him.'

None, indeed—and exquisite, therefore, is the servant standing at the head of the quiet animal, and whom, in an important voice, Mr. Thorpe requests to 'let him go.' With more geniality, but not with more finesse, did Goldsmith paint this class of self-deceivers. We love and pity the immortal Beau Tibbs. Mr. Thorpe's vivacity in all that relates to horse-flesh is almost a good point in his character; he has a heart, even though it is but a jockey's heart. Say anything, or speak of anyone to him, and immediately comes the question—'Does he want a horse? Here is a friend of mine, Sam Fletcher, has got one to sell that would suit anybody. A famous clever animal for the road,' &c.

Catherine Morland herself is led away in the same natural manner by her favourite subject: Mrs. Radcliffe's romances. She talks quite learnedly about the south of France, for she has been there with Emily and Valancourt, and, by the same power of association, a fine English evening becomes just such another as that on which St. Aubin died.

This delicate and yet direct power of character is still more forcibly displayed in *Sense and Sensibility*, a far better tale than *Northanger Abbey*, but not one of Miss Austen's best. The two heroines of this tale are somewhat deficient in reality. Elinor Dashwood is Judgment—her sister Marianne is Imagination. We feel it too plainly. And the triumph of Sense over Sensibility, shown by the different conduct they hold under very similar trials, is all the weaker that it is the result of the author's will.

Elinor is attached to an amiable but reserved young man, Edward Ferrars, who seems to love her, but who never speaks of love. Marianne has given her heart to John Willoughby. He is as free as Edward

Ferrars is shy—he intimates love much more plainly than that bashful young man, but he is just as silent on the important subject. Time unfolds the peculiar temper of either sister, and their sad mistake. Edward Ferrars cannot speak of love to Miss Dashwood, for, years before, he had entered into a foolish and secret engagement with a pretty, vulgar girl, from whom he cannot break with honour; and John Willoughby will not speak of love to Marianne, for he only means to spend his time pleasantly with her, and has not the least intention of making her his wife.

But neither the sisters nor their troubles are the real attraction of the tale. We wish them well, but they cannot interest or agitate. The charm of this story lies, as usual, in the most delicate portraiture of character that exists. There is no caricature, no exaggeration, no strong light or shadow—nothing but every-day men and women, with their selfishness; their good-nature, their small vices, and very small minds. One stroke of the pen sets them before us. The respectable, worldly Mr. Dashwood, who first generously resolves to give his poor half-sisters a thousand pounds a-piece—who cuts down the sum to five hundred—then this to an annuity for their mother—then, as that mother is young, and might live long, to a present of fifty pounds now and then—then, as fifty pounds is really a large sum, to kindness, which costs nothing—and who, when circumstances do not allow that cheap gift, is happy in his mind at having intended it, is admirably brought before us, not merely by those successive meannesses, but much more so by his luke-warm goodwill. Some writers would have shown him insolent, brutal, or, at least, indifferent and cold as his conduct. Miss Austen knew the windings of human nature too well to fall into this error.

'His manners to *them*, though calm, were perfectly kind; to Mrs. Jennings most attentively civil; and on Colonel Brandon's coming in soon after himself, he eyed him with a curiosity which seemed to say that he only wanted to know him to be rich, to be equally civil to *him*.'

Colonel Brandon has two thousand a-year, and, in Mrs. Dashwood's opinion at least, shows a significant admiration of his sister Elinor. Delighted to think that she can become rich without being a burden to him, the fond brother exclaims:—

' "Two thousand a-year!" and then, working himself up to a pitch of enthusiastic generosity, he added, "Elinor, I wish, with all my heart, it were *twice* as much, for your sake." '

After this we know Mr. Dashwood. The wealthy man whose civility is yielded to an income, the rich brother who wishes his sisters rich husbands, and liberally doubles their future income by that cheap process, stands before us for ever in all his respectable baseness.

And yet, and by a masterpiece of skill and temper on the part of the author, we cannot dislike him. With the keenest insight into the meanness of human motives, Miss Austen preserved the greatest command over her really formidable powers. She seldom or never draws a character we can hate; she is too calm, too dispassionate, too self-possessed to be bitter or eloquent. Delicate irony is her keenest weapon; this is very prettily shown in Marianne, who is the secret object of Colonel Brandon's admiration. His praise of her music is quiet, but Marianne 'was reasonable enough to allow that a man at five-and-thirty might well have outlived all acuteness of feeling, and every exquisite power of enjoyment. She was perfectly disposed to make every allowance for the Colonel's advanced state of life, which humanity required.' To be taxed with this gentleman's affection Marianne considers 'an unfeeling reflection on the Colonel's advanced years, and on his forlorn condition as an old bachelor.' Equally wise is her remark concerning the impossibility there is in a woman of seven-and-twenty feeling or inspiring affection; as to second love, it is a fiction, and as at 'her time of life—seventeen—opinions are tolerably fixed,' there can be no doubt about it.

Sir John Middleton, and his mother-in-law, Mrs. Jennings, give us some equally delicate and still more entertaining traits; both are admirable samples of Miss Austen's great forte: the delineation of commonplace foolishness, especially distinct from eccentricity.

Sir John Middleton's takes the sociable shape. Picnics, visitors, new faces, are his delight. No sooner do the Miss Steeles, two vulgar sisters, arrive at his house, than he goes off to impart the happy news to the Dashwoods, pronouncing his visitors the sweetest girls in the world. 'Sir John wanted the whole family to walk to the park directly and look at his guests. Benevolent, philanthropic man! It was painful to him even to keep a third cousin to himself.'

Mrs. Jennings invites Elinor and Marianne to London, and Sir John Middleton, who is to be in town, is delighted at their acceptance; 'for to a man whose prevailing anxiety was the dread of being alone, the acquisition of two to the number of inhabitants in London was something.' His resentment of Willoughby's inconstancy is shown after Miss Austen's favourite fashion. Willoughby was a keen sportsman, and Sir John is amazed to find his rule of moral excellence reversed. So bold a rider to act thus! Deceitful dog! 'It was only the last time they met that he had offered him one of Folly's puppies! And this was the end of it.'

This is the very spirit of foolishness. What has a man's conduct to woman to do with his riding, and Folly's puppies? Observe foolish people. They never speak otherwise; the simplest logic of conversation is unknown to them. Mrs Jennings is fond of comfort, and her consolation to the distressed Marianne takes the shape of good cheer, as Sir John Middleton's indignation was sportsmanlike. She recommends a certain Constantia wine, the finest that ever was tasted. ' "My poor husband," she says, "how fond he was of it! Whenever he had a touch of his old cholicky gout, he said it did him more good than anything else in the world." '

Here we are perplexed again. What analogy does Mrs. Jennings see between cholicky gout and disappointed love? By what obscure mental process does she come to the conclusion that what is good for the one must needs be good for the other? The disclosure of Edward Ferrars's secret engagement gives her a further opportunity of displaying her singular idiosyncrasy. This young man's marriage is, or ought to be, a matter of no moment to Mrs. Jennings. Yet she hastens to settle his household arrangements for him at once. And Elinor—Elinor, who loves him, whom he loves, and to whom he is lost—is her listener.

' "Lord!" exclaims Mrs. Jennings, "how snug they might live in such another cottage as yours—or a little bigger—with two maids and two men; and I believe I could help them to a housemaid, for my Betty has a sister out of place, that would fit them exactly." '

Betty's sister has taken a great hold of Mrs. Jennings's mind; the prospects of Edward Ferrars and his bride undergo a change, and she at once exclaims:—

' "Two maids and two men, indeed!—as I talked of t'other day— no, no, they must get a stout girl-of-all-work—Betty's sister would never do for them *now*." '

And yet so irresistibly fascinating is Betty's sister, that when there is, as Mrs. Jennings conceives, some chance of Elinor's marrying Colonel Brandon, who is in love with her sister all the time, she cannot resist the tempting opportunity of putting in a good word for her. And after the rejoicing over the supposed marriage, there comes in, as a matter of course:

' "I have just been thinking of Betty's sister, my dear. I should be very glad to get her so good a mistress. But whether she would do for a lady's maid, I am sure I can't tell. She is an excellent house-maid, and works very well at her needle. However, you will think of all that at your leisure." '

Poor Elinor has other matters to think of—her sister's illness and danger, and Edward's marriage. And yet, and we might be sure of it, he is not married. The faithless and unworthy Lucy Steele has deserted him for his rich brother; he is free, free to marry Elinor and be happy, and Marianne, cured of her first unhappy love, cured, too, of her contempt for men of thirty-five, becomes the wife of Colonel Brandon.

There is very little story in *Sense and Sensibility*. Miss Austen knew that she excelled in character, and probably guessed that she might not excel in adventure. Her incidents, therefore, though most judiciously selected, are of the slightest and most subdued kind, and all subordinate to her main object.

Silliness rises to its height in her next tale, *Pride and Prejudice*. Mrs. Bennet is constantly foolish: Mrs. Jennings was only occasionally so. One had fits; the disease is chronic with the other, never violent, never so startling as the Constantia wine and cholicky gout, but steady, persistent, and incurable. Foolish Mrs. Bennet was born, and foolish she will die. Indeed, so quiet is her absurdity that many would have weighed her well ere they put her into a book. She is simply silly—no salient points promise to yield us entertainment in contemplating this lady—no peculiarity of dress, manner, or person, is called in to help out her folly. It runs, too, in the straightest and most worn-out channels. She is naturally anxious to see her five daughters married; the means she takes to effect her object are not singular, and her line of action is circumscribed by circumstances; in ordinary hands she would be a failure, but she can talk, and that is enough for Miss Austen.

Lydia Bennet has inherited the maternal wisdom. She runs away with a man who declines marrying her, till her friends interfere. No one, save Mrs. Bennet herself, can do justice to her feelings on this occasion. Mr. Bennet is gone to town in search of the fugitives, and his brother-in-law, Mr. Gardiner, proposes joining him.

' "Oh, my dear brother!" replied Mrs. Bennet, "that is exactly what I could most wish for. And now do, when you get to town, find them out, wherever they may be; and if they are not married already, *make* them marry. And as for wedding clothes, do not let them wait for that, but tell Lydia she shall have as much money as she chooses to buy them, after they are married. And above all things keep Mr. Bennet from fighting. Tell him what a dreadful state I am in—that I am frightened out of my wits—and have such tremblings, such flutterings, all over me—such spasms in my side, and pains in my head, and such beatings at heart, that I can get no rest by night nor by day. And tell my dear Lydia not to give any directions about her clothes till she has seen me, for she does not know which are the best warehouses." '

The message about wedding clothes to a girl in Lydia's position, and expressed as it is after the request to keep Mr. Bennet from fighting, is a felicitous illustration of Mrs. Bennet's incurable absurdity. But she is not merely silly, she is also wrongheaded. There are no obvious truths for her; it is all mist. Her brother's exertions are successful—Lydia is married—and Mrs. Bennet's mind reverts to the wedding clothes with such exultation that her eldest daughter, Jane, thinks to calm her transports by reminding her that Mr. Gardiner has probably bribed the lover into becoming a husband.

' "Well," cried her mother, "it is all very right; who should do it but her own uncle? If he had not had a family of his own, I and my children must have had all his money, you know." '

The sense of injury to herself and her children, by the birth of her brother's children, which lurks in this speech, is exquisite. But such is Mrs. Bennet's mind. Her husband's estate is entailed—it has come down to him by entail; but that it should go away by entail to their cousin, Mr. Collins, whilst she, Mrs. Bennet, has five daughters, is more than she can understand. She fretfully wonders why it is entailed, and especially why Mr. Bennet will not try to do something or other about it? It is singular and irritating; she does not bring down the subject often, but, when it is introduced, her wonder, her vexation, and her dislike of the heir-at-law, all come in naturally, and in a variety of forms, though not of meaning.

Mr. Collins is another, more strongly drawn, though not more excellent, specimen of folly than Mrs. Bennet. He is young, a clergyman, pompous, servile, and conceited, but by no means ill-natured. Amiable he cannot be, indeed, for it requires judgment to be that, and he has none; but he is not without good intentions, and to make up for being the heir-at-law, he kindly proposes to marry one of Mrs. Bennet's five daughters. He comes down to Longbourn for that purpose, and entertains the family with his worship of Lady Catherine de Bourgh, his noble patroness, neighbour, and friend.

'The subject elevated him to more than usual solemnity of manner, and, with a most important aspect, he protested that he had never witnessed such behaviour in a person of rank—such affability and condescension as he had himself experienced from Lady Catherine. She had been graciously pleased to approve of both the discourses which he had already had the honour of preaching before her. She had also asked him twice to dine at Rosings, and had sent for him, only the Saturday before, to make up her pool of quadrilles in the evening. Lady Catherine was reckoned proud by many people he knew, but *he* had never seen anything but affability in her. She had always spoken to him as she would to any other gentleman—she made not the smallest objection to his joining in the society of the neighbourhood, nor to his leaving his parish occasionally for a week or two, to visit his relations. She had even condescended to advise him to marry as soon as he could, provided he chose with discretion; and had once paid him a visit in his humble parsonage, where she had perfectly approved all the alterations he had been making, and had even vouchsafed to suggest some herself— some shelves in the closets upstairs.'

This noble lady has a daughter, and to Mrs. Bennet's inquiry—' "Is she handsome?" '—Mr. Collins complacently, and with undiminished pomp, replies,—

' "She is a most charming young lady indeed. Lady Catherine herself says that, in point of true beauty, Miss de Bourgh is far superior to the handsomest of her sex, because there is that in her features which marks the young woman of distinguished birth. She is, unfortunately, of a sickly constitution, which has prevented her making that progress in many accomplishments which she could not otherwise have failed of, as I am informed by the lady who superintended her education, and who still resides with them. But she is perfectly amiable, and often condescends to drive by my humble abode in her little phaeton and ponies." '

The man so alive to Miss de Bourgh's surprising condescension, is also blessed with a keen appreciation of his own merits. His choice falls upon Jane, the eldest and handsomest of Mr. Bennet's daughters; but the mother dropping a hint of Jane's preference for some other person, 'Mr. Collins had only to change from Jane to Elizabeth; and it was soon done—done while Mrs. Bennet was stirring the fire.'

Matters do not speed so quickly, however, when Mr. Collins makes his proposal to the lively Elizabeth, not forgetting to mention, in his long harangue, that he has been twice advised by Lady Catherine to marry.

' "It was but the very Saturday night before I left Hunsford— between our pools at quadrille, while Mrs. Jenkinson was arranging Miss de Bourgh's footstool—that she said: 'Mr. Collins, you must marry—a clergyman like you must marry. Choose properly—choose a gentlewoman for my sake; and, for your own, let her be an active, useful sort of person—not brought up high, but able to make a small income go a good way. This is my advice. Find such a woman as soon as you can, bring her to Hunsford, and I will visit her.' " '

This prospect of felicity does not tempt Elizabeth, and Mr. Collins is rejected. He is not surprised—refusal, sometimes repeated twice, and even thrice, is, he knows, a proof of maidenly modesty—a formality he was prepared for. He is startled, however, when Elizabeth assures him that his friend Lady Catherine would not approve of her; *that*, he gravely confesses, would be an objection, but it is impossible, and he promises his kind interference with her ladyship.

Mrs. Bennet's dismay, on learning his rejection, makes him, however, suspect the truth; and when that lady angrily exclaims, ' "Depend upon it, Mr. Collins, that Lizzy shall be brought to reason. I will speak to her about it myself directly. She is a very headstrong, foolish girl, and does not know her own interest, but I will make her know it!" ' the gentleman's selfishness takes alarm, and suggests to him the following admirable reply,—

' "Pardon me for interrupting you, madam—but if she is really headstrong and foolish, I know not whether she would altogether be a very desirable wife to a man in my situation, who naturally looks for happiness in the marriage state. If, therefore, she actually persists in rejecting my suit, perhaps it were better not to force her into accepting me, because, if liable to such defects of temper, she could not contribute much to my felicity." '

Elizabeth persisting in her headstrong folly, Mr. Collins applies to her friend, Charlotte Lucas, and is promptly accepted. Sir William and Lady Lucas give a joyful assent, and 'Lady Lucas began directly to calculate, with more interest than the matter had ever excited before, how many years longer Mr. Bennet was likely to live.' The same thoughts occur to Mrs. Bennet on learning the irritating news, and her wrath about the wretched entail is revived in all its bitterness. Why is estate entailed? Why is that Charlotte Lucas to turn them all out? A visit from her sister-in-law, Mrs. Gardiner, who comes from London with the newest fashions, gives Mrs. Bennet opportunity for complaint and consolation.

'They had been very ill-used since she last saw her sister. Two of her daughters had been on the point of marriage, and, after all, there was nothing of it.'

' "I do not blame Jane," she continued, "for Jane would have got Mr. Bingley if she could. But Lizzy, oh! sister, it is very hard to think that she might have been Mr. Collins's wife by this time, had it not been for her own perverseness. He made her an offer in this very room, and she refused him. The consequence of it is, that Lady Lucas will have a daughter married before I have, and that Longbourn estate is just as much entailed as ever. The Lucases are very artful people indeed, sister. They are all for what they can get. I am sorry to say it of them, but so it is. It makes me very nervous and poorly, to be thwarted so in my own family, and to have neighbours who think of themselves before anybody else. However, your coming just at this time is the greatest of comforts, and I am very glad to hear what you tell us of long sleeves." '

But neither Mrs. Bennet's folly nor Mr. Collins's pompous conceit makes up the story of *Pride and Prejudice*. Pride assumes the shape of the handsome, haughty Mr. Darcy; and Elizabeth Bennet, the lively, spirited girl, is Prejudice. Pride begins by pronouncing Elizabeth not handsome enough to dance with, by despising her family, and by preventing her sister's marriage with the man she loves, and who loves her. Hence the inveterate prejudice and dislike felt by Elizabeth against the offender. Humbled and conquered by love, Mr. Darcy makes Miss Bennet an offer of marriage, which is angrily and indignantly rejected. But wrath, like a summer storm, only clears the air; Mr. Darcy proves that he was not so guilty as he was thought, and though he asks no more for love, he secures esteem. His generous interference in behalf of the runaway Lydia, adds gratitude to regard, and love crowns all. Prejudice is conquered; Pride stoops a second time; Mr. Darcy renews his suit, and is accepted. Mrs. Bennet's emotions on learning this engagement, which follows closely upon that of her eldest daughter, Jane, with Mr. Bingley, Mr. Darcy's friend, are in strange confusion. She had always detested that proud Mr. Darcy, but then it is such a match! What pin money, what jewels, what carriages her daughter will have! Such a charming man—so handsome—so tall! She begs her dear Lizzy will apologise for her having disliked him so much! A house in town—everything that is charming—three daughters married —ten thousand a-year! Mrs. Bennet must go distracted; even the entail, that strange and provoking arrangement, is forgotten.

The same keen and subtle grace, softened by much quiet tenderness, appears in Miss Austen's next, and, in the opinion of many, most perfect novel, *Mansfield Park*. It has scarcely more story, but it has more power than its predecessors. Three handsome sisters have married very differently. One, Lady Bertram, is the wife of a rich baronet; the other, Mrs. Norris, marries a clergyman; and the third, Mrs. Price, a lieutenant of marines, without education, fortune, or connection. A breach follows, which is healed in time by Mrs. Price's eldest child, Fanny, being sent to Mansfield Park, and in some sort adopted by Sir Thomas and Lady Bertram, and reared with their two sons and daughters, all older than herself. Fanny is shy, nervous, and delicate, and attaches herself to the only member of the family who treats her with affectionate kindness, her cousin Edmund, the Baronet's second son. This affection ripens into a love of which she is long unconscious, and which Edmund does not for a moment suspect. Her silent grief, her struggles, her jealousy, spite all his kindness, and such events as may occur in a well-regulated English family, make up the story. Here again characters and feelings take up the room so long allotted to adventure in the world of fiction. Selfishness and egotism prevail, in this tale, over the folly of its predecessors.

The three sisters are selfish, each after a fashion of her own. Lady Bertram is handsome, indolent, kind, and indifferent to all save comfort. She is selfish, without the activity or the eagerness which renders selfishness odious, and converts it into ambition. Her husband goes on a long and momentous journey, and Lady Bertram is surprised to find how well she does without him, 'how well Edmund could supply his place in carving, talking to the steward, writing to the attorney, settling with the servants, and equally saving her from all possible fatigue or exertion in every particular but that of directing her letters.'

Similar is her affection for Fanny; she likes to have her by her, for the young girl is pleasant and useful. She would like her to be happy even, if she could think about it; if her wishes could go beyond her own handsome, lazy self. But her love for kindred can go no farther.

'Three or four Prices might have been swept away, any or all, except Fanny and William, and Lady Bertram would have thought little about it; or perhaps might have caught from Mrs. Norris's lips the cant of its being a very happy thing, and a great blessing to their poor dear sister, Price, to have them all so well provided for.'

The affliction of Lady Bertram, whose eldest son is in danger, and whose two daughters have run away, finds Mrs. Price equally sensitive.

'Mrs. Price talked of her poor sister for a few minutes—but how to find anything to hold Sally's clothes, because Rebecca took away all the boxes and spoilt them, was much more in her thoughts.'

Mrs. Norris, the third sister, is another amusing variety of the family failing. She is a faithful representation of the cheap benevolence which shows itself in contriving the good actions of other people. She suggests the scheme of Fanny's being adopted by her uncle and aunt, and kindly leaves them all the trouble and expense, reaping, however, no small share of the merit. Her affections are not warmer than Lady Bertram's. When her husband dies she consoles herself for his loss by 'considering that she could do very well without him,' and she does not feel his death more than her ladyship feels Sir Thomas's absence; but yet there is a marked difference between the two sisters. Lady Bertram is passively kind; Mrs. Norris is actively so. She never ceases to contrive everything for her neighbours, economy as well as charity, and is so overpowered by viewing the benefits she confers upon them that she cannot help exclaiming aloud at her own benevolence, and taking to herself the merit of every benefit and pleasure which life can bring forth for those around her. With Fanny especially, whom she torments in every possible way, she indulges herself most freely, and the charm of her boasting lies in its sincerity. Thus, after having done her best to keep Fanny from a pleasure party to which Edmund makes her go in his aunt's despite and maugre his mother's reluctance, Mrs. Norris benevolently exclaims,—

' "Well, Fanny, this has been a fine day for you, upon my word. Nothing but pleasure from beginning to end! I am sure you ought to be very much obliged to your aunt Bertram and me for contriving to let you go!" '

With equal sincerity, when the young people contrive private theatricals, which are Fanny's torment, for they show her the man whom she loves, openly devoted to a rival, Mrs. Norris, whose whole mind is bent on economizing for the absent Sir Thomas, congratulates Fanny on what she evidently considers a delightful part of this amusement, being a neglected and forgotten looker-on.

' "Come Fanny," she cried, "these are fine times for you, but you must not be always walking from one room to the other a-doing the lookings on, at your ease, in this way—I want you here. I have been slaving myself till I can hardly stand, to contrive Mr. Rushworth's cloak without sending for any more satin; and now I think you may give me your help in putting it together. There are but three seams; you may do them in a trice. It would be lucky for me if I had nothing but the executive part to do—*you* are best off, I can tell you; but if nobody did more than *you*, we should not get on very fast." '

Mrs. Norris's love of the executive takes every form. Her brother-in-law and his elder son go on business to Antigua, and Mrs. Norris, naturally anticipating some dreadful catastrophe on their way to a goal so remote, kindly settles beforehand how the melancholy intelligence shall be broken by her to the afflicted family. Sir Thomas returns safely, and Mrs. Norris is not asked to break the news; he perversely defrauds her 'of an office on which she had always depended, whether his arrival or his death were to be the thing unfolded.'

The return of the grave master of the house puts an end to the theatrical scheme. We share in the regret of Sir Thomas Bertram's children, for these theatricals were entertaining. The polite struggle for the best parts between the actors, the secret heartburnings and disappointments of Maria Bertram and her sister, both striving for the same man's favour, Mr. Crawford; the male flirt's consummate ease between the two, and the foolish exhilaration of Maria's future husband, Mr. Rushworth, delighted to appear in a pink satin cloak, and never ceasing to talk of the forty-two speeches he has to learn; and especially the suggestor of the scheme, the Honourable John Yates, were most amusingly portrayed.

'He came on the wings of disappointment, and with his head full of acting, for it had been a theatrical party, and the play, in which he had borne a part, was within two days of representation, when the sudden death of one of the nearest connections of the family had destroyed the scheme and dispersed the performers. To be so near happiness, so near fame, so near the long paragraph in praise of the private theatricals at Ecclesford, the seat of the Right Honourable Lord Ravenshaw, in Cornwall, which would, of course, have immortalized the whole party for at least a twelvemonth! And being so near, to lose it all was an injury to be keenly felt, and Mr. Yates could talk of nothing else. Ecclesford and its theatre, with its arrangements and dresses, rehearsals and jokes, was his never-failing subject, and to boast of the past his only consolation.' . . . The play had been *Lovers' Vows*, and Mr. Yates was to have been Count Cassel. ' "A trifling part," said he, "and not at all to my taste, and such a one as I certainly would not accept again; but I was determined to make no difficulties. Lord Ravenshaw and the duke had appropriated the only two characters worth playing before I reached Ecclesford; and though Lord Ravenshaw offered to resign his to me, it was impossible to take it, you know. I was sorry for *him* that he should have so mistaken his powers, for he was no more equal to the baron—a little man with a weak voice, always hoarse after the first ten minutes! It must have injured the piece materially; but *I* was resolved to make no difficulties. Sir Henry thought the duke not equal to Frederick, but that was because Sir Henry wanted the part for himself; whereas it was certainly in the best hands of the two. I was surprised to see Sir Henry such a stick. Luckily, the strength of the piece did not depend upon him. Our Agatha was inimitable, and the duke was thought very great. And upon the whole it would certainly have gone off wonderfully. . . . "

"To be sure the poor old dowager could not have died at a worse time, and it is impossible to help wishing that the news could have been suppressed for just the three days we wanted. It was but three days—and being only a grandmother, and all happening two hundred miles off, I know; but Lord Ravenshaw, who, I suppose, is one of the most correct men in England, would not hear of it." '

Considering it was 'only a grandmother,' his lordship was decidedly hard-hearted, though not so cruel as Sir Thomas Bertram, who, without having even this decent pretence of a dead grandmother, calmly put an end to Mr Yates's second hopes of *Lovers' Vows*.

The more serious characters are no less skilfully drawn. Mr. Crawford is excellent. He is not handsome, but he is agreeable, and the business of his life is to make ladies learn it to their cost. He causes himself to be loved by Maria Bertram, though she is engaged to Mr. Rushworth. He also wins the favour of her sister Julia, and, never committing himself, he has, thanks to the most skilful management, the satisfaction of seeing the two sisters jealous, angry, and miserable for his sake. Time passes—one is married, the other is gone, and Mr. Crawford kindly turns to Fanny, who has seen his behaviour to her cousins, and who despises and dislikes him. She is too gentle to show her feelings, but they give her a coldness more alluring than her beauty, though that Mr. Crawford appreciates. With the luxury of an epicure, he explains his plans to his sister,—

' "I will not do her any harm, dear little soul! I only want her to look kindly on me, to give me smiles as well as blushes, to keep a chair for me by herself wherever we are, and be all animation when I take it and talk to her—to think as I think, be interested in all my possessions and pleasures, try to keep me longer at Mansfield, and feel when I go away that she shall never be happy again. I want nothing more." '

But the old story of the biter bit is once more fulfilled. Mr. Crawford falls seriously in love, and, to his surprise, Fanny will not have him. Her heart is guarded by affection for Edmund, who loves Mary Crawford, an agreeable, selfish, and worldly girl. That love, however, is fortunately ill-fated, and gentle, timid little Fanny is rewarded with the affection of Edmund Bertram.

The variety which Miss Austen displayed in the drawing of

commonplace character woke especially the admiration of the late Lord Macaulay. Without assimilating her range to that of Shakespeare, he compared her to the great master in that respect. 'She has given us,' he justly said, 'a multitude of characters, all, in a certain sense, commonplace—all such as we meet every day. Yet they are all as perfectly discriminated as if they were the most eccentric of human beings.'

This remarkable power Miss Austen carried even in the conception of her heroines. They are all very distinct persons. Emma Woodhouse, whose name gives its title to the last work Miss Austen published, is a very different heroine from the gentle Fanny or the spirited Elizabeth. She has not either the *naïveté* of Catherine or the prudence of Elinor— she is a good, vain, and plotting girl; disinterested for herself, but unduly anxious about her friends, especially about Harriet Smith, a little innocent creature, who falls in or gets out of love at her bidding. The scrapes into which Emma's zeal brings her, first with Mr. Elton, then with Frank Churchill, and finally with Mr. Knightley, the hero of the tale, are very entertaining; and still more so are the discourses of Mr. Woodhouse and Miss Bates.

Mr. Woodhouse, Emma's father, is rather peculiar than ridiculous. He is amiable, polite, hospitable, and kind. Few men of his years and infirm health could pass better in society. But he is weak on one or two matters. He is restlessly unhappy about the possible colds and indigestions of his friends, and even acquaintances, and he is miserable about the calamity of their getting married. His eldest daughter, Isabella, is married—she is a happy wife, a happy mother, but she is 'poor Isabella' for ever with her father. Miss Taylor, Emma's governess and friend, exchanges dependence for a kind husband, an excellent home, and children of her own, but she is 'poor Miss Taylor!' 'Matrimony, as the origin of change, was always disagreeable.'

But whereas people only get married occasionally, they eat frequently, and this is another of Mr. Woodhouse's troubles.

'He loved to have the cloth laid,' we are told, 'because it had been the fashion of his youth, but his conviction of suppers being very unwholesome made him rather sorry to see anything put on it; and while his hospitality would have welcomed his visitors to everything, his care for their health made him grieve that they would eat.'

'Such another small basin of thin gruel as his own was all that he could, with thorough self-approbation, recommend, though he might constrain himself, while the ladies were comfortably clearing the nicer things, to say,—

"Mrs. Bates, let me propose your venturing on one of these eggs. An egg boiled very soft is not unwholesome. Serle understands boiling an egg better than anybody. I would not recommend an egg boiled by anybody else—but you need not be afraid—they are very small, you see—one of our small eggs will not hurt you. Miss Bates, let Emma help you to a little bit of tart—a *very* little bit. Ours are all apple tarts. You need not be afraid of unwholesome preserves. I do not advise the custard. Mrs. Goddard, what say you to *half* a glass of wine? A *small* half glass—put into a tumbler of water? I do not think it could disagree with you." '

His veneration and fondness for his medical man, poor Perry, who is bilious, and has not time to take care of himself; his unseasonable intrusion of Perry's advice and opinions; his confidence in James, his own coachman, and, apparently, the only coachman who really knows what driving is; his admiration for the precocious intelligence of his grandsons, who will come and stand by his chair, and say, ' "Grandpapa, can you give me a bit of string?" ' and one of them even asked for a knife, are all in the same strain of fond, foolish egotism. Mr. Woodhouse is selfish, but amiably selfish—he amuses, and never repels us.

' "Do not tell his father," ' he considerately says, before censuring Frank Churchill;' "but that young man is not quite the thing." ' We know already that Mr. Churchill is a flirt, that he trifles with the affections of one or two ladies, but his error is of a deeper die in Mr. Woodhouse's creed of moral excellence. ' "He has been opening the doors very often this evening, and keeping them open very inconsiderately. He does not think of the draught. I do not mean to set you against him, but, indeed he is not quite the thing." '

Next to Mr. Woodhouse, in this pleasant sort of folly, is Miss Bates. What Perry and health are to Mr. Woodhouse, her niece, Jane Fairfax, is to her. She cannot weary of the subject. Jane Fairfax, her looks, her letters, only two pages crossed, are her delight and the torment of her friends. Then Miss Bates is so good-natured, so grateful for everything, so forgetful of herself, though, unfortunately, so mindful of Jane and her concerns, so loquacious, too, that she is almost too well drawn, too like the tiresome, provoking reality. Harriet Smith is another and wholly different form of that commonplace silliness in which Miss Austen is unequalled. She is gentle, docile, and foolish. Emma can make her feel, think, and act as she pleases. Harriet is secretly attached to a young farmer, but Emma does not approve the alliance, and Harriet discovers that she has no liking for him. Emma decrees that she is to be loved by, and to feel love for, the Rev. Philip Elton, and Harriet obeys, thinks him the first of men, so handsome, so superior, saves his worn-out pencils, makes relics of his discarded sticking-plaster, and sheds a few tears when he marries Miss Hawkins.

But Harriet has a light, cheerful, unsentimental disposition. To go to a party is comfort and consolation. 'To be in company, nicely dressed, to sit and smile and look pretty, and say nothing, was enough for the happiness of the present hour.'

We cannot feel much for Harriet's love-sorrows at any time, and least of all when, not with Emma's advice, she bestows her heart on Mr. Knightley, the hero of the tale, and a very agreeable hero he is. A man of sense, a handsome man, too, though he is seven-and-thirty, and above all, the self-possessed lover of young, pretty, and wilful Emma. There is not much in the progress of their affection, but as much as the cast of Miss Austen's tales allows. Emma's regard for him, her anger at the thought of his marrying, her indignation at hearing him called Knightley by Mrs. Elton, and finally her feelings when Harriet innocently confesses her attachment, and even her hopes, enlighten her. 'It darted through her, with the speed of an arrow, that Mr. Knightley must marry no one but herself.' Mr. Knightley is of precisely the same opinion, and after the first shock, Mr. Woodhouse is convinced how very safe and proper it is to have a son-in-law in the same house with himself. Harriet's feelings, left to themselves, return to her first attachment, and the tale ends with pleasant promises of happiness. Yet in such pictures of human life did not lie Miss Austen's forte—she could not paint happy love. Did she believe in it? If we look under the shrewdness and quiet satire of her stories, we shall find a much keener sense of disappointment than of joy fulfilled. Sometimes we find more than disappointment.

Beyond any other of Miss Austen's tales, *Persuasion* shows us the phase of her literary character which she chose to keep most in the shade: the tender and the sad. In this work, as in *Sense and Sensibility*, and in *Mansfield Park*, but with more power than in either, she showed what can be the feelings of a woman compelled to see the love she most longs for, leaving her day by day. The judicious Elinor is, indeed, conscious that she is beloved; but her lover is not free, and she long thinks him lost. Fanny is her lover's *confidante*, and must be miserable when he is blest, or happy when he is wretched. The position of Anne Elliot has something more desolate still. The opposition of her relatives, and the advice of friends, induce her to break with a young naval officer,

Captain Frederick Wentworth, to whom she is engaged, and the only man whom she can love. They part, he in anger, she in sorrow; he to rise in his profession, become a rich man, and outlive his grief; she to pine at home, and lose youth and beauty in unavailing regret. Years have passed when they meet again. Captain Wentworth is still young, still handsome and agreeable. He wishes to marry, and is looking for a wife. Anne Elliot, pale, faded, and sad, knows it, and sees it—she sees the looks, the smiles of fresher and younger beauties seeking him, and apparently not seeking him in vain.

Here we see the first genuine picture of that silent torture of an un-loved woman, condemned to suffer thus because she is a woman and must not speak, and which, many years later, was wakened into such passionate eloquence by the author of *Jane Eyre*. Subdued though the picture is in Miss Austen's pages, it is not the less keen, not the less pain-ful. The tale ends happily. Captain Wentworth's coldness yields to old love, Anne's beauty returns, they are married, yet the sorrowful tone of the tale is not effaced by that happy close. The shadow of a long disappointment, of secret grief, and ill-repressed jealousy will ever hang over Anne Elliot.

This melancholy cast, the result, perhaps, of some secret personal disappointment, distinguishes *Persuasion* from Miss Austen's other tales. They were never cheerful, for even the gentlest of satire precludes cheerfulness; but this is sad.

Of the popularity of Miss Austen's six novels, of the estimation in which they are held, we need not speak. It is honourable to the public that she should be so thoroughly appreciated, not merely by men like Sir Walter Scott and Lord Macaulay, but by all who take up her books for mere amusement. Wonderful, indeed, is the power that out of materials so slender, out of characters so imperfectly marked, could fashion a story. This is her great, her prevailing merit, and yet, it cannot be denied, it is one that injures her with many readers. It seems so natural that she should have told things and painted people as they are, so natural and so easy, that we are apt to forget the performance in the sense of its reality. The literary taste of the majority is always tinged with coarseness; it loves exaggeration, and slights the modesty of truth.

Another of Miss Austen's excellencies is also a disadvantage. She does not paint or analyze her characters; they speak for themselves. Her people have never those set sayings or phrases which we may refer to the author, and of which we may think, how clever! They talk as people talk in the world, and quietly betray their inner being in their

folly, falsehood, or assumption. For instance, Sir Walter Elliot is handsome; we are merely told so; but we never forget it, for he does not.
He considers men born to be handsome, and, deploring the fatal effect
of a seafaring life on manly beauty, he candidly regrets that 'naval
gentlemen are not knocked on the head at once,' so disgusted has he
been with Admiral Baldwin's mahogany complexion and dilapidated
appearance. And this worship of personal appearance is perfectly unaffected and sincere. Sir Walter Elliot's good looks have acted on him
internally; his own daughter Anne rises in his opinion as her complexion grows clearer, and his first inquiry concerning his married
daughter, Mary, is, 'How is she looking? The last time he, Sir Walter,
saw her, she had a red nose, and he hopes that may not happen every
day.' He is assured that the red nose must have been accidental, upon
which the affectionate father exclaims kindly: ' "If I thought it would
not tempt her to go out in sharp winds, and grow coarse, I would send
her a new hat and pelisse." '

But it was natural that powers so great should fail somewhere, and
there were some things which Miss Austen could not do. She could not
speak the language of any strong feeling, even though that feeling were
ridiculous and unjust. A rumour of Mr. Darcy's marriage with Elizabeth Bennet having reached his aunt, Lady Catherine de Bourgh, she
hurries down to Longbourn to tax and upbraid Miss Bennet with her
audacity, and to exact from her a promise that she will not marry Mr.
Darcy. Elizabeth refuses, and there is a scene, but not a good one. Lady
Catherine's interference is insolent and foolish, but it is the result of a
strong feeling, and, to her, it is an important, a mighty matter, and this
we do not feel as we read. Her assertions of her own importance, her
surprise at Elizabeth's independence, are in keeping, but we want something more, and that something never appears. The delicate mind that
could evolve, so shrewdly, foolishness from its deepest recesses, was
powerless when strong feelings had to be summoned. They heard her,
but did not obey the call.

This want of certain important faculties is the only defect, or rather
causes the only defect, of Miss Austen's works: that everything is told
in the same tone. An elopement, a death, seduction, are related as
placidly as a dinner or ball, but with much less spirit. As she is, however,
we must take her, and what her extraordinary powers wanted in extent,
they made up in depth. In her own range, and admitting her cold views
of life to be true, she is faultless, or almost faultless. By choosing to be
all but perfect, she sometimes became monotonous, but rarely. The

value of light and shade, as a means of success, she discarded. Strong contrasts, bold flights, she shunned. To be true, to show life in its every-day aspect, was her ambition. To hope to make so much out of so little showed no common confidence in her own powers, and more than common daring. Of the thousands who take up a pen to write a story meant to amuse, how many are there who can, or who dare, be true, like Jane Austen?

40. Jane Austen and George Eliot

1866

Extract from an unsigned review by E. S. Dallas of George Eliot's *Felix Holt, the Radical* (1866), *The Times* 26 June 1866, p. 6.

Eneas Sweetland Dallas (1828–79) the reviewer and critic is best-known to us for his remarkable study of literary theory, *The Gay Science* (1866). The extract given here is the opening paragraph to his review, acknowledging Jane Austen's subtly natural technique, but giving George Eliot the palm for her attempt upon greater issues of life.

Hitherto Miss Austen has had the honour of the first place among our lady novelists, but a greater than she has now arisen—a lady who in grasp of thought, in loftiness of feeling, in subtlety of expression, in fineness of humour, in reach of passion, and in all those sympathies which go to form the true artist has never been excelled. In the art of weaving a narrative Miss Austen is still pre-eminent among women. Nothing can be more natural than the way in which she evolves an event, leading up to it with the clearest motives and the most likely accidents, never saying too much, never too little, nothing too soon, nothing too late, sparing of reflection, and letting her characters speak for themselves. George Eliot has not attained this ease of story-telling because she has to deal with subjects far more difficult than Miss Austen ever attempted, with wilder passions, with stronger situations, with higher thoughts. Miss Austen scarcely ever gets out of the humdrum of easy-going respectable life; she can therefore well afford to be calm and neat in arranging every thread of the narrative she has to weave. George Eliot undertakes to set forth the issues of a more tumultuous life, to work out deeper problems, and to play with torrents where Miss Austen played with rills. But if thus dealing with stronger forces she has been as a rule unable to give to her plots the finished ease of movement for which her predecessor is famous, she on the other hand succeeds in veiling any deficiency of story by the wondrous charm of her style. We don't know any Englishwoman who can be placed near her as a writer of prose. There is such a pith in her thinking, such a charm in her writing, such a fresh vigour in the combination of both, that—begin where we will in her volumes—we go on reading, now startled by some strange suggestive thought, now tickled by her humour, now touched by her pathos, and ever fascinated by the results of delicate observation and fine literary polish. Her style is very rich, and not only rich with the palpable meaning which in each individual sentence she has to express, but rich also in those swift, indescribable associations which well chosen words recall, allusions to past reading, the reflected sparkle of past thinking, the fragrance of past feeling.

41. The Victorian 'society' view
1866

Extracts from a pair of unsigned articles, 'Miss Austen', *Englishwoman's Domestic Magazine* (July, August 1866), 3rd series ii, 238-9, 278-82.

In these pages we can detect a strong infusion of late-Victorian society attitudes into criticism which is basically not unperceptive (see Introduction, p.30).

However idealised this picture of her character may be, there can be no doubt from her writings that she was a singularly gifted woman, of refined, and, as would have been said in her day, 'elegant' mind, and that her principles were high and pure. But it is not with her character as a woman so much as her skill as an artist that we have to deal, and we will therefore leave the one in the safe custody of her biographer to treat the other as common property.

She is an additional instance, if one was wanted, of the possibility of acquiring an accurate knowledge of human nature with a limited experience of the world. She, like Charlotte Brontë attained her knowledge by the study of comparatively few specimens; but, unlike Charlotte Brontë, her specimens were of the most ordinary character. Both painted with a severe regard for truth, but their canvases show a startling dissimilarity of result. They both painted what they saw with great labour and fidelity. Charlotte Brontë found nature rough, and strong, and passionate; Jane Austen refined, genteel, and little given to the exhibition of emotion. Charlotte Brontë's experience led her to consider life as a severe struggle in which happiness is only attained by severe personal toil, except in extraordinary instances; Jane Austen as a series of little tea-parties, picnics, and routs, where the road to happiness was accomplished by the short cut of an eligible offer. Charlotte Brontë's implements were a poetic heart and a fervid imagination; Jane Austen's heart was tender, but without sentiment, and her imagination sustained, but quite cool and comfortable. Charlotte Brontë wrote like an inspired woman, Jane Austen like a cultivated lady. Both of them had true genius, and used it to the best of their ability, and the works of both will probably live as long as the English language from their inherent truth to nature—but what a contrast!

The reader, after perusing this paragraph, unless previously acquainted with Miss Austen's works, may not only think the contrast very much in favour of Charlotte Brontë, but even be at a loss to think why Miss Austen should be thought worthy of so high a place in literature as is generally accorded to her. 'Only ordinary specimens of human nature,' 'refined,' 'genteel,' 'little given to emotion,' 'life a series of little tea-parties and picnics,' 'without sentiment,' 'imagination cool and comfortable,' what words are these to apply to a novelist and her works! Too true, we assure you, and if sentiment is a *sine qua non* with you, if you think a book must be dull without thrilling incidents and wonderful characters, Miss Austen did not write for you. But if you can be amused with life-like portraits of people like those you meet every day, if you can laugh at their follies and be interested in their hopes and fears, if you can appreciate subtle strokes of character, delicate shafts of satire, can smile at dry wit and laugh at well-sustained humour, if you can take pleasure in fineness of workmanship and have patience to examine it, then Miss Austen did write for you. We hope there are few people who could read her works without some pleasure and admiration, but to appreciate them at their true worth is impossible without closer examination than ordinary novels require, for as she herself said of them, they are like 'little bits of ivory, two inches wide, worked upon with a brush so fine that little effect is produced after much labour.' They are not books to be skimmed hastily, or their beauties will be lost, and the opinion of the reader may perhaps be summed up in a hasty sentence, as was, we are sorry to say, the opinion of some gentleman or lady who had formerly perused our copy of *Pride and Prejudice*. This novel is perhaps unequalled as a work of art among novels, and contains one of the most charming characters in fiction. But workmanship and beauty were thrown away on one reader at all events, for this was the sentence we have alluded to: 'This I should think was written in the year 1801. Such utter nonsense.' Why the year 1801 should have been fixed as the crisis of absurdity is not more incomprehensible to us than the opinion of the writer.

As we have given the adverse criticism of one man on the works of Miss Austen, it is only fair that we should state that we believe and hope it to be unique of its class. Sir Walter Scott said—'Edgeworth, Ferrier, Austen have all given portraits of real society far superior to anything

which man, vain man, has produced of the like nature.' And again—
'That young lady had a talent for describing the involvements, and
feelings, and characters of ordinary life which is to me the most wonderful I ever met with.' Mr. G. H. Lewes, in a letter to Charlotte Brontë,
calls her 'one of the greatest artists, one of the greatest painters of human
character, and one of the writers with the nicest sense of means to an end
that ever lived.' Both Macaulay and Whately have compared her to
Shakspeare for her power of stamping her characters with individual
life. Indeed, the praise of her works has scarcely been less enthusiastic,
if more discriminate, than that accorded by her biographer to her
character and beauty.

One of the greatest charms to us of Miss Austen's novel is the complete
change of scene they afford: we are transferred at once to an old world
which we can scarcely believe was England only half-a-century ago. If
it were only for the completeness with which she holds the mirror up
to the society in which she lived, they would be of great interest. It
scarcely needs more than a glance at the works of her contemporaries,
such as Madame D'Arblay and Mrs. Opie, to be convinced that life
never could have been such a wretched mixture of false sentiment and
stilted morality as it is there represented. No doubt there was a great
deal of both, but human nature was under all, and this Miss Austen
alone gives us. She shows us real men and women, moving in a somewhat curious and confined atmosphere it is true, but still breathing and
moving and having their being actuated by just the same every-day
hopes and fears as ourselves, and expressing them in much the same
language.

It will depend upon the taste of the reader whether the change to a
different and more formal and quaint atmosphere will prove of interest
to him; to many it will be altogether unpalatable, as it probably was to
that gentleman who commented so tersely upon *Pride and Prejudice;*
but, at all events, to most the accurate representation of that human
nature which is never out of fashion will render these works of Miss
Austen a very interesting study.

There are some people in all ages who seem quite untinged by the
peculiar conditions in which they live, who—as far as we can judge,
would have been much the same under any circumstances—in whom
nature is too strong to endure the trammels of convention, and with
such people Miss Austen's novels are well stocked. There are others
living in all generations who are the very representatives and mouth-

pieces of the time, part and parcel of it, in whom the metal of nature is stamped into current coin, the features and superscription of which are sure to be effaced by the progress of time: of these decayed and decaying types Miss Austen's books also furnish several valuable specimens; there are also the mean between these two, whose natures are only modified by the influence of surrounding circumstances, who, though dressed in the fashions and conforming outwardly to the taste of the time, yet preserve their individual shape nearly unaltered.

We have said so much in praise of Miss Austen's art, that it may be as well before we go further to examine in what it consists. Charlotte Brontë was right, in her own sense, in denying her title to the name of one of the greatest artists of human nature. Lewes was right in his in claiming it for her. Andrea del Sarto is said to have been a greater *artist* than Raphael. Charlotte Brontë was judging by the height of aim, Lewes by completeness of execution. But Charlotte Brontë made the mistake of confusing nature with art. Miss Austen's nature was not of the highest type; she was not poetical, she was not philosophical, she was not even very noble or highminded; she was amiable and ladylike, a person of exquisite taste, delicate humour, and refined sense, and she was not less artistic because she was not sentimental than because she was not broadly humorous, for art must be always limited by nature. But her art was almost perfect in its development within this range.

Her material was the upper middle life in the country of the beginning of the century; her power was composed of observation, insight, taste, humour, and good sense; the rest was cultivation. By continued observation, aided by insight, she collected a regiment of knowledge, and by taste, humour, and good sense, selected the most useful recruits and drilled them into order. Her aim was to give an amusing but faithful picture of the people and life with which she was best acquainted.

To be readable is the first requisite of a novel. The preacher is sure of his congregation, but the novel-writer can exercise no compulsion, and even the preacher's effort is completely thrown away unless the ear of the audience is gained. People read novels for amusement, and will not listen to sermons in disguise, especially in three volumes. It has only been in comparatively the last few years that novel-writers have been found who have been able to use novels successfully as the vehicles of high thought, but in such books the instruction has been the medium through which amusement has been conveyed, not the pill of which amusement was the sugared coating. Still now as ever, to amuse is the *sine qua non* of a novel-writer, whether the writer be Thackeray or Miss Braddon, Kingsley or George Eliot.

But at the time in which Miss Austen wrote, high thinkers—for even Scott was not a high thinker—did not write novels. In spite of the large numbers that were printed, they were held, and not unjustly, in something like contempt, and there were very few who dared to speak out in their praise. Even the novel-writers themselves, following the general prejudice, instead of vindicating their right to a high place in the literary world, condemned novels by the mouths of their characters as the foolish pabulum of idlers, exempting by inference their own works only from their ungenerous censure. In the very first book of Miss Austen, she, with a generosity that sprang from good heart and good sense, bravely and indignantly exclaimed against this unworthy civil war. This young girl, who had seen so little of the world but knew so much, who, brought up in the constrained atmosphere of a country parsonage, emancipated herself from the narrow prejudices of the society in which she lived, saw and recognised the value of the novel, and with unusual sagacity set to work to raise it from its degraded position. Avoiding rivalry, silly sentimentality, and ridiculous romance, she resolved to paint the world as she saw it, and to substitute rational for false amusement. That such a resolution ever occurred to her in this precise form is, of course, conjecture, but that she saw that the position novels held in the opinion of the world was in a great measure the fault of the writers, and determined to found her books on a more real base, is plain from several passages in *Northanger Abbey*, and that she did this without contempt of her rivals or desire to eclipse them is equally plain.

Her subjects were not grand, so much the more pains was it necessary to take to select them; the colours at her command were not vivid, so much the more difficult was it to produce a definite effect; she had not even the command of startling contrasts of light and shade, so much more was the need of delicate graduation of tone. To doff metaphor, the commonplace nature of the characters she knew, and therefore drew, the unsensational life which she lived, and therefore depicted, rendered the employment of unusual art requisite in order to make her work readable.

But if she knew that the first requisite of a novel was to be readable, she was also aware that it should not be the only aim, and that it was one not sufficient to be pursued for itself alone, even in an artistic sense, and certainly not worthy to be pursued at the expense of principle, in a moral one. Her machinery and scenery were not sufficient for tableaux;

she had no villains or saints to make tragedies out of, no personages eccentric enough for farce, so she naturally chose or fell into genteel comedy, and in the same way her society not being such as to call forth the display of strong mental struggles with passion and religion ending in the triumph of virtue, she chose or was forced to content herself with the lesser victories of humility, good sense, and propriety, over pride, sensibility, and romance. And she thus became in effect the inculcator of an elegant morality. And that she did not strain beyond this is one of the greatest secrets of her art and its success: to have gone beyond would have been like striving to play *Othello* at a public theatre with a company of ordinary amateurs. She was content to cultivate her own power without emulating that of any one else; she wrote to amuse, not to instruct, but she took care to write nothing that should not have an instructive tendency. She might be called a moral homœopath: not having the power or desire to give strong doses, she administered her physic in such a diluted form, that the pleasant medium in which it was conveyed was made more wholesome and no less palatable.

In *Northanger Abbey*, her first book, she does not, as may be conjectured, arrive at so high a pitch of art as she afterwards attained. In spite of some very excellent character drawing, the book, on the whole, is crude, the interest insufficient, and the story incompletely worked out. Catherine, the principal character, is a half-educated daughter of a country clergyman, whose favourite reading is a romance of Mrs. Radcliffe. With very kindly satire, the author describes the effect of such reading on an innocent mind ignorant of the world. Catherine pays a visit to Bath on the invitation of the Thorpes, whose knowing vulgarity forms a good contrast to her artless simplicity. By her beauty and genuineness she attracts a Mr. Tilney and his sister, the children of General Tilney, a rich and proud man, who, being deceived as to her fortune by the representations of John Thorpe (the fast Oxonian whom we have already introduced to the reader), thinks she will be a good match for his younger son, and invites her to Northanger Abbey. Here she spends a very pleasant time, and the effect of her romantic reading is humorously brought out during her stay there. She searches with trembling hands an old escritoire in her bedroom, and discovers a secret drawer and a roll of manuscript, which, unlike the roll in the *Romance of the Forest*, turns out to be nothing but a collection of washing bills. An old chest, which she, with her head full of the novel in question, half fears to contain a skeleton, proves a repository of linen. The closed doors of the abbey, which have not been disturbed since the death of the general's wife, disclose on examination nothing but well-furnished apartments, and the general himself, who, from the sternness of his character and his silence on the subject of his wife, she pictures as a dreadful villain of the Radcliffe type, proves nothing but a hard, cold man of the world, who, on discovering his mistake as to the fortune of his visitor, summarily ejects her from the house.

This is all very well done, and the artless beauty of Catherine's character is well sustained; but her lover, Henry Tilney, though he has some quiet humour, is rather a 'stick,' and the other characters are either unpleasant or uninteresting, nor do we think that the principal chain of interest—namely, the progress of the loves of Henry and Catherine—is strong enough, or well finished.

But even in this comparatively crude work there is a considerable amount of art. The plot, simple as it is, is exactly adequate to the story, and in the most natural manner in the world works to bring out the points of the heroine's character. There is no redundancy or waste: almost every paragraph has its use. The principal characters do not monopolise all the interest; they gently lead the way, and the little relief they need is supplied with a nice hand. John Thorpe, if he had appeared oftener in the course of the tale, would have marred its subdued effect; this is also true of his family; useful up to a certain point in showing the contrast between natural refinement and natural vulgarity, they are dropped into the background as soon as the object is attained, and fresh points in the heroine's character require to be shown. Henry Tilney, though he is, we repeat, somewhat of a 'stick,' is a perfect gentleman, and just of that quiet, shrewd temperament which would be likely to discover the beauty of Catherine's character under its outward show of romantic girlishness, and gradually fall in love with her from finding that she is falling in love with him. The book, on the whole, may be considered a clever sketch by a young hand, who is trying her powers on a simple subject, afraid of being ambitious and of spoiling her materials. Its principal deficiencies are breadth, interest, and variety.

In *Sense and Sensibility*, the first work she published, we find a great advance in every respect. Greater breadth, greater variety of character and incident, more interest. In some respects we think it unsurpassed by any of her works. She never drew a more humorous character than Mrs. Jennings, nor a more interesting one than Marianne Dashwood. All the characters are several hair'sbreadths broader than in any other of her books. The book, however, to our mind fails in its intention by making sensibility more attractive than sense. Elinor is too good; one feels inclined to pat her on the back and say, 'Good girl,' but all our sympathy is with the unfortunate Marianne. But for all that, the contrast between the two temperaments, which was, perhaps, the principal aim of the book, is complete, and at the same time subtle and not too violent. The character of Willoughby is one of the best of her male impersonations. But the prevailing merit of *Sense and Sensibility* is the excellent treatment of the subordinate characters, and in their excellence in themselves. As we have given one illustration of her art from her poorest work, we will give another from one of her most insignificant characters.

To gain effect by appearance of broad treatment, and to obtain amusing foils to the more distinguished persons of the drama, it is a great temptation to an artist to render the subordinate characters more interesting and effective by exaggeration, and skill is never more shown than in producing such necessary relief without sacrifice to truth. Others, again, from want of patience or true artistic feeling, are apt to treat such secondary figures with something like contempt, using them as necessary evils, careless of drawing and finish, bestowing all their labour on the principal groups. Miss Austen, the most patient and conscientious of artists, never falls into these errors. If she exaggerates even in appearance, it is only as in the cases where, as we have just shown, her characters are more typical than usual; if she sketches slightly, it is because the character itself is a slight one, not from any want of patience. It is, indeed, in these very slightest characters that her art becomes most obvious on a close examination. They do not obtrude themselves into the centre of the composition, they hold their duly subordinate position, but if we look into them we find each touch laid on with the same regard for truth and the same firm hand. No labour has been spared on account of their comparative insignificance in the general effect. Nor is this labour thrown away by an artist, though the public have not, perhaps, the discernment to appreciate it fully. The effect desired is produced, and the labour has its results in the increased delight of the reader, although he may be quite unconscious of the cause of his additional pleasure. And what is more, such good and thorough work will last, in spite of this want of ready appreciation, when the glamour of false effect has long lost its charm. Those who only write to create excitement sink into oblivion as soon as that excitement is over, but writers who, like Miss Austen, work with a reverence for art in itself, and a disregard of immediate popularity as an aim, and are content to labour in the mine of human nature for their material, cannot fail to find the good ore, and to work it into lasting monuments. Mrs. Radcliffe, a woman of considerable ability, now scarcely affords amusement to the lowest class; but Miss Austen, though she may not be much read by the general public, is, perhaps, more completely appreciated than ever by minds of the highest culture.

Lady Middleton is a good example of those inferior characters on which she has expended so much skill, if not labour—characters of the very slightest structure—mere elementary forms, of which most writers, if they had not disdained to use them, would have made but dreary personifications of abstract stupidity, but which in her hands become lifelike studies of our friends.

Who does not know Lady Middleton? perhaps the veriest nobody that ever was drawn. She is the wife of a baronet (Miss Austen never gets higher than baronets), is handsome, of tall and striking figure and graceful address, but from her first visit it is plain to the Dashwoods, who have settled near the seat of Sir John and Lady Middleton, that, though perfectly well-bred, she is reserved, cold, and has nothing to say for herself beyond the most commonplace inquiry or remark. Having read so much, the reader imagines that the character is not one which will interest him much, and does not care to hear much more of her. Miss Austen knew this, and does not introduce her often, and when introduced she seldom speaks; but, nevertheless, the woman lives in the mind of the reader, and, in spite of her insipid character, affords him some amusement. When she goes out visiting she takes a child with her, to afford a subject of interest, if not of conversation. Her only resource is the humouring of her children. She piques herself on the elegance of her table and of all her domestic arrangements, and from this kind of vanity derives her greatest enjoyment in any of her parties, which are very numerous, as her husband, Sir John, delights in collecting around him more young people than his house will hold. According to her mother, she used to play on the piano extremely well, and was very fond of it, but she has given up music since her marriage. All these, and many other apparently insignificant traits in an insignificant character, yet produce a substantial effect in bringing the lady before the reader. They are all of a piece, and at the end of the book the memory has put them together like the bits of a puzzle, and a complete though faint effect is produced, for they all fit. No incident that is recorded of her but is in perfect keeping. She is not silly, she is not exactly inane—what she is it is difficult to say, but her character would take up a large stock of negatives before you exhausted her deficiencies. She does not make you laugh, but you smile when you hear her one moment calling her husband to order for talking while a lady is singing, and the next asking the fair musician to sing the particular song which she has unfortunately just finished singing. On another occasion, when Sir John has invited two relations of hers whom she has never seen to visit them, quite strangers even to Sir John, who has met them in a morning walk, she, says Miss Austen, 'as it was impossible now to prevent their coming, resigned herself to the idea of it with all the philosophy of a well-bred woman, *contenting herself with merely giving her husband a gentle reprimand on the subject five or six times a day.*' When one of her friends—the fair musician above mentioned—has been disgracefully jilted by a Mr. Willoughby, and is suffering all the agonies of a young, romantic, and enthusiastic girl at the disappointment, she becomes even useful:—

The calm and polite unconcern of Lady Middleton was a happy relief to Elinor's (her elder sister's) spirits, oppressed as they often were by the clamorous kindness of the others. It was a great comfort to her to be sure of exciting no interest in *one* person at least among their circle of friends; a great comfort to know that there was *one* who would meet her without feeling any curiosity after particulars, or anxiety for her sister's health.

Every qualification is raised at times, by the circumstances of the moment, to more than its real value, and she was sometimes worried down by officious condolence to rate good-breeding as more indispensable to comfort than good-nature.

Lady Middleton expressed her sense of the affair about once every day—or twice, if the subject occurred very often—by saying, 'It is very shocking indeed!' and by the means of this continual, though gentle, vent, was able not only to see the Miss Dashwoods from the first without the smallest emotion, but very soon to see them without recollecting a word of the matter; and having thus supported the dignity of her own sex, and spoken her decided censure of what was wrong in the other, she thought herself at liberty to attend to the interest of her own assemblies, and therefore determined, though rather against the opinion of Sir John, that as Mrs. Willoughby—her friend's successful rival— 'would at once be a woman of elegance and fortune, to leave her card with her as soon as she was married.'

Indeed it must have been against her husband's opinion, if he held to his first determination after he heard of the affair, for this is how he expressed himself:—

Sir John could not have thought it possible! 'A man of whom he had always had such reason to think well! Such a good-natured fellow! He did not believe there was a bolder rider in England! It was an unaccountable business. He wished him at the devil with all his heart! He would not speak another word to him, meet him where he might, for all the world!—no, not if it were to be by the side of Barton cover, and they were kept waiting for two hours together. Such a scoundrel of a fellow! such a deceitful dog! It was only the last time they met that he had offered him one of Folly's puppies, and this was the end of it!'

Sir John is as good if not better than his wife, and decidedly more amusing, for which reason we have chosen to prefer the lady in an example which aims to show the author's genius for making even the poorest character interesting by faithful, patient art. The mere coupling of these two together in matrimony is a stroke of genius. They are exactly made to live easily together, though of very opposite characters; they don't trot in step, though at about the same pace, and are each too little occupied with one another to care about precision, or an occasional jolt proceeding from inattention.

Persuasion has been called the latest and best of Miss Austen's works, chiefly, as it seems to us, because in the character of Anne there is the nearest approach to a sentimental attachment. In point of general interest in the story we cannot think that any one would give it a place above either *Mansfield Park* or *Pride and Prejudice*, and we ourselves would place it even lower. Nor do we think that it can be contended that as a rule the characters are so finished or amusing as in most of her books, nor, what is, perhaps, more important, that they are so well connected with each other, being more of separate studies than organised groups. Nevertheless it is certainly true that in the loves of Captain Wentworth and Anne there is more natural romance of a sentimental character than in any other of her love sketches. But we have before said that romance and sentiment are not Miss Austen's strong points, and we hesitate to pronounce the work of an artist the best because she has in it striven to reach a higher point than is usual with her. In the present instance we must do more than hesitate, we must dissent, for her strife has not been to our minds successful, and the train has weakened the whole structure.

After much consideration we decide in giving the palm to *Pride and Prejudice*, as the most thoroughly artistic, satisfactory, and amusing of her novels. In construction the book is nearly perfect; the principal theme—the victory over D'Arcy's pride and Elizabeth's prejudice—sprouts at the beginning, flowers in the middle, and, without forcing, bears fine fruit at the end. All the other characters are arranged with the nicest feeling for graduation and variety: there is not one which has not its own peculiar interest perfectly sustained, yet never obtrusive. All the qualities for which Miss Austen is so justly celebrated are here seen in perfection. The one blot in the book is the character of Lydia—one which, however natural, jars with the refined taste usually displayed by the authoress. The moral preached by it is not a very high one, perhaps: it is shortly this—a rich man should not shut his heart against the attractions of a good, pretty girl because she has a vulgar mother and no fortune to speak of; and good and pretty girls with small fortunes and vulgar mothers should not be in too great a hurry to judge the characters of rich men because they are supercilious in demeanour. However, as far as it goes it is quite unexceptionable, and the method of its illustration is so excellent and diverting that the reader cares nothing whatever about the precept at all.

As regards characters, *Pride and Prejudice* is also on the whole superior to her other works. For dry wit Mr. Bennet has never been surpassed—the king of gentlemanly domestic stoics. For broad humour of a delicate kind we have Mrs. Bennet, a priceless specimen of native vulgarity of mind and manners. For humour ironical there are Lady Catherine de Bourgh and Mr. Collins. In Wickham we have a capital adventurer. Mr. Bingley and Miss Bennet are somewhat insipid, but serve as excellent foils to D'Arcy and Elizabeth, Miss Austen's *chef-d'œuvres*.

We have not much more space to spare, but no notice of Miss Austen's books would be complete without some notice of *Emma*. The great fault of this book is that the stupid, unpleasant, and uninteresting nature of most of the characters is unrelieved by much humour. Mr. Woodhouse is merely an amiable old cosset. Harriet is insipid to a degree; and even Miss Bates—though it will be considered treason by some to say it—becomes a bore. She is *too* natural. Nevertheless, on the book has been expended an immense amount of labour not without effect. Emma herself is, perhaps, the most elaborate character Miss Austen ever drew. Considered as a picture of a young lady early induced to think too much of herself by being the head of a household, and having everything her own way both at home and in the society of the neighbourhood, one cannot too much praise its fidelity to nature. That she should take in hand a pretty, half-educated girl, and patronise her, and endeavour to form her manners, is very natural; and that she should prove to be not quite so wise as she imagines herself, equally so. She not only places her *protégé*, but herself also, in so many awkward predicaments by too fond a belief in her own judgment, that she is obliged at last to open her eyes to her fallibility. The misfortune of the book is that the interest in her *protégé* is so slight that it is of little consequence what becomes of her affections, and that the consequences to herself are so advantageous, and the humiliations of so slight and temporary a character, that the point of the lesson is blunted.

Mansfield Park is a book of much more power, if not so well finished: the characters of Fanny and Mary Crawford are excellently drawn, and form a contrast of much the same stamp as that between Molly and Cynthia in Mrs. Gaskell's last work. In this book there is a character which, though secondary, deserves especial notice—that of Mrs. Norris, the most perfect specimen of genteel meanness that we know of. There is more variety of scene and more skill in devising situations for the development of character also than is usual with her. The getting-up of the play at Mansfield Park is an excellent device, and excellently managed; and the return of Fanny to the squalor of her home after the luxury of Mansfield Park is the greatest social contrast to be found in any of her books. It is a pity that the story is not concluded in a less hurried and unsatisfactory manner, for it contains as good, if not better, material, and certainly better machinery, than even *Pride and Prejudice*.

For many qualities, as we hope we have sufficiently shown, Miss Austen was in her day unrivalled and is now even unsurpassed; but if there is one quality in which she then stood or now stands superior to all writers of her sex, it is in humour. We will not compare her to men, for she never aimed at writing like a man (she is as unapproachable by them as they by her), but as a female humorist she stands almost alone. In satire, humour, wit, and irony, all of a refined and amiable kind, she is excellent; herself a model of refined and cultivated taste, breeding, and sense, even the smallest weakness in any of these points was immediately discerned by her with an infallible but good-natured understanding, and noted for the amusement of her readers. The peculiar refinement which marked the ladies of her day, and which is mirrored in her writings, has been succeeded by another, and, we think, truer refinement, and has lost much of its charm for this generation (though we are sure that it can only increase our reverence for our female ancestors to believe that there were such women as Elizabeth Bennet, Elinor Dashwood, and Anne Elliot), but it is a proof how little that refinement has changed in spirit when we find that the humour which mainly consisted in the exposure of little sins of less cultivated minds against it has still power to make us smile as though committed against one's own pet social code. Thus the power of Miss Austen to make us smile as she does is an inverse tribute to that delicate, lady-like taste which she must have possessed in so great a degree, and, thus explained, we prefer to rest her highest claim to celebrity on her humour.

To conclude, and for a moment leave the consideration of Miss Austen's genius in itself, to judge it by a larger standard. We must admit that its principle characteristic is moderation. She has been called 'the most ladylike of artists,' an expression which in itself conveys a sense of moderation. Her love is nothing more rash than a deep attachment based on esteem, a chastened affection which does not catch fire under a thousand a year; her poverty is 'genteel poverty,' the hardship of reduced circumstances; her mirth seldom rises above a smile; her tears are all women's tears, and soon wiped. Her morality is what may be termed *elegant*, never severe nor zealous, religion she eschews, the domestic stoicism of Mr. Bennet is her nearest approach to philosophy, and romance and enthusiasm are to her alike untinged with poetry, and seem but the effusions of thoughtless youth.

From this quality spring all her beauties and defects. She paints faithfully what she sees, and never tries beyond. She sees and paints just as much of nature as we all see without reflecting upon it every day. Within this limit she is absolute.

The great deficiency in her books is a want of interest in the principal characters; there is scarcely one who enlists our sympathy, and we may say none in any of her books which raises our feelings above esteem or respect. Here her moderation is carried to an excess. Fanny, in *Mansfield Park*, is perhaps an exception; but she is never sufficiently tried to make us thoroughly appreciate her. She is a sweet-tempered, right-feeling girl, who behaves in the most proper way in a dependent position, and very carefully conceals her attachment to Edmund Bertram; she has also a great deal to bear in seeing his attachment to another, and we might have been quite miserable about her except for the certainty that matters would come right in the end; but our sympathy is excited more by the position in which she is placed than on account of our love for the character; we like her very much and would be very sorry if her rival had defeated her, but more because we *know* she is a better girl than Mary Crawford, and deserves to be made happy, than because we feel for her as a sister.

Miss Austen's brain does not seem to have any maternal love for its children: it treats them somewhat like a man of the world. As long as they do nothing dishonourable and make advantageous matches he is satisfied. She treats them all impartially and according to their merits. She seems to look on the world as a curious observer exercising her faculties for the delight they afford herself, and making notes silently for literary purposes. She seems to have cared more for her art than her subjects or any higher consideration, and if we regret it as detracting from the interest of her works, we must at the same time confess that it added greatly to their success and their value as studies of nature. Her subtle strokes of satire and wit would have been thrown away if the pictures were too much coloured with emotion. Tears obscure the sight, strong passions destroy the judgment, and loud laughter drowns the voice of common sense and dry wit.

42. Mrs. Oliphant on Jane Austen
1870

Extract from an unsigned article, 'Miss Austen and Miss Mitford', *Blackwood's Edinburgh Magazine* (March 1870), cvii, 294–305.

Margaret Oliphant (1828–97), the novelist and historical writer, was one of the principal reviewers for *Blackwood's*. The occasion for this article was the publication of the *Memoir of Jane Austen* (1870) by J. E. Austen-Leigh. Mrs. Oliphant's account of the novels is, like that of Mrs. Kavanagh, perceptive and challenging (see Introduction, pp. 30–1). At the point where this extract commences, Mrs. Oliphant is comparing the varying range of society and action presented in the works of these two women-novelists.

Lady Catherine de Bourgh and the housekeeper at Pemberly—conventional types of the heaven above and the abyss below—are the only breaks which Miss Austen ever permits herself upon the level of her squirearchy; while Miss Mitford's larger heart takes in all the Joes and Pollys and Harriets of a country-side, and makes their wooings and jealousies as pleasant to us as if they were the finest ladies and gentlemen. To be sure, Miss Austen's ladies and gentlemen are seldom fine; but they are all to be found in the same kind of house with the same kind of surroundings. Their poverties, when they have any, are caused in a genteel way by the entail of an estate, or by the premature death of the father without leaving an adequate provision for his lovely and accomplished girls. The neglect which leaves the delicate heroine without a horse to ride, or the injury conveyed in the fact that she has to travel post without a servant, is the worst that happens. If it were not that the class to which she thus confines herself was the one most intimately and thoroughly known to her, we should be disposed to consider it, as we have said, a piece of self-denial on Miss Austen's part to relinquish all stronger lights and shadows; but perhaps it is better to say that she was conscientious in her determination to describe only what she knew, and that nature aided principle in this singular limitation. Of itself, however, it throws a certain light upon her character, which is not the simple character it appears at the first glance, but one full of subtle power, keenness, finesse, and self-restraint—a type not at all unusual among women of high cultivation, especially in the retirement of the country, where such qualities are likely enough to be unappreciated or misunderstood.

Mr Austen Leigh, without meaning it, throws out of his dim little lantern a passing gleam of light upon the fine vein of feminine cynicism which pervades his aunt's mind. It is something altogether different from the rude and brutal male quality that bears the same name. It is the soft and silent disbelief of a spectator who has to look at a great many things without showing any outward discomposure, and who has learned to give up any moral classification of social sins, and to place them instead on the level of absurdities. She is not surprised or offended, much less horror-stricken or indignant, when her people show vulgar or mean traits of character, when they make it evident how selfish and self-absorbed they are, or even when they fall into those social cruelties which selfish and stupid people are so often guilty of, not without intention, but yet without the power of realising half the pain they inflict. She stands by and looks on, and gives a soft half-smile, and tells the story with an exquisite sense of its ridiculous side, and fine stinging yet soft-voiced contempt for the actors in it. She sympathises with the sufferers, yet she can scarcely be said to be sorry for them; giving them unconsciously a share in her own sense of the covert fun of the scene, and gentle disdain of the possibility that meanness and folly and stupidity could ever really wound any rational creature. The position of mind is essentially feminine, and one which may be readily identified in the personal knowledge of most people. It is the natural result of the constant, though probably quite unconscious, observation in which a young woman, with no active pursuit to occupy her, spends, without knowing it, so much of her time and youth. Courses of lectures, no doubt, or balls, or any decided out-of-door interest, interferes with this involuntary training; but such disturbances were rare in Miss Austen's day. A certain soft despair of any one human creature ever doing any good to another—of any influence overcoming those habits and moods and peculiarities of mind which the observer sees to be more obstinate than life itself—a sense that nothing is to be done but to look on, to say perhaps now and then a softening word, to make the best of it practically and theoretically, to smile and hold up one's hands and

wonder why human creatures should be such fools,—such are the
foundations upon which the feminine cynicism which we attribute to
Miss Austen is built. It includes a great deal that is amiable, and is full
of toleration and patience, and that habit of making allowance for
others which lies at the bottom of all human charity. But yet it is not
charity, and its toleration has none of the sweetness which proceeds
from that highest of Christian graces. It is not absolute contempt either,
but only a softened tone of general disbelief—amusement, nay enjoyment, of all those humours of humanity which are so quaint to look at
as soon as you dissociate them from any rigid standard of right or
wrong. Miss Austen is not the judge of the men and women she collects
round her. She is not even their censor to mend their manners; no
power has constituted her her brother's keeper. She has but the faculty
of seeing her brother clearly all round as if he were a statue, identifying
all his absurdities, quietly jeering at him, smiling with her eyes without
committing the indecorum of laughter. In one case only, so far as we
can recollect, in the character of Miss Bates in *Emma*, does she rise
beyond this, and touch the region of higher feeling by comprehension
of the natural excellence that lies under a ludicrous exterior. It is very
lightly touched, but yet it is enough to show that she was capable of a
tenderness for the object of her soft laughter—a capability which
converts that laughter into something totally different from the gentle
derision with which she regards the world in general. Humankind
stands low in her estimation, in short, as a mass. There are a few pleasant
young people here and there to redeem it, or even an old lady now and
then, or in the background a middle-aged couple who are not selfish,
nor vulgar, nor exacting. But there is a great deal more amusement to
be got out of the mean people, and to them accordingly she inclines. . . .

[Section omitted, derived from *Memoir.*]

Nothing but a mind of this subtle, delicate, speculative temper,
could have set before us pictures which are at once so refined and so
trenchant, so softly feminine and polite, and so remorselessly true. . . .

[Section omitted, largely on Miss Mitford.]

Miss Austen began her literary work at so early an age that its
extreme skill and refinement, as well as the peculiar point of view from
which she regarded the world, becomes more and more wonderful. It
is a very difficult thing to realise how a brain of one-and-twenty could

have identified such a family as the Bennets, such a character as Mr
Collins, and could have willingly filled up her background with figures
such as those of the female Bingleys, Wickham, Lady Catherine, and
the rest. Nothing could be more lifelike, more utterly real. The household is not described, but rises vividly before us as if we had visited it
yesterday, with all its rusticity and ignorance, its eager thirst for pleasure,
and incapacity to perceive the bad taste and futility of its own efforts.
The first wonder that occurs to us is how Jane and Elizabeth should
have found a place in such a family. The eldest is all sweetness and grace
and beauty; the second brightly intelligent, quick to perceive, and
equally quick to take up false impressions, but clever and affectionate
and honest to the highest degree; while every one else in the house is
a study of absurdity and vulgarity of one sort or another. Miss Austen
had too much genius to fall into the vulgar error of making her heroes
and heroines all perfect, and relieving them against a background of
unalloyed villany; but her actual conception of the world, as shown in
her first completed work, is not much less elevated. The background
is full, not of villains, but of fools, out of the midst of whom the heroes
and heroines rise in all the glory of superior talents and more elevated
character. The power that is spent in setting forth these fools—their
endless variety—the different shapes in which conceit, and vanity, and
selfishness, and vulgar ambition display themselves—the wonderful
way in which they amalgamate and enhance each other, now and then
rising into the successes of triumphant cunning, or sinking to pure folly
once more,—is set before us with a skill which is quite marvellous. It is
all so common—never rising above the level of ordinary life, leaving
nothing (so think the uninstructed) to imagination or invention at all—
and yet what other hand has ever been able to detach such a group
from the obscure level of their ordinary fate? Mr Collins, for instance,
who is the heir of Mr Bennet's entailed estate, and who, with a certain
quaint sense of justice which enhances his self-importance, comes prepared to propose to one of the daughters, whom he is obliged to deprive
of their inheritance. We give so much explanation, with a certain shame
at the very possibility that Mr Collins should want a formal introduction
to any portion of the British public; but yet it is true that the young
ones are not so well up in the relationships of the Bennets as we could
wish them to be. The sublime and undisturbed complacence of his
arrival, when he compliments Mrs Bennet on having so fine a family
of daughters, 'and added that he did not doubt her seeing them all in
time well disposed of in marriage,' is inimitable. ' "I am very sensible,

madam, of the hardship to my fair cousins," ' he says, ' "and could say much on the subject, but I am cautious of appearing forward and precipitate. But I can assure the young ladies that I come prepared to admire them. At present I will not say more, but perhaps when we are better acquainted——" ' When he receives Elizabeth's refusal to marry him with undisturbed complacency, attributing it to ' "your wish of increasing my love by suspense, according to the usual practice of elegant females," ' the situation rises to one of the most genuine comedy, and our only regret is that Mr Collins's adventures have never been adapted for the stage.

Miss Austen does not even let her victim escape her when he is married and has left the central scene. She pursues him to his home with the smile growing a little broader in her eyes. 'Elizabeth was prepared to see him in all his glory; and she could not help fancying that in displaying the good proportions of his room, its aspect and its furniture, he addressed himself particularly to her, as if wishing to make her feel what she had lost in refusing him.' His pompous assurance that 'he has no hesitation in saying' that his goddess and patroness, Lady Catherine, will include his cousin in her invitations—his triumph when the party is asked to dinner—the pride with which he takes his seat at the foot of the table by her ladyship's command, looking 'as if he felt that life could furnish nothing greater'—the 'delighted alacrity' with which he carved and ate and praised—his game at cards with his august patroness after dinner, in which 'he was employed in agreeing to everything her ladyship said, thanking her for every fish he won, and apologising if he thought he won too many,'—are all so many touches which add perfection to the picture; and when we take our parting glance of Mr Collins, watching the country road from his 'book-room,' and hastening to inform his wife and her friends every time Miss de Bourgh drives by in her phaeton, we feel that the power of consistent remorseless ridicule can no further go. There is not a moment's faltering, nor the ghost of an inclination on the part of the author to depart from her wonderful conception. He stands before us tall and grave and pompous, wrapt in a cloud of solemn vanity, servility, stupidity, and spitefulness, but without the faintest gleam of self-consciousness or suspicion of the ridiculous figure he cuts; and his author, with no pity in her heart, walks round and round him, giving here and there a skilful touch to bring out the picture. It is amazing in its unity and complete-ness—a picture perhaps unrivalled, certainly unsurpassed, in its way. It is, we repeat, cruel in its perfection.

Whether it is not too cruel to make the wife of this delightful Mr Collins share so completely in his creator's estimate of him is a different matter. 'When Mr Collins could be forgotten there was really a great air of comfort throughout, and by Charlotte's evident enjoyment of it Elizabeth supposed he must be often forgotten'—the unflinching narrative goes on. 'The room in which the ladies sat was backward, and Elizabeth at first had rather wondered that Charlotte should not prefer the dining-parlour for common use—it was a better-sized room and had a pleasanter aspect; but she soon saw that her friend had an excellent reason for what she did, for Mr Collins would undoubtedly have been much less in his own apartment had they sat in one equally lively; and she gave Charlotte credit for the arrangement.' This is rather diabolical, it must be owned, and there is a calmness of acquiescence in the excellent Charlotte's arrangements which it takes all the reader's fortitude to stomach. It is possible that the very youth of the author may have produced this final stroke of unexampled consistency; for youth is always more or less cruel, and is slow to acknowledge that even the most stupid and arrogant of mortals has his rights.

Mr Collins, however, is one of the most distinct and original portraits in the gallery of fiction, and we accept him gladly as a real contribution to our knowledge of humankind; not a contribution certainly which will make us more in love with our fellow-creatures, but yet so lifelike, so perfect and complete, touched with so fine a wit and so keen a perception of the ridiculous, that the picture once seen remains a permanent possession. And when we are told that the Bennet family, with all its humours—the father who is so good and sensible, and yet such an unmitigated bear; the mother whom he despises and ridicules without hesitation, even to his heroine-daughters who accept his sarcastic comments as the most natural thing in the world; the stupid pompous Mary, the loud and noisy, heartless and shameless Lydia—are all drawn with an equally fine and delicate touch, we have not a word to say against it. We acknowledge its truth, and yet we rebel against this pitiless perfection of art. It shocks us as much as it could possibly have shocked Mr Darcy, to allow that these should be the immediate surroundings of the young woman whom we are called upon to take to our hearts. We blush for the daughter who blushes for her mother. We hate the lover who points out to her, even in self-defence, the vulgarities and follies of her family. A heroine must be superior, it is true, but not so superior as this; and it detracts ever so much from the high qualities of Elizabeth when we see how very ready she is to be moved by a sense of the inferiority of her mother and sisters, how ashamed she is of their ways, and how thankful to think that her home will be at a distance from theirs.

Curiously enough, it would seem that Miss Austen herself felt for this same Elizabeth, and for her alone, the enthusiasm of a parent for a child. 'I have got my own darling child from London,' she writes to her sister, in a little flutter of pleasure and excitement. 'Miss B—— dined with us on the very day of the book's coming, and in the evening we fairly set at it and read fully half the first volume to her, prefacing that having intelligence from Henry that such a book would soon appear, we had desired him to send it as soon as it came out; and I believe it passed with her unsuspected. She was amused, poor soul! *That* she could not help, you know, with two such people to lead the way, but she really does seem to admire Elizabeth. I must confess that I think her as delightful a creature as ever appeared in print, and how I shall be able to tolerate those who do not like *her* at least I do not know.' In a letter she adds—'Fanny's praise is very gratifying. My hopes were tolerably strong of her, but nothing like a certainty. Her liking Darcy and Elizabeth is enough; she might hate all the others if she would.' This is as curious a piece of revelation as we know, and proves that the young woman who had just given so original a work to the world was in reality quite unaware of its real power, and had set her heart upon her hero and heroine like any schoolgirl. Our beloved Mr Collins, upon whom the spectator would be tempted to think a great deal of pains and some proportionate anxiety must have been expended, evidently goes for very little with his maker. It is her lovers she is thinking of, a commonplace pair enough, while we are full of her inimitable fools, who are not at all commonplace. This curious fact disorders our head a little, and makes us ponder and wonder whether our author is in reality the gentle cynic we have concluded her to be, or if she has produced all these marvels of selfish folly unawares, without knowing what she was doing, or meaning anything by it. Genius, however, goes a great deal deeper than conscious meaning, and has its own way, whatever may be the intentions of its owner; and we but smile at the novelist's strange delusion as we set aside Elizabeth and Darcy, the one a young woman very much addicted to making speeches, very pert often, fond of having the last word, and prone to hasty judgments, with really nothing but her prettiness and a certain sharp smartness of talk to recommend her; and the other a very ordinary young man, quite like hosts of other young men, with that appearance of outward pride and *hauteur* which is so captivating to the youthful feminine imagination, though it must be admitted that he possesses an extraordinary amount of candour and real humility of mind under this exterior. It is curious to realise what a shock it must have given to the feelings of the young novelist when she found how little her favourite pair had to do with the success of their own story, and how entirely her secondary characters, in their various and vivid originality, carried the day over her first.

Sense and Sensibility, which was really the first of Miss Austen's publications, as well as the first production of her youthful brain, has fewer salient points. There is nothing in it that can approach within a hundred miles of the perfection of Mr Collins. The Miss Steeles are simply vulgar and disagreeable, and we can scarcely be grateful for the vivid drawing of two persons whom we should be sorry ever to see again, and who really contribute nothing to our amusement, except so far as the fluttered sensibilities of the eldest in respect to 'the Doctor' are concerned. No doubt the foolishness of Sir John Middleton, who is so much afraid of being alone that the addition of two people to the population of London is a matter of delight to him; and of his wife, whose folly is concentrated in adoration of her children; and Mrs Palmer, who laughs loudly at her husband's insolence, and calls heaven and earth to witness how droll he is,—are amusing enough in their way; but Marianne's sensibility is not amusing, and we find it utterly impossible to take any interest in her selfish and high-flown wretchedness. Elinor's sense and self-restraint, though so much superior in a moral point of view, are scarcely more enlivening; and the heroes are about as weak specimens of the genus hero as one could desire to see: that, however, would be immaterial but for the absence of the rich background with its amazing multiplicity of character; for Shakespeare himself cannot always confer interest upon his *jeune premier*, the first gentleman of the story. The same criticism may be applied to *Mansfield Park*, which is the least striking of the whole series, and though full of detached scenes, and still more of detached sentences, quite wonderful in their power of description, is dull and lengthy as a whole, and not agreeable.

But Miss Austen is herself again when she comes to the story of *Emma*, which, next to *Pride and Prejudice*, is, in our opinion, her best work. *Emma* was the work of her mature mind. She was but one-and-twenty when she created Mr Collins, and surrounded the heroine whom she regarded with a girl's sympathy with so many repulsive and odious, yet perfectly-depicted, characters. Perhaps there was something of the inexperience and ignorance of youth in this device—the natural impulse to exalt the favourite, and win all the more love for her by encircling her with people whom it was impossible to love. Our novelist had left her youth behind her, and her first home, and all the early conditions of her life, before Emma Woodhouse became her heroine; and there is a sweetness about this book which is not to be found in any of the others. There is scarcely one character in *Pride and Prejudice* for whom we can feel any kindly sympathy, except, perhaps, Jane, the soft, pretty elder sister, who is little more than a shadow upon the full and vigorous landscape. But in *Emma* there is nobody to be hated, which is a curious difference. Kindness has stole into the authoress's heart. The malicious, brilliant wit of youth has softened into a better understanding of the world. Mr Woodhouse is very trying in his invalidism, and we sympathise deeply with his visitors when the sweetbread and asparagus are sent away from their very lips as not cooked enough, and gruel, thin, but not too thin, is recommended in its place; but on the whole we like the courteous, kindly, troublesome old man: and Miss Bates, no doubt, is a person we would fly from in dismay did she live in our village; and had she belonged to the *Pride and Prejudice* period, no doubt she would have been as detestable as she was amusing. But other lights have come to the maturer eyes, and the endless flutter of talk, the never-ending still-beginning monologue, the fussy, wordy, indiscreet, uninteresting old maid is lighted up with a soft halo from the heart within. Instead of impaling her on the end of her spear, like Mr Collins and Mrs Bennet, her author turns her outside in with an affectionate banter—a tender amusement which changes the whole aspect of the picture. It is not that the fun is less, or the keenness of insight into all the many manifestations of foolishness, but human sympathy has come in to sweeten the tale, and the brilliant intellect has found out, somehow, that all the laughable beings surrounding it—beings so amusingly diverse in their inanity and unreason —are all the same mortal creatures, with souls and hearts within them. How Miss Austen came to find this out, we cannot tell. But it is pleasant to see that she had made the discovery. In *Emma* everything has a softer touch. The sun shines as it never shone over the Bennets. This difference of atmosphere, indeed, is one of the most remarkable points in the change. We suppose we are told sometimes that it was a fine day in *Pride and Prejudice*, but so far as our own perceptions go, the sky is very leaden, and there is little of the variety and vicissitude of nature in the monotonous landscape. We have a feeling that the Bennet girls were always muddy when they walked to Meriton, and that the wind, which blew in their faces and sometimes improved their complexions, was a damp ungenial sort of wind. But in *Emma* the sun shines, and the playful soft breezes blow, and the heroine herself, with all her talents and quickwittedness, is as absurd as heart could desire, and makes such mistakes as only a very clever girl, very *entêtée* and addicted to her own opinion, very wilful, and unreasonable, and hasty, and charming, could be expected to make. Miss Austen no longer believes in her, or gives her all the honours of heroine, as she did to her Elizabeth, but laughs tenderly at her *protégée*, and takes pleasure in teasing her, and pointing out all her innocent mistakes: one after another she falls into them, and scrambles out, and falls once more—and is overwhelmed with distress, and hates herself, and dries her eyes, and takes the bit in her teeth and is off again. We do not wonder that Mr Knightley finds it a dangerous amusement to watch, and try to guide her in her vagaries; and no doubt he had a hard time of it when he had finally secured her, in that period that comes after Miss Austen gives her up to him, but, we don't doubt, liked it all the same.

And it is impossible to conceive a more perfect piece of village geography, a scene more absolutely real. Highbury, with Ford's shop in the High Street, and Miss Bates's rooms opposite, the parlour on the first floor, with windows from which you can see all that is going on, and, indeed, call to your friends down below, and hold conversations with them. And the vicarage lane at one end of the town, which is muddy, and where the young vicar from his study can see the young ladies passing on their way to their cottage pensioners, and has time to get his hat and umbrella and join them as they come back. And Hartfield, with its pretty shrubberies, standing well out of the town, a dignified conclusion for the walks of the ladies, whom Mr Woodhouse is so glad to see; and Randalls further on, with its genial sanguine master, and the happy, quiet, middle-aged wife, who has been Emma's governess, and is still 'poor Miss Taylor' to Emma's father. Nothing could be more easy than to make a map of it, with indications where the London road strikes off, and by which turning Frank Churchill, on his tired horse, will come from Richmond. We know it as well as if we had lived there all our lives, and visited Miss Bates every other day.

Miss Austen's books did not secure her any sudden fame. They stole into notice so gradually and slowly, that even at her death they had not reached any great height of success. *Northanger Abbey*, perhaps her prettiest story, as a story, and *Persuasion*, which is very charming and full of delicate touches, though marked with the old imperfection which renders every character a fool except the heroic pair who hold their place in the foreground—were published only after her death, the MS. having been sold for ten pounds to a careless country bookseller, from whom it was repurchased after the others had risen into fame. We are told that at her death all they had produced of money was but seven hundred pounds, and but a moderate modicum of praise. We cannot say we are in the least surprised at this fact; it is, we think, much more surprising that they should at length have climbed into the high place they now hold. To the general public, which loves to sympathise with the people it meets in fiction, to cry with them, and rejoice with them, and take a real interest in all their concerns, it is scarcely to be expected that books so calm and cold and keen, and making so little claim upon their sympathy, would ever be popular. 'One of the ablest men of my acquaintance,' says Mr Austen Leigh, 'said in that kind of jest which has much earnest in it, that he had established it in his own mind as a new test of ability whether people could or could not appreciate Miss Austen's merits.' The standard is real enough. A certain amount of culture and force of observation must be presupposed in any real independent admiration of these books. They are not the kind of books which catch the popular fancy at once without pleasing the critic —a power sometimes possessed by very imperfect and unsatisfactory performances; neither do they belong to that highest class of all which takes every variety of imagination by storm, and steps into favour without any probation. They are rather of the class which attracts the connoisseur, which charms the critical and literary mind, and which, by dint of persistency and iteration, is carried by the superior rank of readers into a half-real half-fictitious universality of applause. Perhaps the effort has been more successful in the case of Miss Austen than it has been with any other writer. Her works have become classic, and it is now the duty of every student of recent English literature to be more or less acquainted with them. Authority was never better employed. 'The best judges' have here, for once, done the office of an Academy, and laureated a writer whom the populace would not have been likely to laureate, but whom it has learned to recognise. . . .

[The article continues with a biographical discussion on Jane Austen and Miss Mitford.]

43. The Victorian 'historical' View
1870

Unsigned article, 'Jane Austen', *St. Paul's Magazine* (March 1870), v. 631–43.

Like No. 42, this article was occasioned by the publication of the *Memoir*. R. W. Chapman considered whether the review might not have been written by Trollope, then editing the *St. Paul's Magazine*; but, apart from anything else, the arguments advanced in the article (see Introduction, p. 30) do not match Trollope's known views.

More than half a century has elapsed since the spirit of Jane Austen left its mortal frame, and her bright smile ceased to charm the eyes, and her pleasant voice ceased to charm the ears, of those who loved her. She was forty-two years of age when she died, in the year 1817. She had lingered some time in ill-health before her final departure, and when her sister, watching by her bed, asked her at the last hour if there was anything she wanted; she replied, 'Nothing but death!' Her kindred mourned her loss; from them the cherished friend was withdrawn, but her works remained for posterity, and the authoress still lives among us. Her fame as a novelist was slowly won, and will be long maintained; it will be maintained so long as a taste endures for what is true in conception and faultless in execution. The sobriety of her fiction, which prevented it from making any sudden sensation, secures to it a permanence of approbation; and the appearance of her biography probably excites a deeper interest at the present day than it would have done had it been given to the world immediately after her decease. Mr. Austen Leigh, her biographer, is the son of her eldest brother James, and is the Vicar of Bray. He was the only one of his generation who attended her funeral, and he was but a boy then. His recollections are, therefore, far from copious, and are such as a child would store up of any affectionate aunt, apart from such impressions as the intellect of a greatly gifted woman would make upon a more mature observer. Jane Austen was to him the good aunt, who was full of amusing stories, and could not only tell an old fairy tale better than any one else, but who could add to its incidents, and pursue the subjects of the narrative into further perplexities, and weave more bright gossamer threads to gleam across the region of enchantment. For this reasons he and his sisters were fond of clustering about her knees, knowing nothing then of the works which she laid aside for their sake.

But the fact that they did not know this must be accepted as an indication of a temper sweet and strong enough to resist the pressure of composition and the vexation of a child's interruption. What else there is to tell is gathered from other sources, but it is of a negative character; and the idea of the authoress is rather drawn from what she was not than from what she was.

Her girlhood was passed in the parsonage-house of Steventon, her father being the pastor. It was situated in a pretty district of the county of Kent, and Jane Austen rarely emerged from the circle of family connections and her own immediate neighbourhood. She had one sister, Cassandra, who was the object of her warmest affection, and five brothers, two of whom rose to eminence in the naval profession. Her life was very quiet, affording no subjects for the excitement of emotion, leaving ample time for composition, and by the narrowness of its sphere of action inducing a habit of minute observation. There was no large field of view open to her, there was nothing, either in the natural or artificial life about her, to stimulate her imagination to any fine excess, or to rouse any deep, any bitter, or any exalted passion within her. She lived a comfortable life in a comfortable house, full of pleasant influences and cheerful affections. The ways of the family were not much disturbed by public events, and it was only when her brothers were at sea, fighting their country's battles, that the troubles of the time awakened any strong interest in Jane Austen's mind. Her delight was in the exercise of her powers of observation and reflection, and in the humour which grew out of them or accompanied them. It was her special vocation to make fresh combinations out of the peculiarities of character coming under her immediate notice; and thus to create something new out of something old, and so to bring the diverse parts together in perfect harmony as to make the new thing seem true. In the art, which turns fiction into truth, no writer has ever excelled her. Her just sense of proportion never deserts her, no one portion of her work is ever suffered to bear down another, the action is always easy, the progress of the narrative is always smooth, the writer never gets in the way of her characters, they are never interfered with by un-necessary reflections, the business of the scene is never disturbed by useless interjections from the dramatist. Her personages live their own lives in a perfectly natural manner, and the love stories which arise out of their juxtaposition are such as belong to the ordinary course of things. Only one character through the six novels written by Miss Austen is moved by any very impetuous emotion. It is that of Marianne, in *Sense and Sensibility*, and it is exhibited to be rebuked. For the most part, the men and women love each other rather because circumstances throw them together, than from any passionate predilection. As a balance to the indiscretion of Marianne, however, there is one man whose passion out-runs his prudence; this is Darcy, in the novel of *Pride and Prejudice*. But even when her characters are somewhat carried away by their feel-ings the authoress maintains her own propriety, and there is a total absence of the delirious excitement which distinguishes the novel writing of the present day. The wild pulsation, the stormy embracing, the hand-pressure which bruises, the kiss which consumes, all these things, the essentials of the fiction of our period, are absent from Jane Austen's pages; the strongest expression there permitted to a lover is 'dearest,' and the most ardent exhibition of passion is a shake of the hands.

The novels of *Mansfield Park* and *Pride and Prejudice* contain incidents which, in the hands of M. Octave Feuillet, or M. Edmond About, or M. Cherbuliez, or their host of English imitators, would bring into play every variety of feverish emotion. Maria Rushworth who, under the bewilderment of personal vanity fostered by private theatricals, leaves her husband to follow the fortunes and fickle affections of Mr. Crawford, would not be suffered to do it in the novel of our period without a vast amount of agitating detail. Her veins would throb with fire, her brain would swell to bursting, her wealth of hair would uncoil its golden mass and heavily sweep her dainty feet; her seared brow would plunge and hiss in ice cold fountains a thousand times before the fatal step was taken; and Lydia Bennet, the silly vulgar girl, in *Pride and Prejudice*, who, stricken by a passion for the military, elopes with Captain Wickham of the Militia without a promise of marriage, would offer to modern fashionable writers a subject for infinite commiseration and tender sentiment,—her feet would fail beneath the weight of her feelings, her slender frame would yield beneath the overwhelming force of her passion, the solid ground would dissolve beneath her, the great chasm would open, her blood would chill, her cheek would pale; she would be as one struggling in a nightmare, as one sliding down the purple depth of a crevasse, on a million occasions before she fell the prey to an unrelenting destiny. Instead of all which we have these events quietly dismissed by Jane Austen with merely decent phrases of regret.

Tears are only sparingly bestowed on the heroines, and they are such as a little eau-de-cologne or cold water judiciously served speedily obliterates. Anne, in the novel of *Persuasion*, has more regret for the loss of her lover whom she has given up to please her friends, and more tenderness of disposition than belongs generally to Miss Austen's women, but her sorrow never reaches any great climax, and the certainty of a serene conclusion is always present. Those, then, who seek for distraction from the disquiet, or relief from the monotony, of life, by any exaltation of the imaginative powers, by any deep pathos or stirring passion, will not find their desire fulfilled by Miss Austen; but such as take delight in a pleasant vein of irony permeating the ordinary scenes of ordinary life, and marking all its follies, vulgarities, vanities, and baseness, with unfailing precision, will find every one of the Austen novels abundant in the special truth, and in the satire which they relish.

Miss Austen's own favourite authors were the poets Crabbe and Cowper, and Richardson, the great novelist, whom she appears to have studied continually, reading over and over again the letters of Miss Byron and Sir Charles Grandison. We are not told whether she admired equally his greatest work, the work which must make his memory immortal, *Clarissa*; but we may rather infer from there being no mention made of her intimate acquaintance with this book, that it was less a favourite with her than its immediate successor, and indeed the Grandison has more affinity with her sympathies than the Harlowe novel. In neither work, however, is there much of the quality of truth which distinguishes Miss Austen's own works. Richardson gives an air of exactness and fidelity to his narratives by a great abundance of detail, but the men and women who wear the dresses and do the actions so minutely described, for the most part, want the breath of life within them. The dialogue is clever, the sketches of the personal habits of the characters are skilful, but the characters themselves are very artificial, their sentiments are strained, and they evidently play to an audience. Richardson's real ascendancy as a writer consists in the true conception of a noble passion, and in the construction of a great ideal of beauty and purity. It is by moving the mind of his readers to high admiration and to sympathy with a sublime endurance, that Richardson has won the imperishable crown,—not by his disquisitions upon the tails of Sir

Charles Grandison's grey horses, or the polite behaviour of the hero at his wedding breakfast.

Clarissa, as an ideal of feminine elevation of character, has obtained an universal fame. Different ages and different nations have united to pay her a just homage. France, Germany, Russia, all countries where literature is known, know her afflictions and appreciate her great soul. It is probably through her influence that Richardson's other works hold their ground, although the novel of *Sir Charles Grandison* with many faults has many merits, and contains in the story of Clementina one little piece of genuine pathos.

Miss Austen at a very early age amused herself with the dagger and bowl school of romance writers in the spirit of satire.

Northanger Abbey was an offshoot from these juvenile burlesques, which were her first essays in literature. The inequalities of many clever writers arise from their failing to perceive the exact limits of their genius. The perfection of Miss Austen is due to her accurate knowledge of her own boundaries. This is very well shown in a letter addressed to Mr. Clarke, Librarian to the Prince Regent. The Prince Regent was a cordial admirer of the Austen novels, and kept a set of them in every one of his residences, and he desired Mr. Clarke to wait upon the authoress when she was staying in London for a time in the year 1815. She was then nursing her brother Henry, who was very ill, in Hans Place, and the court physician, Sir Henry Halford, attended him. Through the physician the Prince Regent's appreciation of her works was first made known to Jane Austen, and it is very probable that he carried anecdotes of the authoress to the prince in her vocation of nurse and sister which augmented the Regent's admiration. Mr. Clarke informed her that the Prince Regent would esteem it a favour to have one of the novels dedicated to himself. Accordingly such a dedication was affixed to *Emma*, which was at that time in the press. Mr. Clarke, in the course of his correspondence with Miss Austen upon this subject, suggested to her the introduction of an enthusiastic literary high-minded English clergyman into one of her works of fiction, a request which she answered in the following terms:—

I am quite honoured by your thinking me capable of drawing such a clergy-man as you gave the sketch of in your note of November the 16th. But I assure you I am NOT. The comic part of the character I might be equal to, but not the good, the enthusiastic, the literary . . .

And, again, when the same Mr. Clarke pressed upon her attention a possible historical romance, 'founded on the House of Coburg,' she wrote in reply,—

I could no more write a romance than an epic poem. I could not sit seriously down to write a serious romance under any other motive than to save my life, and if it were indispensable for me to keep it up and never relax into laughter at myself or at others, I am sure I should be hung before I had finished the first chapter.

The same discriminative power which enabled Miss Austen to see what she was incapable of doing showed her also what her strength was within its proper sphere, and, in writing to her sister concerning the novel of *Pride and Prejudice*, she said,—

Miss B. dined with us on the very night of the book's coming, and in the evening we fairly set at it and read half the first volume to her. She was amused, poor soul! That she could not help being with two such people to lead the way, but she really does seem to admire Elizabeth. I must confess that I think her as delightful a creature as ever appeared in print. . . . Upon the whole, I am quite vain enough and well satisfied enough. The work is rather too light and bright and sparkling, it wants shade, it wants to be stretched out here and there with a long chapter of sense if it could be had; if not, of solemn specious nonsense; an essay on writing, a critique on Walter Scott, or the history of Buonaparte, or something that would form a contrast and bring the reader with increased delight to the playfulness and epigrammatism of the general style.

This was written under the excitement of the first appearance of Elizabeth in public. At a later date, in cool reflection, Miss Austen would hardly have called the heroine of *Pride and Prejudice* 'as delightful a creature as ever appeared in print;' for her raillery is not without vulgarity, and her vanity and self-satisfaction extend beyond the proper development of those feminine qualities. It is a common fault with Miss Austen's young women that they are remarkably addicted to the contemplation of themselves and their own qualities with special reference to the effect they produce upon men. It is the first aim to be the object of a man's attention,—this desire not springing from a strong preference for some particular man, but from the general ambition of distinction in this kind. Emma wonders whether Frank Churchill will distinguish her before she has seen him, and Elizabeth is greatly fluttered and occupied with thoughts of Mr. Wickham after the first conversation with him, and she is described as going to the ball prepared to win what remains of his heart, without his having given any sign of having a heart at all. Most of the women throughout these novels are ready to arrive at the last conclusion a woman should come to with regard to a man's inclinations towards herself, at the very first possible opportunity, and all the feminine discussions recorded in these volumes generally hover about this single topic. Even the men, who might be supposed to be engrossed with other pursuits, take the village flirtations into anxious consideration, and seem to have few more important interests in life. But this is probably a true picture of village life in England half-a-century ago, and perhaps even now, though the feminine sphere of thought and action has greatly enlarged with the progress of education, something of the same kind of small gossip, and small agitation, and mean rivalry, and base detraction, might go on wherever there existed a contracted circle, holding within its bounds several young people of different families and opposite sex, with parents to watch over their interests. Only at the present day a girl of higher mind would make an occasional exception to the rule, employing her intellect upon better things, and not, as is the case with Emma, using her superior intelligence to do base things with superior vigour.

At the present day it is inconceivable that a clever girl, with a fine disposition, such as Miss Austen intends to represent in Emma, should go through such a course of meanness as her friendship with the weak-minded Harriet Smith exhibits, or should be guilty of such evil-thinking and evil-speaking as her jealousy of Jane Fairfax calls forth. Without any foundation for suspicion but what is afforded by the anonymous present of a pianoforte to Jane Fairfax, and by the casual remark from Frank Churchill,—Emma's favourite,—that a certain Mr. Dixon, lately married to Jane's dearest friend, Miss Campbell, preferred Jane's music even to Miss Campbell's, Emma constructs the theory of an amorous passion on the part of Mr. Dixon for Miss Fairfax, and supposes it to result in the gift of the pianoforte, and to be the cause of Jane's retirement to the village of Highbury.

The confidant of Emma's suspicion is Frank Churchill, a young careless coxcomb, little fitted to receive any sort of confidence from any young woman. Nor are these damaging suggestions made in the excitement of a single conversation, to be dropped on subsequent reflection. No; they are renewed and repeated through many chapters on to the very end, when it turns out that the young man who has seemed to listen to them willingly was himself privately engaged to the subject of these indelicate and injurious insinuations. On one occasion, when Emma is half ashamed of her own suggestions, Frank Churchill says,

'Leave shame to her;' and Emma replies, 'I think she is not wholly without it.' Miss Austen saw faults in Emma, and in one of her letters she speaks of her as a heroine whom none but herself,—the authoress,—will like; but she does not appear to estimate the magnitude of this one fault. Nor does the pettiness of her dealings with Harriet Smith seem so evident to her as it should be; nor does she give any indication of surprise that her heroine should be fancying herself in love with Frank Churchill, and given up to the desire for his attentions, and be at the same time actually in love with George Knightley. Few things can be more offensive than Emma's chase after lovers for Harriet Smith; than her pursuit of Mr. Elton, the coxcombical curate, in her behalf; and her subsequent attempt to engage for her the preference of that very Frank Churchill whom she so long intended for herself. The trivial, miserable business of providing suitors for Harriet Smith, and the rejection of one honest young farmer who is much too good for her, but whom Emma persuades her to refuse on the plea that he is not a gentleman, occupy Emma's time and meditations very largely, and form the subject of many dialogues between her and the friend of her choice; and in her patronage of that common boarding-school girl who first loves Robert Martin, and then Mr. Elton, and then George Knightley, there is no less vulgarity of feeling than there is cruelty in the injustice with which her jealousy pursues the one young lady in the neighbourhood whose beauty and good breeding and superior education place her in a position of rivalry with herself. Emma's treatment of the young farmer, Robert Martin, exhibits the same low order of feeling as her question to Frank Churchill concerning Jane Fairfax, 'You know Miss Fairfax's situation in life, I conclude—what she is destined to be?'—alluding in a tone of detraction to Jane's intention of going out as a governess, an intention which proceeded from a high sense of honour, and which any right-minded girl would have known how to appreciate. But Emma is always Emma. She is a living being, and therefore those faults which would offend us in an actual acquaintance, sting us with equal keenness when we come in contact with them in the course of our progress through this novel.

In Miss Austen's fictions it is not the image of sorrow, of suffering, or want, which induces commiseration in the reader; but the exhibition of petty aims, vain strivings, low intellects, and mean jealousies, which excites pain, as it augments our appreciation of the weakness of human nature and the narrowness of life and thoughts when contracted to certain conditions. There is, however, much less of this small village, or watering-place, or country neighbourhood kind of existence to be found in England now than there was in Miss Austen's days.

Railways have made movement general if not universal. Few people remain rooted to any one spot. London is no longer unknown to the country. Travelling made easy to all classes has enlarged the circle of every individual experience. All the means of intercourse between man and man have increased and are increasing rapidly; ideas are in constant circulation; postage is cheap. No place is too isolated for the reach of magazines; no town, no country house is condemned solely to the interests of its own limits in space. Even the watcher at the solitary lighthouse has his newspaper or his railway library, and the most lonely manor house has its box from Mudie, to supply to the minds of the inhabitants food for meditation in the suggestions of gifted men and women with varied themes of thought, and beautiful pictures of fancy, so that it is no longer necessary to canvass the possible affections of the nearest curate, or the ways and means of the doctor's wife and daughter, or to quiz the farmer's son. The true object of education is the enlargement of thought and the promotion of worthy pursuits and wholesome subjects of interest; for the growth of these signifies the suppression of paltry agitations and evil speaking. As literature and education increase in any circle, jealousy and slander will diminish. It is the increase of knowledge among the wealthier classes which has stimulated their sympathies for the poorer, and, in the course of the present century, distinguished writers of fiction exhibiting the affections and sorrows of the poor, have awakened in the rich a sensibility of which they were at one time thought incapable. Miss Austen's biographer, who is remarkable for his candour, has pointed attention to the evident indifference among all the ministers of the church represented in her works to those duties which every clergyman now considers it essential that he should endeavour to fulfil. Yet Miss Austen's father and grandfather were both in orders, and she had ample opportunities for studying all the avocations of a Christian teacher. But in her time there was great apathy generally among the privileged classes concerning the trials and troubles of those born to poverty. There were, of course, exceptions to the rule, but it is a happy reflection that in the present time the exception is the indifference, and that each day's progress is marked by some amelioration in the condition of the indigent classes of society. There were, no doubt, pioneers to this better state of things in days earlier than Miss Austen's, and Goldsmith's *Vicar of Wakefield*, and parson in the *Deserted Village*, and George Herbert's Curate, must be accepted as types of the benevolent working ministers known to each of these charming writers, the one living in the reign of George III, the other of the two Charles Stuarts.

The exceptionally good, however, was not Miss Austen's stimulus in writing, as we have seen from her own letter, and as we know from the internal evidence of her novels. Her special power lay in the satire of the mean and the ridiculous, and this may serve as an instrument of good, if it succeeds in making the contemptible repulsive. The danger in reading too much of Miss Austen, to the exclusion of other works of fiction, would consist in the low estimate of humanity likely to arise from such a study, and from the starving of the higher imaginative faculties; as the danger in reading too much romance would consist in the undue exaltation of the fancy above the level of ordinary life, in the excitation of desires which this world cannot gratify, and the distaste for the real, which is induced by a yearning after the visionary.

The novelist who has best united the true with the ideal, who has achieved the most natural amalgamation of the romantic and the real, is Sir Walter Scott. There is hardly a phase of humanity which he has not touched skilfully; his comprehensive glance travels over distant ages, and far-off lands; he extends to all humanity the hand of good fellowship; he recognises the evil as an offset to the good; he has no varnish for vice, but he has a tenderness for the foibles which he satirises, and a genuine pathos underlies his genial humour. He has a rare pictorial power; he calls up processions from the long past, and gives life to history; he has an unbounded wealth of fancy. With one hand he can shower barbaric pearl and gold, while with the other he can gently open the door of the lonely hut, and show the interior of the poor peasant's life. He can tell his story for him with the manly unaffected sympathy which awakens tenderness. He can teach the lettered and learned to understand the ways and thoughts of the ignorant and simple; he can persuade feminine fastidiousness to contemplate the sorrowful and the sore with unaverted head and with the desire to save and to heal; he can transport the thoughts of the hard-worked artisan from the suffocation of his dark dwelling-place to the freedom of the mountain-side. He surrounds his reader with healthy influences, with the poet's love of beautiful nature, with the stir of active life, with heroic impulses, and high ambition. He does it all without apparent effort; the ease of his narrative occasionally approaches negligence, but his simplicity is never forced, and his style is never slovenly. An eminent writer has described it well in speaking of 'its sweet, careless music.' His fancy flows like the running brook through the mountain gorges, and lingers in the valleys among flowery ways, and among the darker aspects of life stays as a well-spring of hope, reflecting what light there is from heaven.

It may be urged with truth that Walter Scott has not produced any one character of such complete reality as the feeble Mr. Woodhouse, the caustic Mr. Bennet, the inane Lady Bertram, the chattering Miss Bates, of Miss Austen; his portraits are less elaborately finished, and reveal themselves with less subtlety than hers; but, then, what an immense gallery of human likenesses he has exhibited. It is not to be denied that some of them are mere sketches, invested with no great personal interest, and this is mostly the case with his lovers, male and female, out of whose perplexities his story is built up; but the larger number are portraits vigorously conceived and executed, showing the true lineaments of humanity; and however Miss Austen may excel in the completeness of her representation of a narrow sphere of existence, Scott's is the fairer interpretation of human life, because he gives true suggestions, if not complete pictures, of all its moods, as they vary, according to the infinite variety of time and circumstance.

There is the same kind of difference between Walter Scott and Miss Austen as between Victor Hugo and Balzac. Not that these four writers bear any actual resemblance the one to the other, but that the mutual relation between the two French resembles that which exists between the English writers. Victor Hugo is less real than Scott, but also Balzac is less real than Miss Austen. Balzac is a more exact delineator of individual character than Victor Hugo, but Victor Hugo is the greater interpreter of general humanity.

Jane Austen's discriminative power, which was her strongest quality, showed her at once that the author of *Marmion* was the author of *Waverley*. She recognised the poet in his mask, and she spoke on the subject without any shadow of doubt. She assumed in sport a terror of the new romance writer, and wrote thus to one of her correspondents:—

Walter Scott has no business to write novels, especially good ones. It is not fair. He has fame and profit enough as a poet, and ought not to be taking the bread out of other people's mouths. I do not mean to like 'Waverley' if I can help it, but I fear I must. I am quite determined, however, not to be pleased with Mrs.——'s should I ever meet it, which I hope I may not. I think I can be stout against anything written by her. I have made up my mind to like no novels really but Miss Edgeworth's, E.'s, and my own.

If Scott had rested upon his poems he would never have known what the extent of profit and fame could be for a thoroughly successful writer. The appearance of his romances made a new era in the history of literature; the talk of the town was the last volume out; all the interest of society not absorbed in the chapters of the novel was centred in the doubt which existed as to its authorship. Some vain persons, by judicious silence and averted looks, sought to be suspected themselves of that greatness in ambush, and one or two succeeded in the attempt. Most other works of fiction dwindled into insignificance by the side of these brilliant productions. Miss Austen's popularity, however, had not reached such a height as to suffer any evident diminution by the rise of Sir Walter Scott's. Her way lay in a different direction, and she still quietly pursued it. Being in no actual need of money she could afford to wait, and her excellent judgment took the right estimate of her own merits, and assured her that they would be sufficiently recognised in due time. Few writers have known so little of the sufferings which are supposed to be the badge of their tribe. She was easily contented, a small modicum of general approbation satisfied her, and what she coveted most was that of her own family. She was willing, like the mole, to make her ingenious structures in the dark. Yet these structures seem to have been the aim and end of her life. She appears to have been born expressly to write her six novels and then to die; her biographer records few emotions beyond the pleasure she had in these creations. Her death was premature; it was the close of a blameless life, and such a life is unhappily rare among women of genius.

On the death of Miss Austen's father, in the year 1801, the family removed to Bath, and afterwards to Southampton, but finally they settled down quietly at Chawton, a property which was left to Jane's second brother, Edward, who had been in early days adopted as a son by his cousin, Mr. Knight, and who had taken the name of Knight in consequence.

It was at Steventon and at Chawton that Jane Austen composed all her novels; the tranquillity of home was perhaps necessary to her for the act of creation; she certainly did not write anything more than a few letters during her residence at Southampton and Bath; but her subsequent works show the result of energies stimulated and observation enlarged during that interval of seeming idleness, for at Chawton she composed the novels of *Persuasion*, *Mansfield Park*, and *Emma*.

Miss Austen's style is good,—not indeed graceful or melodious, but simple and unaffected, and generally correct; although a bit of awkward construction occasionally occurs, as in the following sentence, 'This was obliged to be repeated before it could be believed'. But the easy-going, thoroughly ungrammatical English which distinguishes the female novelists of the present day had not been invented in Miss Austen's time. She gives the right cases to her relative pronouns, and she does not substitute adjectives for adverbs; and this is a degree of accuracy quite startling to readers accustomed to the slovenly feminine style of our time, in which such phrases as 'the man who I met in the wood,' and 'I did not preach like he did,' are of such frequent occurrence that these errors in grammar may not unreasonably be supposed to be intentional. For if there were not some special agreement on the subject between the female writers of this age, how could it happen that the same faults continually appeared in the pages of so many of them? It is true that others occasionally arise by way of novelty; but these are a constant quantity, their presence is inevitable, and must be accepted as a necessity. It is possible that the perpetrators of such inaccuracies having achieved in many cases considerable grace of style, in spite of them, look upon them with fondness, and that they are prepared to condemn correctness in grammar as a needless pedantry. But if they believe their grace to be due to their disorder, they are mistaken; the grace exists in spite of the departure from rule, not because of it; and the same writers, if they would take time to consider the order of the English language, lax though it be in its own nature, would find a considerable gain in force from the use of discipline. And also they will do well to remember that the tendency of negligence is to increase as it goes on, and that a very little more of licence would lead to the confusion of their meaning.

The power and beauty of language depend upon its symmetry, and true harmony cannot be obtained without attention to the science of its music. A fair fabric of lace, or a pretty piece of woven tissue, may be fair and may be pretty still, though in tatters; but the tatters will not be pronounced to be an improvement by any candid person, although it might happen that a trader, desiring to sell such imperfect goods, might choose to assert that the holes proved in a beautiful manner the lightness and elegance of the material. The highest power will never result from slovenly work; and those writers among women who are qualified to stand by the side of the most eminent men,—those who have reached the impregnable heights, and won the imperishable crown,— have not scorned the laws of order, and among their other great powers have exhibited the power of restraint. George Eliot, to whom none will deny the highest excellence, is disciplined as she is forcible in her style; and because of her force and her accuracy, the world at large,—

women no less than men,—proclaimed upon the first appearance of her works that their author must certainly be a man. But the author of *Adam Bede, The Mill on the Floss, Silas Marner,* and *The Spanish Gypsy,* stands revealed a woman, and the whole host of female writers may rejoice in her as their head; they may follow her example in some sort; they may work with some kind of care, acknowledging the responsibilities of their vocation; and they may certainly avoid the violation of their mother-tongue.

The women of France are not ungrammatical or careless writers; but it must be allowed that the French language is more complete in its grammar than the English, and does not admit of the same amount of irregularity in its writers. The French are also a more precise and methodical people in all their undertakings. Whatever they do is done with the idea of organisation, whether it is the arrangement of an establishment for baths or for bouillons, or the management of a railway buffet or of a military enterprise; and this sense of order is the secret of the success they attain in many works wherein other nations fail. It is the secret of all perfect and permanent success.

Miss Austen's letters are as remarkable as her novels for clearness and accuracy of style, and for light touches of humour enlivening ordinary themes. The following extract may be accepted as a fair specimen of her playful manner;—

MY DEAR E——,

One reason for my writing to you now, is that I may have the pleasure of directing to you 'Esq.' I give you joy of having left Winchester. Now you may own how miserable you were there; now it will gradually come out,—your crimes and your miseries,—how often you went up by the mail to London, and threw away fifty guineas at a tavern; and how often you were on the point of hanging yourself, restrained only, as some ill-natured aspersion upon poor old Winton has it, by the want of a tree within some miles of the city . . .

Publishers in Miss Austen's times made no fewer mistakes than they are wont to make now. One of them kept *Sense and Sensibility* by him for many years, frightened at having given ten pounds for it; and was very willing to return it to her brother Henry for the same sum, when Jane Austen sent him to make terms for its recovery. As Thackeray's *Vanity Fair* in our own time with difficulty found a publisher, we have no reason to express surprise. Nor should it be forgotten that of the numerous progeny of novels which the publishers help into the world, many die in the birth, and most expire in their first year. The greater part of novels belong to the ephemeral class of literature. Representing the manners of their time, or reflecting the special taste of their time, they cease to please when those manners pass away or when that taste alters; but such as contain in their characters or their scenes either the essence of truth or of poetical beauty will not quickly perish. The *Vicar of Wakefield* is still universally read. Scott's romances are recovering the place which a reaction from excessive popularity at one time forfeited for them; and Jane Austen's works,—though not devoured by young ladies of our period with the same greediness as the new stories just come from Mudie's,—are still taken down by 'the girls' from the maternal shelf, when there is nothing else to be had, and are read,—by them,—with tranquil interest. But they are pondered over with most attention and most appreciation by men of thought and literary education.

44. Richard Simpson on Jane Austen
1870

Unsigned review of the *Memoir, North British Review* (April 1870), lii, 129–52.

Simpson (1820–76) was a Shakespearian scholar and writer on Roman Catholic matters, a Catholic himself. Nominally a review of the *Memoir*, the article is one of the high points in the understanding of Jane Austen (see Introduction, pp. 2–31).

Although Miss Austen has left a great name in literature, she never belonged to the literary world. Her gallery of portraits was not like that of Miss Burney, selected from a motley crowd of artists and authors, noble patrons and plebeian listeners, which frequented a father's concerts or drawing-rooms, or was gradually drawn within the net of literary correspondence and acquaintance. She never aspired higher than to paint a system of four or five families revolving round a centre of attraction in a country mansion, or a lodging at Bath, or a house in a country town. This was, indeed, the only society she knew. Her name therefore, though great in a history of literature, counts for nothing in the history of men of letters. She stood by herself, and not only may but must be studied apart from them. Not they, but their books, influenced her—their writings, not their company and conversation. She belongs to them as a student and follower: as a model for them to follow, her influence only began to be felt after her death. During her life she neither belonged to their order nor drew inspiration from their society. She was born in 1775 at the rural parsonage of Steventon, where she lived nearly a quarter of a century. Before she was sixteen she wrote many tales, nonsensical but spirited. After that age, she practised herself in burlesquing the silly romances of the period. She wrote *Pride and Prejudice* when she was twenty-one, *Sense and Sensibility* when she was twenty-two, and *Northanger Abbey* when she was twenty-four. She then, on the death of her father, removed to Bath and Southampton, the only places where she had experience of urban society; and there she wrote nothing. Her second period of literary activity began in her second country home at Chawton, in Hampshire, whither her family moved in 1805. She published *Sense and Sensibility* in 1811, *Pride and Prejudice* in 1813, *Mansfield Park* in 1814, and *Emma* in 1816; and she had prepared for the press *Northanger Abbey* and *Persuasion* before her death in 1817.

If she had no personal help from her contemporaries, she cannot be said to have derived much from books. The record of her studies is brief. Her favourite authors in history were Goldsmith, Hume, and Robertson. She was not wholly uninterested in politics; but it was only the politics of a couple of centuries before her day. She could be enthusiastic for Charles I and Mary Queen of Scots; but she lived and wrote through the period of the French Revolution and the European war without referring to them once, except as making the fortunes of some of her naval characters. She was well acquainted with the Essayists of the beginning of her century, the *Spectator*, the *Rambler*, and the rest. Richardson was a favourite with her; so was Dr. Johnson; and in poetry Crabbe and Cowper were her special delight. Her handwriting was beautiful, her needlework delicate. She was neat-handed in any operation that required steadiness and precision. She was the life of her family, which belonged to the higher rank of gentry whom she paints in her novels. She had two brothers sailors, both of them distinguished in the navy, to whose influence we may trace her knowledge of and enthusiasm for the service. And this is about all that we know of the outward circumstances amidst which she wrote her novels. But this information is enough to lead to a knowledge of her method of working, and of her theory of art. It is clear that she began, as Shakespeare began, with being an ironical censurer of her contemporaries. After forming her prentice hand by writing nonsense, she began her artistic self-education by writing burlesques. One of her works, *Northanger Abbey*, still retains the traces and the flavour of these early essays. By it we may learn that her parodies were designed not so much to flout at the style as at the unnaturalness, unreality, and fictitious morality, of the romances she imitated. She began by being an ironical critic; she manifested her judgment of them not by direct censure, but by the indirect method of imitating and exaggerating the faults of her models, thus clearing the fountain by first stirring up the mud. This critical spirit lies at the foundation of her artistic faculty. Criticism, humour, irony, the judgment not of one that gives sentence but of the mimic who quizzes while he mocks, are her characteristics. If she had set herself to imitate her models seriously, as the Seicentisti imitated Cicero, or Miss Burney copied Dr.

Johnson, she would never have reached the heights she actually attained. She might have spoiled an intelligible style; she might have clothed her thoughts in a garb totally unfit for them; she might have written much earnest sentiment; but she would never have displayed the subtle humour, the fine sense of the incongruous, the constant presence and alertness of mind, which her writings are full of. Nature has many methods of educating her children. She derives wisdom sometimes from a wise exemplar, sometimes from a foolish foil. Sometimes a man 'takes virtuous copies to be wicked:' sometimes he learns prudence by laughing at the shallow follies of others. For 'the dulness of the fool is the whetstone of the wits.' It was in such manner that Miss Austen schooled herself into an unimpeachable conformity to nature, not by direct imitation of nature, but by looking through, and amusing herself with, the aberrations of pretended imitators. It is the same kind of wonder how she gleaned her 'theoric,' as how Henry V gleaned his,

> Since his addiction was to courses vain,
> His companies unlettered, rude, and shallow;

and his distinguished and imperial ideas grew in him while consorting with men like Poins, who thought as every one else thinks, and kept the roadway of commonplace without declining to the right hand or to the left. In this growth through contradictions we see the highest exercise of the critical faculty. And such in her sphere was Miss Austen's growth; she was a critic who developed herself into an artist.

That the critical faculty was in her the ground and support of the artistic faculty there are several reasons for believing. The first reason is her notable deficiency in the poetical faculty. Perhaps there is no author in existence in whom so marvellous a power of exhibiting characters in formation and action is combined with so total a want of the poetical imagination. Heywood has been called a prose Shakespeare; Miss Austen much more really deserves the title. Within her range her characterization is truly Shakespearian; but she has scarcely a spark of poetry. Her nephew, who has lately written her biography, gives some lines of hers in memory of Mrs. Lefroy, which only show that in serious poetry her model was Johnson, or Cowper in his more prosaic moods, and that the serious imitation of such a model deprived her of all humour, all delicacy of analysis, all subtlety of thought or language, and led her into affectations and commonplaces which in her novels she would have scornfully criticised. She could, however, write pointed epigrams and tolerable charades; in fact she was just so far a poet as a critic might be expected to be. She even seems to have had an ethical dread of the poetic rapture. At least she makes the latest and more carefully drawn of her heroines declare 'that she thought it was the misfortune of poetry to be seldom safely enjoyed by those who enjoyed it completely; and that the strong feelings which alone could estimate it truly were the very feelings which ought to taste it but sparingly.'

And secondly, the paramount activity of the critical faculty is clearly seen in the didactic purpose and even nomenclature of her novels. *Pride and Prejudice* and *Sense and Sensibility* are both evidently intended to contrast, and by the contrast to teach something about, the qualities or acts named in the titles. In *Persuasion* the risks and advantages of yielding to advice are set forth. *Northanger Abbey* exhibits the unreality of the notions of life which might be picked out of Mrs. Radcliffe's novels; and *Mansfield Park* and *Emma*, though too many-sided and varied to be easily defined by a specific name, are in reality just as didactic as the rest. This didactic intention is even interwoven with the very plots and texture of the novel. The true hero, who at last secures the heroine's hand, is often a man sufficiently her elder to have been her guide and mentor in many of the most difficult crises of her youth. Miss Austen seems to be saturated with the Platonic idea that the giving and receiving of knowledge, the active formation of another's character, or the more passive growth under another's guidance, is the truest and strongest foundation of love. *Pride and Prejudice, Emma,* and *Persuasion* all end with the heroes and heroines making comparisons of the intellectual and moral improvement which they have imparted to each other. The author has before her eyes no fear of the old adage, 'Wise lovers are the most absurd.' Many of her novels are simply expansions of Shakespeare's ballad which tells of the lordling's daughter loving her tutor, then of his being eclipsed by a knight, and then of the lady's perplexities, and her final decision in favour of her first love:

Then lullaby, the learned man hath got the lady gay.

Her favourite ideal was to exhibit this intelligent love in its germ, to eclipse it for a season by the blaze of a great passion, to quench this glare, and to exhibit the gentle light of the first love reviving and waxing greater till it perfects itself in marriage. So far was she from agreeing with Marlowe's 'mighty saw,'

He never loved that love not at first sight,

that she expressly writes one of her novels, *Sense and Sensibility*, to controvert the view, to show that the sudden passion is not the lasting affection, and to make true love rather an adjunct of the sober common sense than of the impetuous and passionate side of the soul. In *Pride and Prejudice* too she says, 'if gratitude and esteem are good foundations of affection,' then her heroine is a proper lover; but 'if the regard springing from such sources is unreasonable or unnatural in comparison of what is so often described as arising on a first interview, and even before two words have been exchanged,' then nothing is to be said for her, except that she had tried the love at first sight, and found it a failure. In this we see clearly enough her habitual exaltation of judgment over passion, of the critical over the poetical and imaginative faculties. And this is perhaps even more perceptible in the manifest irony of her whole mass of compositions. As was the bounden duty of a novelist, she concentrated her forces on bringing her heroes and heroines together, and marrying them off happily. But she generally gives us to understand that a sufficient amount of happiness might have been secured for them in other ways. Indeed, in *Mansfield Park* she speculates on what would have followed if Henry Crawford had not run wild, and if the hero had consequently married the anti-heroine, and the heroine the anti-hero; and she anticipates that they would have been happy enough. But more than this. Her plots always presuppose an organized society of families, of fathers and mothers long married, whose existence has been fulfilled in having given birth to the heroes and heroines of the stories. Now, these people are almost always represented as living together in fair comfort; and yet there is scarcely a single pair of them who have not, on the usual novelist's scale of propriety, been wofully mismatched. Sense and stupidity, solidity and frivolity, are represented as in everyday life cosily uniting, and making up the elements of a home with the usual average of happiness and comfort. Miss Austen does not absolutely tell us that the special ends which she takes so much trouble to bring about are anything short of the highest happiness, or that such happiness could possibly be obtained by any other means. On the contrary, she appears as earnest as other novelists for the success of her favourites. But there is enough in her evident opinions, in her bywords, in her arguments, to prove to any sufficiently clear sight that it would be, after all, much the same whether the proper people intermarried, or whether they were mismatched by some malevolent Puck. Dr. Johnson thought it nonsense to say that marriages were made in heaven, and held that any woman and any man might, if they determined upon it, live well enough together, and settle down into the prosaic happiness of a comfortable couple. In similar manner Miss Austen believed in the ultimate possible happiness of every marriage. The most ill-assorted couples may get used to one another. Even Willoughby, the nearest approach to a rascal that her benevolent judgment allowed her to paint, is ultimately not unhappy in a marriage that yoked him with a woman he disliked, and separated him for ever from the only one he loved. There are only two marriages in all the six novels that really end badly; and only one of these comes into the action of the story,—Rushworth's marriage with Maria in *Mansfield Park*. Thus the great coil Miss Austen makes to bring the right people together is really much ado about nothing. A story is told of a London curate, who, seeing many couples before him, told them to 'sort themselves,' and proceeded to marry them. Two pairs found themselves mis-sorted. The curate, not knowing much of canon law, thought the case difficult, and tried to arrange matters as they stood; and the two couples were with little difficulty, and no ill consequences, persuaded to 'bide as they were.' In *Mansfield Park*, Miss Austen tells us that this might easily have been managed. Yet she of course devotes all the machinery of the novel to bring together the true hero and heroine. Now, what is this other than taking a humourist's view of that which as a novelist she was treating as the summum bonum of existence? That predestination of love, that preordained fitness, which decreed that one and one only should be the complement and fulfilment of another's being—that except in union with each other each must live miserably, and that no other solace could be found for either than the other's society—she treated as mere moonshine, while she at the same time founded her novels on the assumption of it as a hypothesis. Her biographer and nephew supposes, as a reason of her never marrying, that her notions of love were too exalted for her to find a man who could satisfy her. Those who can only judge upon the evidence derived from her novels must be led to the belief that in her idea love was only an accident of friendship, friendship being the true light of life, while love was often only a troublesome and flickering blaze which interrupted its equable and soothing influence. Friendship, to judge from her novels, was enough for her; she did not want to exaggerate it into passionate love. In it she in fact seems to have found sufficient tenderness and support to satisfy her cravings; she was contented with her home, with her brothers and sister, and did not want a husband. This gave her a great advantage for describing the perturbations of love. She sat apart on her rocky tower, and watched the poor souls struggling in the waves beneath. And her sympathies were not too painfully engaged; for she knew that it was only an Ariel's magic tempest, and that no loss of life was to follow. Hence she could consider the struggles of the mariners with an amused and ironical complacency, and observe minutely all the hairbreadth escapes of their harmless peril. Accordingly her view of the life she described was that of a humourist, but of a very kindly one. She did not precisely think that all she dis- cribed was vanity and vexation of spirit. But she thought that, in ordinary language, and especially in that of romance-writers, it was screwed up to a higher tension than the facts warranted. She was con- scious that as a novelist, she was speaking somewhat in Cambyses' vein, and that the earnestness of her language was a little outdoing the truth of things. This consciousness gave her a superiority to her subject, which is one element in solving the secret of her wonderful power over it. She is so true because she is consciously exceeding the truth. Others may believe in the stability of raptures, and in the eternity of a momen- tary fancy; she knows exactly what they are worth; and, though she puts into the mouths of her puppets the language of faith, she knows how to convey to her readers a feeling of her own scepticism. The most she does is to allow that 'the cure of unconquerable passions and the transfer of unchanging attachments must vary very much as to time in different people.' Hence that disproportion between her language and her judgment, which constitutes the crucial test of her humour. Hers is not humour of the strongest and vividest kind, which awakens the indirect reminiscence of the Infinite through the disproportion of language and imagery to the finite things which they profess to express. It is not the method of Cervantes, magniloquent on trifles, nor of Swift, trifling away magnificence, both of which methods imply a tacit allusion to a common measure, unseen but felt, which equalizes all finite magnitudes by the overwhelming transcendence of its infinity. Her humour is only partial, investing with more importance than they have things of which she owns the importance; but her pervading critical judgment, which never allows her feelings to run away with her, qualifies her humour, and couples her with such writers as Lamb and Thackeray, rather than with the novelists of the type of Scott.

As a writer she has little resemblance to Lamb. She cannot vie with him in probing a question by a play upon words. But she anticipated his love of the absolutely natural, and his humourous view of the ordinary relations of life. She had too good a memory, too precise a judgment, to allow of that play of the imagination which distinguished him. His peculiar fancy was one that was founded on a defect of mem- ory. He asked by what fatality it was that everything he touched turned into a lie, that he had a 'lying memory?' There is in genius a compensation for defective memory. Horne Tooke supposed that the only reason why the child might be more fluent than the man was that the child was not troubled by the choice of words, but spoke in the words that came foremost. Lamb's stuttering want of fluency was even more mental than physical. The memory refused to supply the right word, or the right circumstance; but his fancy stepped in with an image or a suggestion which was worth many times more than the direct truth which he was looking for. His genius furnished a wrong word, or a wrong idea, which was found more apposite, more fitting, more subtle in its truth, more true, than the commonplace right. This source of humour there is no trace of in Miss Austen. Her incongruities are all well considered and pre-arranged: 'Miss Bingley's congratulations to her brother on his approaching marriage were all that was affectionate and insincere.' Such collocations so evidently proceed on theory, that any one who chooses to take the trouble can acquire the knack. They differ from Lamb's as, to the ordinary imagination, a natural though uncommon event differs from one that is 'supernatural and causeless.' She sat too self-collected in that central calm which is at the heart of all agitation to allow her imagination to run away with her. Her faculties were poised; their action and reaction were equal; she had them all well in hand. In this respect she differed from Thackeray, whom she much more nearly resembled than Lamb. Thackeray declares that he could give no account why he made his characters speak as they did or act as they did. They seemed to guide his pen, not he their course. They influenced him as independent persons suggesting their autobiographies to his fancy, not as puppets created by himself, whom he could make to do what he pleased. In him the poet transcended the critic, and the imagination sometimes outstripped the judgment. Not so with Miss Austen. She felt herself to be thoroughly mistress of her own creations; and though, she treated them all as sufficiently personal to have subsequent histories which she would recount to the members of her own family, yet she showed how well she knew them by defining them. We can define what we create: the works of nature, or of other minds, or of our own minds under the inspiration of uncontrolled impulse, escape the defining power. Miss Austen knew what she wanted her characters to say, what they were going to say, and why they said it. With all their nature, there is very little mystery in them. And whatever residuum of mystery there might be the author always manages to clear up with the bull's-eye of her bright common-sense before she comes to a conclusion.

One more instance of the action of her critical faculty must be mentioned. It is well known that Macaulay has given her a place, far indeed below, but nearest to, Shakespeare, for her power of composing characters. She does not give any of them a hobby-horse, like Sterne, nor a ruling passion, like Pope, nor a humour, like Ben Jonson, nor a trick, like Mr. Dickens. They are all natural, all more or less commonplace, but all discriminated from one another beyond the possibility of confusion, by touches so delicate that they defy analysis, and so true that they elude observation, and only produce the effect by their accumulation. She exhibits no ideal characters, no perfect virtue, no perfect vice. She shows strength dashed with feebleness, feebleness braced with some fibres of strength. Even Mrs. Norris, the only one of her characters who is thoroughly and consistently selfish, ends by placing herself in a situation of trouble and sacrifice, in undertaking to be the guardian of her degraded niece. Willoughby, the nearest to a villain of her developed characters (Mr. Elliot in *Persuasion* is rather described than seen), gives so plausible an account of himself that he is thoroughly forgiven by those whom he has most injured; and Wickham, the modified villain of *Pride and Prejudice*, has so much charm about him that his sensible and epicurean father-in-law is almost disposed to like him better than his other and more honourable sons. Miss Austen has a most Platonic inclination to explain away knavishness into folly. Wickedness in her characters is neither unmixed with goodness, nor is it merely a defect of will; she prefers to exhibit it as a weakness of intelligence, an inability of the common-sense to rule the passions which it neither comprehends nor commands. It is her philosophy to see not only the soul of goodness in things evil, but also to see on the face of goodness the impress of weakness and caducity. This is one reason which obliges her to compound her characters. Another is even stronger. It is her thorough consciousness that man is a social being, and that apart from society there is not even the individual. She was too great a realist to abstract and isolate the individual, and to give a portrait of him in the manner of Theophrastus or La Bruyère. Even as a unit, man is only known to her in the process of his formation by social influences. She broods over his history, not over his individual soul and its secret workings, nor over the analysis of its faculties and organs. She sees him, not as a solitary being complete in himself, but only as completed in society. Again, she contemplates virtues, not as fixed quantities, or as definable qualities, but as continual struggles and conquests, as progressive states of mind, advancing by repulsing their contraries, or losing ground by being overcome. Hence again the individual mind can only be represented by her as a battle-field, where contending hosts are marshalled, and where victory inclines now to one side, now to another. A character therefore unfolded itself to her, not in statuesque repose, not as a model without motion, but as a dramatic sketch, a living history, a composite force, which could only exhibit what it was by exhibiting what it did. Her favourite poet Cowper had taught her,

By ceaseless action all that is subsists.

And she herself explains that the society in the dullest country neighbourhood, however confined, is not unvarying, because 'people alter so much that there is something new to be observed in them for ever.' With her even constancy may be a perpetual inconstancy, for it must be perpetually finding fresh reasons for loving, fresh manifestations of qualities to be loved.

Thus each of her characters, like Shakespeare's Richard II, 'plays in one person many people,' contains within him 'a generation of still breeding thoughts,' none of which is 'self-contained,' but all 'intermixed,' each modified by something else. And neither in the drama of the soul nor in the drama of life did she allow herself to carry her composition of forces too high, or to make the problem too complicated for her analysis. The heroic passions she never touched; all her characters, as Macaulay owns, are commonplace. And heroic combinations of characters are equally beyond her range. Dramatic she is, but it is only within the lines of the domestic drama. She defined her own sphere when she said that three or four families in a country village were the thing for a novelist to work upon. Each of these 'little social commonwealths' became a distinct personal entity to her imagination, with its own range of ideas, its own subjects of discourse, its own public opinion on all social matters. Indeed there is nothing in her novels to prove that she had any conception of society itself, but only of the coterie of three or four families mixing together, with differences of intellect, wealth, or character, but without any grave social inequalities. Of organized society she manifests no idea. She had no interest for the great political and social problems which were being debated with so much blood in her day. The social combinations which taxed the calculating powers of Adam Smith or Jeremy Bentham were above her powers. She had no knowledge how to keep up the semblance of personality in the representation of a society reckoned by averages, and no method of impersonating the people or any section of the people in the average man. Her clergymen even have very little of their calling about them; there is little attempt to delineate clerical manners as such, except so far as they may be quizzed or caricatured in the solemn inanities of Mr. Collins, and the touchy parochial dignity of Mr. Elton. The other clergymen are a little more serious and learned than the non-clerical characters; but their classification goes no further. They are members of the family, or the coterie of families, with more or less of distinction from their office; but there is no distinctive social force incarnate in them, nor does the official social weight which they carry become interwoven in the web of their characters. In some of her novels she places her coterie of families in Bath, or even in London; and then Bath society comes in as a picturesque background; but it is only pictorial; it has no more to do with the development of her drama or the explication of her characters than the woods and the hills which she is much more fond of describing. There is not the least attempt to bring public opinion to bear on any one. Some of the characters are said to show too much or too little deference to public opinion; but it is only spoken of, not represented. It is an abstract notion, a word not a thing, an idea not a force. Yet if it had been within the sphere of her power she might have made excellent opportunities for using it. She delights in introducing her heroines in their girlhood, shapeless but of good material, like malleable and ductile masses of gold. We have the flower in the germ, the woman's thought dark in the child's brain, the dream of the artist still involved in the marble block which some external force is to chip and carve and mould. She must have known the force of public opinion in doing work of this kind; and she would no doubt have dramatized public opinion, and exhibited its workings, if she had possessed any such knowledge of it as is displayed by George Eliot or by Mr. Browning. She was perfect in dramatizing the combination of a few simple forces; but it never struck her to try to dramatize the action and reaction of all.

Platonist as she was in her feelings, she could rise to contemplate the soul as a family, but not as a republic. The disturbances in it were not insurrections or revolutions, but only family quarrels; and the scapegrace passion did not necessarily lose the affections of the family ruler. There is no capital punishment, not even transportation or imprisonment for life, in her ethical statute-book. There lives no faculty within us which the soul can spare, says Wordsworth. It was the same in her code: 'every qualification is raised at times, by the circumstances of the moment, to more than its real value;' good-breeding is now and then more opportune than good-nature. The same favour which she shows to younger brothers in the plots of her novels she distributes in her philosophy to the qualifications of the mind which usually only play secondary parts in the symphony of life. It may be strange to attribute to the girl who wrote *Pride and Prejudice* and *Sense and Sensibility* a conscious philosophy which had reasoned out and affirmed all these conclusions; but they were just those which her favourite Cowper would lead her into. There is in fact a great similarity in their views; and the estimate of what people should live for, as insinuated in her novels, is adequately expressed in his lines:

> He that attends to his interior self,
> That has a heart and keeps it; has a mind
> That hungers, and supplies it; and who seeks
> A social, not a dissipated life,
> Has business.

It is true then to say that the perfection, within their limits, of her delicately compounded characters is quite of a piece with her theories, and that artistic instinct need not be postulated to account for what may be a product of judgment; so that even where her originality is most unquestioned and her power most manifest it is a moot point whether she is a born or a made poet.

If her possession of the poetic genius is denied, her literary eminence certainly becomes more remarkable than it would otherwise be. Genius is unaccountable; it comes and goes without our being able to know whence or whither. It is called inspiration, to show how little it is in the power of the man that has it. But of all the characteristics of Miss Austen the most striking is the perfect power she had over her wit. She certainly did not exemplify Boileau's rule:

> Notre Muse, souvent paresseuse et stérile,
> A besoin, pour marcher, de colère et de bile.[1]

She is never carried away, hardly even carried on, by passion or indignation. She is always perfectly calm, perfectly self-conscious. Her great characteristic is patience, which is notoriously a surrogate genius, the best substitute for it which nature has contrived.

> I worked with patience, which means almost power,

says Mrs. Browning. 'The little bit, two inches wide, of ivory on which I work with so fine a brush, as produces little effect after much labour,'

---

[1] 'Our Muse, often lazy and unproductive, needs gripe and anger in order to get going.'

was Miss Austen's way of describing her method. Whateley called it Dutch-painting. But her own comparison of it to miniature-painting on ivory is more just. It is as far from the boorish tastes of Teniers as from the sublime gloom of Rembrandt, while it has all the minute attention to detail of the most accomplished miniature-painter. She lived more than forty years, and yet only wrote six novels which she thought fit to print. She has left many manuscripts, which her family refuses to publish, on the ground of their not being worth it. None of them were intended for publication; they were exercises, not studies. What she wrote was worked up by incessant labour into its perfect form. She did not cast her statues in one jet, nor mould them with a few strokes on the anvil. She had no Cyclopean force of poetical production. She was patient as Penelope at her web, unpicking at night much that she had laboriously stitched in the day. This patience, joined to that imperious necessity of creating which is probably the distinctive difference of the active artistic nature, is what chiefly characterizes her. Rogers was perhaps nearly as patient; but he concentrated his attention not on imitating nature but on perfecting his obedience to the rules of art. He used his file so perseveringly that he had little but filings to present to the public. Miss Austen, with equal patience and perseverance, watched the growth of character, amassed a multitude of minute traits, and arranged them in the order of their growth. She was continually adding to her store, replacing less characteristic traits by more telling ones, and improving herself in the knowledge of nature.

He who maintains that judgment was the foundation-stone of Miss Austen's genius ought to be prepared to trace in her writings the development of the quality. Inspiration or instinct is subject to no rules of growth. Judgment is a quality which must grow with the accumulation of the materials on which it feeds. The comparison of the novels of Miss Austen's youth with those of her maturity would probably have more clearly betrayed the growth of her mind if they had not all been finally prepared for the press in the last seven years of her life. Hence it is that we have to look for her mental development rather in their general construction than in their details. Her six stories divide into two trilogies. The early one consists of *Pride and Prejudice, Sense and Sensibility,* and *Northanger Abbey:* the later, of *Mansfield Park, Emma,* and *Persuasion.* Many readers must have felt tempted to consider the latter trilogy a kind of reproduction of the former, in the light of a maturer knowledge. The moral and intention of the stories is very similar; the same general types of character are introduced; they are borne through similar vicissitudes;

and they come to similar ends. In the former set the art is simpler, less concealed, more easily discovered: in the latter, both passion and humour are rather more developed. But it does not appear that the author was conscious of anything that she could correct in her earlier works; indeed, the two characters in *Pride and Prejudice*, Darcy and Elizabeth, seem to have been her favourites all her life. In all the novels the plots are equally natural; there is nothing sensational, nothing even improbable. The events gow out of one another; and the characters of the actors are the sufficient reasons of the acts which are related. The action is such as is necessary to display the characters, not such as is invented for the purpose of mystifying and surprising the reader. Since she did not write for the press, but simply to satisfy her own artistic cravings, and to embody her own ideals, there was no temptation for her to go out of her way to catch the vulgar taste by surprises and catastrophes, and no reason why she should not over and over again vary the same air, or present the same ideas in different settings. As in society she found variety in the development of the same mind, so does she create variety in her novels by different presentments of a conception fundamentally one.

It is generally supposed that a moral purpose spoils a fiction. This opinion is only partially true. When a writer describes the reaction of different characters on each other, he can scarcely escape the intention of showing his preference for some type of character or some rule of conduct over another. And it seems no compliment to his intelligence to say that if he foresees the superiority he is about to exemplify, and allows his intention to make it one of the conditions of his work, it will spoil his creation. Small-minded writers who interest themselves for some narrow and sectarian idea, and write a story to recommend it, are necessarily as forced and unnatural as such apologists would be in any other kind of argument. But this does not apply to those who attack a prevalent superstition—for mental narrowness never becomes wider by being widely spread—or try to enforce a general truth against special prejudices. And it is quite clear that Miss Austen did work with this intention. She avows it. She wrote her first novel with a polemical bias against the sudden flash of love which poets and novelists had agreed to make the great characteristic of the passion, at least in its heroic stage. She wrote her second to prove how entirely the sentimental preoccupations which the study of poetry might produce in the young mind are refuted by the logic of facts, and are found inapplicable to real life. The concluding moral of *Sense and Sensibility* is: 'Marianne Dashwood was born to an extraordinary fate. She was born to discover the falsehood of her own opinions, and to counteract, by her conduct, her most favourite maxims. She was born to overcome an affection formed so late in life as at seventeen, and with no sentiment superior to strong esteem and lively friendship voluntarily to give her hand to another.' In *Northanger Abbey* the same polemical intention is pushed even to the verge of caricature. The heroine is a girl who thinks that Mrs. Radcliffe's novels give a real picture of life, and who expects to find in a gentleman's house which was once an abbey all the traces of the romantic crimes and mysterious wickedness which Mrs. Radcliffe would have domiciled in its moss-grown walls. Her aspirations all run on the road of Gray's lines:

> Hail horrors, hail! ye ever gloomy bowers,
> Ye Gothic fanes, and antiquated towers!

Such is the clearly acknowledged polemical intention of her first trilogy of tales. And the two first of the second trilogy carry on and develop the same habit. *Mansfield Park* is another attempt to show that true love is that which is founded on esteem, not on passion, and that passion should rather be the crown of the edifice than its foundation. It exactly contradicts the romantic ideal of *Romeo and Juliet*. Shakespeare exhibited the grand passion kindled in the eyes and breaking forth into a conflagration which devoured all former passions, and even life itself. This is the heroic, tragic way of treating love. Miss Austen would have made Romeo find out that Juliet was not worth having; and his former love for Rosaline would have revived, all the sweeter from the contrast with the sulphurous trial which the passing passion would have left behind it. This is the domestic and ironic way of treating love—a way which Miss Austen considers to be both more true and more amusing, since it exhibits such a contrast between aspirations and facts 'as time is ever producing between the plans and decisions of mortals, for their own instruction and their neighbours' entertainment.' As *Mansfield Park* is thus a kind of supplement to *Pride and Prejudice*, so is *Emma* the complement of the two other novels of the first trilogy. Emma, the heroine, like Marianne Dashwood and Catharine Morland, is a young lady full of preconceived ideas, which she has not, however, like Marianne and Catharine, borrowed from the traditional romance of poets and novelists, but which are the product of her own reflections upon her own mental powers. Her prejudices are natural, not artificial; she fancies herself cleverer than she is, with an insight into other hearts which she does not possess, and with a talent for management which is only great enough to produce entanglements, but not to unravel them. These ideas of hers govern the plot; and she is cured of them by the logic of events. At the same time, her esteem for the mentor who stands by her and tries to guide her through her difficulties gradually ripens into love; the scholar gratefully marries her master; and the novel ends, as usual, with a retrospect in which both teacher and taught find themselves equal gainers each from the other, even intellectually, and the Platonic ideal is realized, not merely through the heart, but through the intelligence. *Persuasion*, the last and altogether the most charming of the novels, stands in the same relation to an earlier sketch. In Anne Elliot we have a reproduction of the same character of 'sense' that was first displayed by Elinor in *Sense and Sensibility*. It cannot be denied that it is in some degree a retraction of former theories. It seems written to show that, whatever may have been the author's apparent meaning, she never intended really to separate the heart and the head, intellect and passion. In this novel, therefore, she traces the course of a love founded equally upon esteem and passion, interrupted by the interference of friends, and kept unsoldered for eight years by the heat of the man's anger at his unmerited rejection. Anne Elliot is Shakespeare's Viola translated into an English girl of the nineteenth century. Like Viola, she never tells her love, or rather never talks of it after its extinguishing, but sits like patience on a monument smiling at grief; the green and yellow melancholy feeds on her, and wastes her beauty. Like Viola, too, she meekly ministers to the woman who is unknowingly her rival. Miss Austen must surely have had Shakespeare's *Twelfth Night* in her mind while she was writing this novel; for not only is the general conception of the situation the same, but also the chapters which she wrote during the last months of her life are directly founded upon Shakespeare. They contain Anne's conversation with Captain Harville on the different characteristics of men's and women's love, through overhearing which Wentworth, the hero, is convinced of her constancy, and comes forward again, after his long estrangement.

> There is no woman's sides
> Can bide the beating of so strong a passion
> As love doth give my heart; no woman's heart
> So big to hold so much; they lack retention.

So says the Duke; and Viola, disguised as Cæsario, replies,

> In faith they are as true in heart as we,

and gives the example of her supposed sister pining in thought. 'Was not this love indeed?' she asks.

> We men may say more, swear more; but indeed
> Our shows are more than will.

Similarly, Captain Harville believes that as men's bodies are the strongest so are their feelings capable of bearing most rough usage, and riding out the heaviest weather. 'Your feelings may be the strongest,' replies Anne, 'but the same spirit of analogy will authorize me to assert that ours are the most tender. Man is more robust than woman, but he is not longer lived, which exactly explains my view of the nature of their attachments. . . . All the privilege I claim for my sex (it is not a very enviable one; you need not covet it), is that of loving longest, when existence or when hope is gone.' This is the song of the dying swan, in which she makes ample recantation for all her heresies, more apparent than real, against the Majesty of Love; in it she displays a poetical vein which her previous writings hardly justified one in suspecting. It is exquisitely beautiful, in spite of the affected logical precision which gives too great a prosiness to the expression to allow it to take the poetical rank which its ideas deserve.

There is then a decided growth in the general intention of Miss Austen's novels; she goes over the same ground, trying other ways of producing the same effects, and attempting the same ends by means less artificial, and of more innate origin. The same may be said of the details of her works—for instance, of the characters. Macaulay, as we have seen, fixes upon her clergymen as an instance to show how she could discriminate men of the same class and position from one another. The instance is not well chosen, because the principle of classification is one which depends on the organization of society which she never deeply studied. If she had understood the clergy better, and had formed her own theories about their duties and place in society or in the commonwealth, she would very likely have made her clergymen more typical. As it is, they no more form a class apart than her baronets. She had no more idea that a clergyman as such had his own ways of talking and acting than that a baronet had them. She gave them credit for a little more regularity of conduct, a little more love of books, and a little more activity among the poor, than the rest of men. Bertram, Tilney, and Ferrars would be equally natural as laymen; and it is only by giving them a provision to marry upon, or by impressing the imagination of the ladies they are in love with, that their ordination affects their characters as developed in the stories. It is only in Collins and in Elton that the official self-consciousness of the clergyman is strongly brought out, and in each case as a foil to show off some weak fibre in the mind or the character. We should rather examine a natural than an artificial set of characters if we wish to find out her subtle means of discriminating one from another. Macaulay declares that they are so subtle as to defy analysis. But Miss Austen is so pellucid a writer, her whole soul displays itself in so kindly and unreserved a way, that if it is ever possible to analyse an artistic synthesis into its first elements it should be so in her case. Her biographer refers to her fools as a class of characters in delineating which she has quite caught the knack of Shakespeare. It is a natural class, better defined than most natural classes are, and less difficult to analyse. It ought therefore to serve very well to test her manner of working. In reality her fools are not more simple than her other characters. Her wisest personages have some dash of folly in them, and her least wise have something to love. And there is a collection of absurd persons in her *stultifera navis*,[1] quite sufficient to make her fortune as a humourist. She seems to have considered folly to consist in two separate qualities: first, a thorough weakness either of will or intellect, an emptiness or irrelevancy of thought, such as to render it impossible to know what the person would think of any given subject, or how he would act under it; and often, secondly, in addition to this, fixed ideas on a few subjects, giving the whole tone to the person's thoughts so far as he thinks at all, and constituting the ground of the few positive judgments arrived at, even in subject-matter to which the ideas in question are scarcely related. The novels do not give a single instance of the fool simple in all the purity of its idea. Mrs. Palmer, in *Sense and Sensibility*, comes the nearest to it, but in her case her thorough womanly good-nature gives a solid nucleus to a character which in order to be perfect ought to have only *pepo loco cordis*, a pumpkin for a heart. Intellectually however she is a nullity; and Miss Austen's method of positively representing a mere negative is ingenious and happy. It is one solution of the great problem of art, the universal form of which is, how to represent the realities of the natural scale in the imitations of the artificial scale—how to imitate the song of birds on the gamut of the pianoforte, or the coloured lights of nature with the unluminous colours of the palette. Mrs. Palmer's nullity is represented first by her total want of intellectual discrimination. Her good-nature furnishes her with a perpetual smile; and any event, any word, that

[1] 'Ship of fools'.

should cause either pain or pleasure to a person of sense, has no other effect upon her than to broaden the smile into a laugh. When she talks, her entire want of discrimination is shown in her failure to see the contradition of contradictories. Her indignant speech about Willoughby is a typical utterance:—'She was determined to drop his acquaintance immediately, and she was very thankful that she had never been acquainted with him at all. She wished with all her heart that Combe Magna [Willoughby's place] was not so near Cleveland [her husband's], but it did not signify, for it was a great deal too far off to visit; she hated him so much that she was resolved never to mention his name again, and she should tell everybody she saw how good-for-nothing he was.' There are foolish sayings of which a clever man might be proud; if any real Mrs. Palmer could in fact string together contradictions so readily she would soon lose her character as a mere simpleton. The method does not make Mrs. Palmer look so thoroughly inane as she is intended to be. Mr. Frank Matthews was once playing Bottom the weaver, and in the speech 'ear hath not seen, eye hath not heard,' etc., by some inadvertence put the words right, and then by a greater inadvertence corrected himself, and put the words wrong. The effect was ludicrous—a natural fool finding it much more unnatural to be foolish than wise, and painfully retracing his steps when he had inadvertently followed common sense. Something of the same effect of want of naturalness attends the elaborate self-contradictions of Mrs. Palmer. In the later novel, *Emma*, where perhaps Miss Austen perfects her processes for painting humourous portraits, the negative fool is much better represented in Miss Bates. Miss Bates has enough of womanly kindness and other qualities to make her a real living person, even a good Christian woman. But intellectually she is a negative fool. She has not mind enough to fall into contradictions. There is a certain logical sequence and association between two contradictories, which it requires mind to discover: Miss Bates's fluent talk only requires memory. She cannot distinguish the relations between things. If she is standing in a particular posture when she hears a piece of news, her posture becomes at once a part of the event which it is her duty to hand down to tradition: 'Where could you possibly hear it? For it is not five minutes since I received Mrs. Cole's note—no, it cannot be more than five—or at least ten—for I had got my bonnet and spencer on just ready to come out—I was only gone down to speak to Patty again about the pork—Jane was standing in the passage—were you not, Jane?—for my mother was so afraid that we had not any salting-pan large enough,' etc. etc., for it might go on for ever. Any reader can see that here is the same fortuitous concourse of details which makes up Mrs. Quickly's description of Falstaff's promising her marriage—the sea-coal fire, and the green wound, and the dish of prawns—in the speech which Coleridge so justly contrasts with Hamlet's equally episodical, but always relevant, narrative of his voyage towards England.

The fool simple is soon exhausted; but when a collection of fixed ideas is grafted upon him he becomes a theme for endless variations. Mrs. Bennet, in *Pride and Prejudice*, Miss Austen's earliest work, is one of this kind. She is no sooner introduced than she is defined. She is 'a woman of mean understanding, little information, and uncertain temper.' That makes up the fool negative. Her positive qualities are these: 'When she was discontented, she fancied herself nervous. The business of her life was to get her daughters married; its solace was visiting and news.' Her fixed ideas of the happiness of catching any young man for any of her daughters, of the iniquity of an entail which prevented their succeeding to her husband's estate, and of her weak nerves, make up the staple of her talk, always amusing because never to the purpose. Another fool of the same novel is Mr. Collins, somewhat of a caricature, and therefore easier to analyse. He is a man of mean understanding, and a bore to boot; that is, he esteems himself worthy to be always occupying a place in the notice of those with whom he associates, and he thinks it incumbent upon him always elaborately to explain his motives, and his reasons. At the same time he has some sense of the necessity of humility, and lays claim to this virtue by always speaking of himself and his belongings as 'humble' and by the most expansive display of humility towards his patrons, and towards any one of a rank above his own. To his own personal claims he adds the official claim derived from his being a rector in the Church of England, which gives him occasion to obtrude his advice, always wrong, in the various vicissitudes of the tale. The contrast between his empty head and heart and his fixed ideas constitutes the diversion of the portrait. He is perfect when he exhorts a father to forgive his erring daughter like a Christian, and never to speak to her again.

However good these characters may be, it cannot be denied that they have in them much of the element of farce. Miss Austen in her later series of novels has given us new and improved versions of them; for example, Mr. Woodhouse in *Emma*, a mere white curd of asses' milk, but still a man with humanity enough in him to be loveable in spite of, nay partly because of, his weakness and foolishness. His understanding is mean enough. His invalid's fixed ideas, which divide all that is into two kinds, wholesome and unwholesome, his notion of the superiority of his own house and family to all other houses and families, his own doctor to all other doctors, and his pork to all other pork, and his judgment of all proposals and events by their effect in bringing persons nearer to, or driving them further off from, the centre of happiness which he enjoys, show that the portrait is one of the same kind as that of Mrs. Bennet, but improved by the addition of a heart. In a similar way we may compare with Mr. Collins Sir Walter Elliot in *Persuasion*. He is at bottom a fool, with two fixed ideas to guide all his judgments. Vain of his own rank and good looks, these two points form his scale of comparison and rule of judgment for all men and all things: 'I have two strong grounds of objection to the navy. First, as being the means of bringing persons of obscure birth into undue distinction, and raising men to honours which their fathers and grandfathers never dreamed of; and, secondly, as it cuts up a man's youth and vigour most horribly; a sailor grows old sooner than any other man.' Sir Walter is a character constructed in the same way as Mr. Collins, with simpler means and less caricature. Altogether, he is a less factitious and artificial personage than Mr. Collins, who is rather built on the lines habitually adopted by Mr. Dickens. Miss Austen, in her earlier fools, seems scarcely as yet to have realized the Aristotelian maxim that all things, even stones, fishes, and fools, pursue their proper end. Now, Mr. Collins's fixed ideas have nothing to do with his objects in life. They govern his talk and his behaviour, but not his conduct. Sir Walter Elliot, however, is superior to Mr. Collins in making his ideas his rule of life; so his portrait becomes equal in absurdity, but superior in naturalness.

There is another class of fools whom Miss Austen treats with special distinction. These people are sometimes acute enough mentally; the meanness is in their moral understanding rather than in their intellect. The conversation between John Dashwood and his wife in the opening of *Sense and Sensibility*, where she proves to him that his promises of generous conduct to his sisters, made to his dying father, do not require him to deprive himself or his children of anything that would otherwise be theirs, becomes in Miss Austen's humourous narrative a melancholy masterpiece of stupid casuistry, without conscience to build on, and of the surreptitious substitution of interest for duty. Again, Miss Thorpe the flirt, and young Thorpe the fast Oxford man, in *Northanger Abbey*, are fools rather on their moral than on their intellectual side. But in the earlier novels there is no such systematic attempt to connect wicked-ness with a deficiency of moral understanding as there is in the later ones. There is no endeavour to show that Wickham, the villain of *Pride and Prejudice*, or Willoughby, the villain of *Sense and Sensibility*, lacks the understanding of what virtue is. But in the much more subtle portraits of Crawford and his sister, in *Mansfield Park*, it is brought home to us throughout that their levity and want of principle is an ignorance—that, in spite of their intellectual brilliancy and good-nature, there is a want of moral understanding, analogous to the want of intelligence in the fool. So Mrs. Norris, in *Mansfield Park*, a bustling, managing, sharp, and odious woman, proves to be not only wrong, but also, and in a still higher degree, foolish, by the thorough collapse of her method, and the complete failure of all her undertakings. In the earlier novels wickedness is wickedness; in the later it is ignorance also.

One more characteristic should be noticed. Miss Austen, in construct-ing her chief characters, sometimes lets her theory run away with her. For instance, Darcy, in *Pride and Prejudice*, is the proud man; but he is a gentleman by birth and education, and a gentleman in feeling. Would it be possible for such a man, in making a proposal of marriage to a lady whose only fault in his eyes is that some of her connections are vulgar, to do so in the way in which Darcy makes his overtures to Elizabeth? It is true that great pains are taken to explain this wonderful lapse of propriety. But, all the explanations notwithstanding, an im-pression is left on the reader that either Darcy is not much of a gentle-man as he is represented, or that his conduct is forced a little beyond the line of nature in order the better to illustrate the theory of his bio-grapher. The same criticism is applicable to the most elaborate of the novels, *Emma*. The heroine's suspicions about the relations between Miss Fairfax and Mr. Dixon may be natural; but her decision in believing without proof what she suspected, and her open and public reproaches to the lady, are violently opposed to the general notion of feminine grace and good-nature which the character is intended to embody. Here again, theory seems to be pushed a little beyond the line not of possibility but of consistency. In the novels where these exaggera-tions are avoided, the heroes and heroines are inclined to be somewhat too didactic, so much so as to be sometimes priggish. It is only in the last novel, *Persuasion*, where all these faults are avoided. The strength of mind of the heroine is maintained throughout, in spite of the apparent weakness of her early behaviour to the hero; and the intellectual superiority and moral constancy of the hero are maintained in spite of the temporary weakness and folly into which he is betrayed by his anger and vexation. The aberrations of both are perfectly natural, and thoroughly consistent with the ideal which they profess to embody.

There is great analogy between the character of Miss Austen and the characteristics of her novels—for example, her unconsciousness of her artistic merits, as manifested by the surprise she felt at the very moderate success she lived to enjoy, and her wonder at receiving £150 as the profits of one of her novels. Her powers were a secret to herself. And in a similar way she makes love a secret even to the lover. Her Beatrices and Benedicks only discover their mutual attraction by their failures to love elsewhere. The proof is a negative one. 'Worse essays proved thee the best of loves.' The star of love on its rising is enveloped in mists; and the mists are dispersed not by its own beams, but by the heat of a meteoric love which crosses its path, and bursts, and clears the air. The false glare is extinguished, and the immortal and unquenchable light which had long been shining in secret is revealed to consciousness. In the novels Elton is Harriet Smith's meteor, Churchill Emma's, Crawford Fanny Price's, Miss Crawford Edmund Bertram's, Louisa Captain Wentworth's, Wickham Elizabeth Bennet's, Willoughby Marianne Dashwood's. It is the commonest form of her love-histories. She makes the love of fancy, the sudden love engendered in the eyes, blaze up to supersede and eclipse the germ of idea or rational love; but this germ borrows heat from the fire which would destroy it, and becomes the stronger and brighter flame which puts out all rival fires.

Hints given in Miss Mitford's letters, however strenuously controverted, seem to show that in early days there was something offensive in Miss Austen's manner and conduct. It may be that both Emma and Darcy contain autobiographical elements. There is an air of confession in the conception of each. We find in the novels a theory that, as love is educated by contradiction, so is love the great educator of the mind through sorrow and contradiction. Dante describes philosophy as the *amoroso uso de sapienza*: wisdom without it talks but does not act wisely. He who acts without love acts at haphazard; love alone shows him how and where to apply his principles, chiefly by the agony it gives him when he wounds it by wrong applications of them. Emma's wisdom nearly ruins her happiness, till she finds that wisdom is nothing unless it is directed by love. Darcy too by his similar love of managing almost ruins the prospects of his friend and himself. With all the importance which Miss Austen attributes to education, she never forgets its double aspect, theoretical and practical. But the practice must be directed by love. Love is however only a tardy teacher; it teaches as the conscience teaches, or as the dæmon of Socrates taught him, by the penalties it exacts for error. Πάθει μάθος,[1] as Æschylus says. If Miss Austen ever was a flirt, as Mrs. Mitford reported, it was most likely rather in Emma's style; not with any idea of engaging men's hearts in order to disappoint them, but with a view to show her disengaged manners, and the superiority of which she was conscious. The shade of priggishness with which her earlier novels are tinged is perhaps most easily explicable on this supposition.

But in any case, after all possible deductions, Miss Austen must always have been a woman as charming in mind as she was elegant in person. What defects she had only prevented her being so good as to be good for nothing. If her sympathies were somewhat limited, this was only because her society was limited. Perhaps the assertion that she had no powers of portraying or understanding society as such should be modified in favour of one special class, whose outward life singularly influences its general character. She thoroughly understood the naval officer, whom she could study at home, in her brothers. Her naval officers are really social portraits. A clergyman's daughter, she yet regarded the clergyman's position with a half-quizzical eye. She let the church stand in the churchyard, and did not attempt to transplant it into her novels. But the naval officer was a favourite personage in her later novels; Admiral Croft, Captain Wentworth, Captain Harville, Captain Benwick, Captain Price, and William Price are all admirable portraits, perfectly distinct, and yet all saturated with their professional peculiarities. She even, in Captain Price's case, did what Pope pronounced to be impossible, reconciled the 'tarpaulin phrase' with the requirements of art and civility. Out of these bounds her language never strays. She is neat, epigrammatic, and incisive, but always a lady; there is no brandy and cayenne in her farrago—no 'opinions supercélestes et mœurs souterrains,'[2] as Montaigne says. There is no overstepping her own faculties; if she did not know, she felt, that every man, ever so little beyond himself, is a fool. She obeyed the adage, 'ne gladium tollas mulier.'[3] She spun out the feminine fibre of the sons of Mars and Neptune, but meddled neither with the sword nor with the trident. She is altogether an example for the aspiring artist. She shows what patience, perseverance, modest study, and a willingness to keep her

---

[1] 'Wisdom comes through suffering', *Agamemnon*, 177.
[2] 'Unworldly opinions and worldly morality.'
[3] 'The woman does not bear arms.'

compositions for the test of time, could do for a genius not very com-
manding in its own nature. Her example preaches with the mediæval
poet,

> Ars compensabit quod vis tibi magna negabit.

Art will make up for want of force. Altogether, she is a luminary not
beyond the spell of ordinary human magic,

> A being not too wise or good
> For human nature's daily food.

But this is no more than a New Zealander might have said of the
missionary whom he was about to eat. Miss Austen should have some
more distinctive appraisement. In the gallery of authors hers is one of
the most graceful and kindly figures. There is not a quality in her which
is repulsive, not one which calls for suspension of judgment or the
allowance usually claimed for the eccentricities of genius, not one so
transcendent as to raise her above imitation or emulative hope. Hers is a
magnetic attractiveness which charms while it compels. As she has a
way of melting love into intelligence, so her intelligence becomes in
turn amiable. Montalbemert's first literary essay was the biography of
a woman who, in a different sphere, and for different reasons, exerted
this kind of influence over his mind; and he adopted as his own the
title which the simple devotees of Germany from Tauler downwards
have given to die liebe H. Elisabeth, la chère Sainte Elisabeth. Might
we not for like reasons borrow from Miss Austen's biographer the title
which the affection of a nephew bestows upon her, and recognise her
officially as 'dear aunt Jane'?

45. Unsigned notice of *Northanger Abbey* and *Persuasion, Blackwood's Edinburgh Magazine*

May 1818, n.s.ii, 453–5

We are happy to receive two other novels from the pen of this amiable and agreeable authoress, though our satisfaction is much alloyed, from the feeling, that they must be the last. We have always regarded her works as possessing a higher claim to public estimation than perhaps they have yet attained. They have fallen, indeed, upon an age whose taste can only be gratified with the highest seasoned food. This, as we have already hinted, may be partly owing to the wonderful realities which it has been our lot to witness. We have been spoiled for the tranquil enjoyment of common interests, and nothing now will satisfy us in fiction, any more than in real life, but grand movements and striking characters. A singular union has, accordingly, been attempted between history, and poetry. The periods of great events have been seized on as a ground work for the display of powerful or fantastic characters: correct and instructive pictures of national peculiarities have been exhibited; and even in those fictions which are altogether wild and monstrous, some insight has been given into the passions and theories which have convulsed and bewildered this our 'age of Reason'. In the poetry of Mr Scott and Lord Byron, in the novels of Miss Edgeworth, Mr Godwin, and the author of *Waverley*, we see exemplified in different forms this influence of the spirit of the times,—the prevailing love of historical, and at the same time romantic incident,—dark and high-wrought passions,—the delineations, chiefly of national character,—the pursuit of some substance, in short, yet of an existence more fanciful often than absolute fiction,—the dislike of a cloud, yet the form which is embraced, nothing short of a Juno. In this raised state of our imaginations, we cannot, it may be supposed, all at once descend to the simple representations of common life, to incidents which have no truth, except that of universal nature, and have nothing of fiction except in not having really happened,—yet the time, probably, will return, when we shall take a more permanent delight in those familiar cabinet pictures, than even in the great historical pieces of our more eminent modern masters; when our sons and daughters will deign once more to laugh over the Partridges and the Trullibers, and to weep over the Clementinas and Clarissas of past times, as we have some distant recollection of having been able to do ourselves, before we were so entirely engrossed with the Napoleons of real life, or the Corsairs of poetry; and while we could enjoy a work that was all written in pure English, without ever dreaming how great would be the embellishment to have at least one half of it in the dialect of Scotland or of Ireland.

When this period arrives, we have no hesitation in saying, that the delightful writer of the works now before us, will be one of the most popular of English novelists, and if, indeed, we could point out the individual who, within a certain limited range, has attained the highest perfection of the art of novel writing, we should have little scruple in fixing upon her. She has confined herself, no doubt, to a narrow walk. She never operates among deep interests, uncommon characters, or vehement passions. The singular merit of her writings is, that we could conceive, without the slightest strain of imagination, any one of her fictions to be realized in any town or village in England, (for it is only English manners that she paints,) that we think we are reading the history of people whom we have seen thousands of times, and that with all this perfect commonness, both of incident and character, perhaps not one of her characters is to be found in any other book, portrayed at least in so lively and interesting a manner. She has much observation,—much fine sense,—much delicate humour,—many pathetic touches,—and throughout all her works, a most charitable view of human nature, and a tone of gentleness and purity that are almost unequalled. It is unnecessary to give a particular account of the stories here presented to us. They have quite the same kind of merit with the preceding works of their author. As stories they are nothing in themselves, though beautiful and simple in their combination with the characters. The first is the more lively, and the second the more pathetic; but such is the facility and the seemingly exhaustless invention of this lady, that, we think, like a complete mistress of a musical instrument, she could have gone on in the same strain for ever, and her happy talent of seeing something to interest in the most common scenes of life, could evidently never have been without a field to work upon. But death has deprived us of this most fascinating companion, and the few prefatory pages which contain a sketch of her life, almost come upon us like the melancholy invitation to the funeral of one whom we had long known and loved.

She was the daughter of a clergyman of the name of Austen, 'a scholar and a ripe one,' whose care of her education was soon rewarded by the early promise which she displayed. It was not, however, till after his death that she published any of her works; 'for though in composition she was equally rapid and correct, yet an invincible distrust of her own judgment induced her to withhold her writings from the public till time and many perusals had satisfied her that the charm of recent composition was dissolved.' She lived a quite and retired life with her mother and sister, in the neighbourhood of Southampton, when early in 1816 she was attacked by the disease which carried her off. It was a decline, at first deceitfully slow, and which her natural good constitution and regular habits, had given little room to dread. 'She supported all the varying pain, irksomeness and tedium attendant on decaying nature, with more than resignation,—with a truly elastic cheerfulness. She retained her faculties, her memory, her fancy, her temper, and her affections warm, clear, and unimpaired to the last. Neither her love of God nor of her fellow creatures flagged for a moment.' The following passages from a letter written a few weeks before her death, are the best representation of her happy state of mind. 'My attendant is encouraging, and talks of making me quite well. I live chiefly on the sofa, but am allowed to walk from one room to another. I have been out once in a sedan chair, and am to repeat it, and be promoted to a wheel chair as the weather serves. On this subject I will only say further, that my dearest sister, my tender, watchful, indefatigable nurse, has not been made ill by her exertions. As to what I owe to her, and to the anxious affection of all my beloved family on this occasion, I can only cry over it, and pray to God to bless them more and more.' She then turns off in her lively way to another subject. 'You will find Captain —— a very respectable, well meaning man, without much manners,—his wife and sister all good humour and obligingness, and, I hope, (since the fashion allows it,) with rather longer petticoats than last year.'

Such was this admirable person, the character of whose life fully corresponds with that of her writings. There is the same good sense, happiness, and purity in both. Yet they will appear very defective to that class of readers who are constantly hunting after the broad display of religious sentiments and opinions. It has been left for this age to discover that Mr Addison himself was scarcely a Christian: but we are very certain, that neither the temper of his writings, nor even that of Miss Austen's, (novels as they are, and filled with accounts of balls and plays, and such abominations,) could well have been formed without a feeling of the spirit of Christianity.

APPENDIX: EARLY EDITIONS OF THE NOVELS OF
JANE AUSTEN

An account of the contemporary publishing history of the six novels is given in the Introduction (pages 4–5); also of the 1832–3 reprints (pages 20–21), and the French and American editions (pages 26–27).

Sense and Sensibility: 1811, 1813 corrected second edition, 1815 *Raison et Sensibilité* (and 1828), 1833 in Bentley's Standard Novels series, 1833 Philadelphia, 1844, 1846, 1847, 1849, 1851.

Pride and Prejudice: 1813, 1813 second edition, 1817, 1822 *Orgueil et Préjugé, Orgueil et Prévention,* 1832 Philadelphia (as *Elizabeth Bennet*), 1833 in Bentley's Standard Novels series, 1839, 1844, 1846, Boston 1848, 1851.

Mansfield Park: 1814, 1816 corrected second edition, 1816 *Le Parc de Mansfield,* 1832 Philadelphia, 1833 in Bentley's Standard Novels series, 1846, 1851.

Emma: 1816,[1] 1816 Philadelphia, 1816 *La Nouvelle Emma,* 1833 in Bentley's Standard Novels series, 1833 Philadelphia, 1841, 1849, 1851

Northanger Abbey: 1818,[2] 1824 *L'Abbaye de Northanger,* 1833 in Bentley's Standard Novels series, 1833 Philadelphia, 1848, 1850.

Persuasion: 1818,[1] 1821 *La Famille Elliot* (and 1828), 1832 Philadelphia, 1833 in Bentley's Standard Novels series, 1848, 1850.

Collected editions: 1833, 1837, 1838 Philadelphia, 1856.

[1] *Emma* was published in December 1815, with 1816 on the title-page.
[2] *Northanger Abbey* and *Persuasion* were published together as a four-volume set in December 1817, with 1818 on the title-page.

Bibliography

This short select bibliography is of works listing or describing the nineteenth-century criticism of Jane Austen.

CHAPMAN, R. W., *Jane Austen: A Critical Bibliography* (1955): quotes early private comments, though does not list early reviews.

DUFFY, J. M., jnr., *Jane Austen and the Nineteenth-Century Critics of Fiction 1812–1913:* unpublished dissertation, University of Chicago (1954): relates the course of Jane Austen's reputation to criticism of the novel in general.

HOGAN, C. B., 'Jane Austen and her early public', *Review of English Studies* (1950) n.s.i.: our most important source for information regarding the documentation of Jane Austen's contemporary and near-contemporary reception.

KEYNES, G., *Jane Austen: A Bibliography* (1929): lists a quantity of nineteenth-century periodical criticism unmentioned by Chapman; also fuller bibliographical information on the early editions of the novels.

LINK, F. M., *The Reputation of Jane Austen in the Twentieth-Century* (with an annotated enumerative bibliography of criticism from 1811 to June 1957), unpublished dissertation, Boston University (1958).

WATT, I., *Jane Austen: a collection of critical essays* (1963), with an interesting Introduction.

Select Index

In preference to a straightforward alphabetical listing of contents I have grouped the index references as follows: I Periodicals and journals from which material has been quoted. II Critics and reviewers. III Authors compared with Jane Austen. IV References to the novels of Jane Austen, where there is significant comment.

I

II

An index of reviewers and critics including the names of those who passed informal comment; but not listing the members of the Austen

SELECT INDEX

family, their friends and acquaintances who contributed to Nos. 5 (a)
and 7, the Opinions of *Mansfield Park* and *Emma* (see notes on pages
48, 55).

Austen, Francis, 15
Austen, H., No. 13; 7, 15, 16, 52, 73
Austen-Leigh, J. E., *Memoir of Jane Austen*, 1–2, 16, 21, 30–1, 32, 215, 216, 225, 226, 234, 241, 243, 246, 265
Bessborough, Lady, 7
Branstone, Mrs., 7
Brontë, C., No. 28 (a, b); 21, 24–5, 124, 160–1, 203
Browning, E. B., 25
Byron, Lady, 7–8
Cage, C. 16
Carlyle, Mrs., 24
Chasles, Philatre, 26
Clarke, J. S., 52, 230–1
Coleridge, S. T., No. 22 (d); 23
Cooper, J. F., 26–7
Dallas, E. S., No. 40; 2, 198
Darcy, Lady, 9
Eliot, George, ? No. 34; 140
Edgeworth, M., 11, 17, 19, 22, 149
Emerson, R. W., 28
Farrer, R., 32
Ferrier, S., 15
FitzGerald, E., end-note to No. 37
Frampton, Lady, 12
Gifford, W., 8, 13
Guiton, Mrs., 15
Harding., D. W., 18–9, 32–3
Hastings, W., 7
Herries, Miss, 16
James, H., 31–2

Kavanagh, J., No. 39; 29–30, 176
Kirk, J. F., No. 33; 142
Knapp, S., 27
Lascelles, M., 32
Lefroy, A., 6
Lewes, G. H., Nos. 27, 30, 32, 36; 2, 14, 22, 24, 25, 28–9, 36, 124, 126, 128, 202, 203
Lister, T. H., No. 20, ? No. 25; 22, 23, 25, 27, 135–6
Longfellow, H. W., No. 22 (f)
Lytton, E. B., No. 22 (c); 22, 146
Macaulay, T. B., No. 26; 22, 24, 122, 125, 130, 148, 162–3, 192, 195, 202, 249, 250, 257, 258
Mackintosh, J., No. 22 (a)
Macready, W., No. 23; 22–3, 118
Marshall, J., 27
Martineau, H., 23–4
Mitford, M. R., No. 6; 8, 10, 15, 54
Montolieu, I. de, 26
Morpeth, Viscount, No. 24; 23
Mudrick, M., 33
Murray, J., 5, 8, 13, 53, 58
Newman, H., No. 22 (e); 23
Oliphant, M., No. 42; 30–1, 215
Pollock, W., No. 37; 29, 167
Prince Regent, 14–5, 52, 230–1
Robinson, H. C., No. 15; 8–9, 85
Romilly, A., 12
Sclater, Mrs., 16
Scott, W., Nos. 8, 17; 2, 3, 6–7, 11, 16, 19, 21, 22, 25, 27, 29, 58, 135, 148, 149, 156–7, 161, 195, 201–2

274

III

An index of writers whose work is compared by critics and reviewers with that of Jane Austen.

IV

The novels of Jane Austen, listing important entries and particularly interesting discussions of individual characters. Publication history, 4–5, 20–1, 269.